MEGHAN

MEGHAN

— A Hollywood Princess —

ANDREW MORTON

GRAND CENTRAL
PUBLISHING

NEW YORK   BOSTON

Grand Central Publishing
Hachette Book Group
1290 Avenue of the Americas, New York, NY 10104
grandcentralpublishing.com
twitter.com/grandcentralpub

First Edition: April 2018

Grand Central Publishing is a division of Hachette Book Group, Inc. The Grand Central
Publishing name and logo is a trademark of Hachette Book Group, Inc.

The publisher is not responsible for websites (or their content) that are not
owned by the publisher.

The Hachette Speakers Bureau provides a wide range of authors for speaking events.
To find out more, go to www.hachettespeakersbureau.com or call (866) 376-6591.

Library of Congress Cataloging-in-Publication Data has been applied for.

ISBNs: 978-1-5387-4735-3 (hardcover), 978-1-5387-4734-6 (ebook)

Printed in the United States of America

LSC-C

10 9 8 7 6 5 4 3

To Carolyn and all our friends in Pasadena

Contents

Prologue

The Stars Were Aligned

When the American actor Rachel Meghan Markle walks down the aisle at St George's Chapel in Windsor Castle on May 19, 2018, she will be making history.

In the last important royal wedding for a generation, Prince Harry's glamorous bride will be the first biracial divorcée ever to marry a member of the British royal family. Their union, blessed by Her Majesty the Queen, will make the monarchy seem more inclusive and relevant in an ever-changing world.

During the service the eight hundred guests at the grand affair might hear a low hum competing with the singing of the choir. It will be the sound of the Duke of Windsor, who gave up his throne in 1936 so that he could marry a twice-divorced American, spinning in his grave, located nearby at Frogmore, on the grounds of Windsor Castle.

He was prevented from making the love of his life his queen because Wallis had two former husbands still living. The only time Wallis was admitted into Windsor Castle was in her coffin in April 1986 for her funeral service at St. George's Chapel. In the 1950s the queen's younger sister, Princess Margaret, faced the same predicament, choosing duty before the love of her divorced paramour, Group Captain Peter Townsend.

If nothing else, the wedding of the second son of Prince Charles and the late Diana, Princess of Wales shows how much and how far the royal family—and the British nation—have changed and evolved during the reign of Queen Elizabeth II. It is a union and an occasion redolent with symbolism.

Since the romantic traumas surrounding Edward VIII and Princess Margaret, the royal family, like the rest of the world, has accepted, albeit reluctantly, the fact that divorce no longer carries the social stigma it once did. Yet even in the early 1980s when Prince Charles was scouting the shires for a bride, the notion of a divorced American marrying into the royal family was unthinkable. Then the priority was to find a white Anglo-Saxon Protestant aristocratic virgin.

He found one in the winsome shape of Lady Diana Spencer, and the constitutional catastrophe of their marriage—and rancorous divorce—has caused the older generation of royals and their supporters to take pause before commenting on the chosen companion of the younger members of the family. Nor was the parting of the future king and queen a unique occurrence inside the royal family. The queen's sister, Princess Margaret; her daughter, Princess Anne; and her beloved second son, Prince Andrew, divorced their marital partners. All were enveloped in varying degrees of scandal, most notoriously when Andrew's wife, the Duchess of York, known as Fergie, was photographed having her toes sucked by her so-called financial adviser next to a swimming pool in the south of France.

That Meghan divorced after a brief two-year union with a film producer has hardly raised an eyebrow, let alone created a constitutional crisis. After all, the future king, Prince Charles, is a divorcé who married his former mistress, Camilla Parker Bowles, also divorced, in April 2005 in a civil ceremony just over the road from St. George's Chapel—all very modern. Divorce, race, and a racy past—the House of Windsor now welcomes all comers. As Prince Harry succinctly put it during their engagement interview, the "stars were in alignment."

It is an observation Harry's uncle, Prince Andrew, the Duke of York, may reflect upon as he watches Megan Markle make her stately procession down the aisle. For Prince Andrew it is not just the stars but the decades that are out of alignment. Just thirty-six years ago, almost to the week, the prince, a red rose between his teeth, ran down the gangway of his ship, HMS *Invincible*, to be greeted by his proud parents, the Queen and the Duke of Edinburgh.

Back then he was the world's most eligible bachelor and a fully certified war hero, risking his life during the Falklands conflict between Britain and Argentina, which left more than nine hundred dead and thousands wounded.

A few weeks later, in August 1982, he secretly flew to the private Caribbean island of Mustique, where the queen's sister, Princess Margaret, had a property, Les Jolies Eaux. He and his American girlfriend, Kathleen "Koo" Stark, the daughter of Hollywood producer Wilbur Stark, had, according to first reports, flown under the assumed names of "Mr. and Mrs. Cambridge."

When she first arrived in London in 1975 Kathleen wanted to be an actor and starred in a tepidly erotic rite-of-passage movie titled *Emily* directed by an arty aristocrat, the Earl of Pembroke. As pictures were circulated of Koo in various stages of undress, hysteria gripped the mass media and even some members of Parliament.

Their romance continued long after their holiday, and the early revelations about her film role. She met the Queen, and Princess Diana considered her the perfect match for Andrew. She told me: "Sweet Koo adored him. She was terribly good to have around. Very gentle and looked after him. All her energies were directed at him. Very quiet. They suited each other so well."

Yet the stigma of that movie, one of her first, ultimately

poisoned her relationship with Andrew. Forevermore known as a "porn actress"—nothing could be further from the truth—Koo and Andrew's love affair was doomed. But for a fifth-rate movie, Kathleen may have been the first American to marry into the royal family since Wallis Simpson.

By contrast Meghan Markle has taken acting roles where she has been filmed snorting cocaine, teaching housewives the art of striptease and having sex in a storeroom. She appeared semi-naked in so many scenes in the long-running TV drama *Suits* that she complained that scriptwriters were deliberately crafting scenarios to show off her body.

(Meghan might note that while the palace has ordered her website, The Tig, which contained intelligent and well-written essays about gender equality and race, to be scrubbed from the internet, videos of her very unprincesslike behavior remain for all to see.)

While Meghan is not the first mixed-race woman to marry into European royalty—that honor goes to Panamanian-born Angela Brown, now Princess Angela of the tiny but wealthy country of Liechtenstein—she is the first divorced biracial American to take her place in the House of Windsor.

Though race has aroused plenty of debate in her own country—inevitably because of America's past as a nation practicing slavery and segregation—race relations have been largely ignored in conjunction with the royal family.

Ironically, when the engagement was announced in November 2017, moviegoers in America and Britain were enjoying *Victoria and Abdul*, the story of Queen Victoria's friendship with an Indian attendant Abdul Karim. His presence at court excited so much animosity that when the queen died in 1901, her successor, King Edward VII, personally supervised his eviction and deportation back to India. Victoria's daughter Beatrice erased all references

to Karim in her mother's voluminous diaries. As historian Car-
olly Erickson observes in *Her Little Majesty*, "For a dark-skinned
Indian to be put very nearly on a level with the queen's white
servants was all but intolerable, for him to eat at the same table
with them, to share in their daily lives was viewed as an outrage."

Though the present queen does not, as author Penny Junor
argues, recognize color, only 6 percent of the 1,100 people
employed by the palace are from ethnic minorities, and only
around thirty are in senior positions. While this ethnic imbal-
ance is also reflected in the senior ranks of the civil service, it has
been argued that the royal family has missed an opportunity to
take the lead on race.

It is a subject that Meghan has not shied away from discussing, and she will already be well aware that people of color do not
feature noticeably inside the palace. Perhaps it is an issue she may
decide to involve herself in after she settles into royal life.

As Trevor Phillips, former head of the Equality and Human
Rights Commission, notes, the way in which Meghan handles
herself will send out an important message to minorities. "It is
a very big deal that she has talked of her pride in her ethnicity.
For people of colour that will be seen as a very positive, modern
approach and immensely welcome."

Not only is she part of the discussion about race in Britain, but
her racial background informs attitudes in the US. The biracial
soon-to-be-royal is considered part of the Loving generation, the
cohort that gets its name from the Virginia couple Richard and
Mildred Loving, who were arrested in 1958 and put in jail for the
crime of miscegenation. Until the 1967 Supreme court judgment
in *Loving v. Virginia*, interracial marriage was against the law in
some states.

In the 1970s there were about 65,000 black and white married
couples in the United States. By the 1980s, a little over a decade

after the Loving ruling, that number had doubled to 120,000. A significant jump, but one has to keep in mind that the population was around 240 million at the time.

With a white Republican father and a black Democrat mother, Meghan has found herself at the center of an active discussion about the place of mixed-race individuals in society. Thus, Meghan's narrative is that of a woman trying to find herself not just as a woman but to define her place in society, a world where she is seen as neither black nor white.

Looking to the future, she will also have to define herself as part of the far smaller world of royalty.

Even though Meghan is very much her own woman, it is interesting that those who taught her or knew her spontaneously mention the D-word in the same breath as Meghan. Comparisons with Diana are inevitable; Meghan's secret solo visit in February 2018 to comfort the survivors of the Grenfell Tower inferno in Kensington, West London, revives memories of Diana's trips to the homeless on London's South Bank. Her social work visiting AIDS patients, the homeless, and those on their last lonely journey was therapeutic, as healing for her as it was for those she comforted.

While Meghan is empathetic, certainly, but also self-possessed, sophisticated, poised, and charismatic. She is a woman who is camera-ready, not camera-shy.

Long before Prince Harry was mentioned in conjunction with Meghan, her alma mater, Immaculate Heart in Los Angeles, regularly screened the 2015 speech she made at the United Nations Women conference on gender equality as inspiration for the current generation of female students.

It is said that to be an effective congressman, member of Parliament, or president, it is preferable to have enjoyed a successful career outside the political world so that when you walk into the chamber or the White House, it is not so intimidating. This is where Meghan finds herself. She has arrived at the gates of the palace fully formed: a successful actor, a popular blogger, and an acknowledged humanitarian.

She can boast a bloodline of slaves and kings, servants and swordsmen. Hers has been a remarkable journey, a journey that began—where else—the city of dreams, Los Angeles.

1

In Search of Wisdom

For years she was troubled by a nagging question at the back of her mind: *Where does my family come from, what is my history?* For Rachel Meghan Markle—known as "Bud" and "Flower" by her family—it was an endlessly perplexing issue. The fact that her mother, Doria Ragland, was an African American and her father, Thomas Wayne Markle, was a white Pennsylvanian only added to the confusion.

As a member of the so-called Loving generation, those mixed-race Americans born after 1967 when miscegenation—that is, marriage between races—was no longer a crime, Meghan felt she had to find her place, where she belonged, in both the black and the white worlds. In the hierarchy of color that still defines place, position, and proximity in American society, she was light-skinned and therefore seen as "whiter" than her black cousins. From birth she loved both white and black skin, not a familiar occurrence in American society. So, along with her perplexity came a fluidity, a readiness to view the world from different perspectives, from both sides.

She had listened wide eyed as her uncle Joseph had told and retold the story of the Raglands' cross-country drive from

Cleveland, Ohio, to Los Angeles in a borrowed car when her mother, Doria was a babe in arms. Their adventure turned nasty when they pulled into a one-horse town in Texas in the teeth of a blizzard. They were looking for a room for the night, but soon realized they were not wanted in the redneck town. One guy pointed off into the snow and yelled: "The highway is that way. Get going. You are not welcome here." Another version of the story has them picking up Kentucky Fried Chicken from the "colored" door at the rear of the restaurant.

While it may be family lore—the road from Cleveland to Los Angeles goes nowhere near the Lone Star state—for Meghan's uncle, then around seven or eight, it represented his first real experience of racism. As Meghan was to learn, the history of her mother's family was one of exploitation, discrimination, and injustice. Some of it she would experience firsthand, such as when she felt the rush of blood to her cheeks when someone in a parking lot used the N-word to her mother because she did not leave briskly enough. It was a word that her humble ancestors—slaves who worked on the cotton plantations of Georgia—would have heard on a daily basis.

It is no wonder that Meghan was left bewildered by her family tree. Tracing her family back through her mother's line is a difficult business. Prior to emancipation, evidence about the lives of black people in the South was inevitably scarce. There were few written records, and most information was passed on by word of mouth. What we do know is that for years the family was the property of a Methodist, William Ragland, whose family originated from Cornwall in the southwest of England, before emigrating to Virginia and then North Carolina. Ragland lived in Chatham County, North Carolina, with his slaves before moving to the rural town of Jonesboro in Georgia, where land was regularly given away by the authorities in lotteries to encourage settlement. Traditionally, slaves were only known by a first name, given to them by their owner, and on occasion they also took their owner's surname. The scanty records that are available show that the first "black Ragland"—that is to say, a direct ancestor of Meghan—was born in Jonesboro in 1830. This was Richard Ragland, who married a woman named Mary. Though much of his life was spent in enforced servitude, at least his son, Stephen, who was born in 1848, lived to see the emancipation that came when the Union, the anti-slave Northern states lead by President Abraham Lincoln, triumphed over the pro-slave Confederacy in 1865. At the end of the war, Stephen Ragland became a sharecropper and remained in Jonesboro, according to records unearthed by Massachusetts-based genealogist Elizabeth Banas. But this was merely slavery by another name, as the overwhelming majority of what was produced by sharecroppers was taken by the white landowners in rent and other dues, leaving an average sharecropper such as Stephen Ragland constantly in debt.

Though freed at the end of the Civil War, it was not until the 1870 census that former slaves could officially register a name for themselves. Stephen Ragland stuck with his former master's surname and his given name—not quite as romantic as "Wisdom," the name Meghan believes her great-great-great-grandfather Ragland chose when he was given the chance to make a fresh start. As she wrote: "Perhaps the closest thing to connecting me to my ever-complex family tree, my longing to know where I come from, and the commonality that links me to my bloodline, is the choice that my great-great-great grandfather made to start anew. He chose the last name Wisdom."

Sadly, the professional genealogists and researchers who have carefully investigated her history point out that the records, albeit sketchy and contradictory, show that he kept his original name. They also reveal that his first wife was named Ellen Lemens, and that the couple married on August 18, 1869, and went on to have four children: Ann (who was also known as Texas), Dora, Henry, and Jeremiah, born in either 1881 or 1882, who is Meghan's great-great-grandfather. Based on census and tax records it seems that for some years Stephen and Ellen continued to live on the plantation of white former slave owner Lemuel Ragland and his wife, Mary. In fact, when Lemuel Ragland died on May 19, 1870, Stephen Ragland was recorded in the census as working for the widow Mary, then age sixty. Other family members living in the vicinity, probably in the same plantation bunkhouse or rough-hewn wooden shacks, included Vinny and Willy Ragland, as well as Charles, Jack, Jerry, Mariah, and Catherine Lemens.

For a time the extended Ragland family lived in the vicinity of Jonesboro, the town now famous as the setting for the epic novel about the American Civil War, *Gone with the Wind*, before moving the short distance to Henry County, an agricultural district noted for its rich soil and premium cotton. Stephen and his sons, Henry and Jeremiah, worked the land as either sharecroppers or hired hands. However, beyond the cotton profits, Henry County also had a darker reputation, as an outpost of the Ku Klux Klan, which was formed in Tennessee in the spring of 1866. The Klan's first action in the county was to lynch former slave Dave Fargason during a local conflict centering on educating black children. Stephen's son Henry Ragland was also later confronted by a gang of armed white men but managed to escape with his life. Local historian R. H. Hankinson observes that soon afterwards the KKK was disbanded—although it remained hazardous to be black in the vicinity.

The threat of violence and grinding poverty prompted many to migrate north or west in search of a better life. Sometime after the turn of the century Stephen Ragland's daughter Ann and her husband, Cosby Smith, whom she married in 1892, together with their six children decided to make the three-thousand-mile journey to start a new life in Los Angeles in the days when oil and oranges were more important to the town's economy than making movies.

Their decision to move inspired Stephen's youngest child, Jeremiah, and his wife, Claudie Ritchie, daughter of the wonderfully named Mattie Turnipseed, and their growing brood to leave Georgia as well. Around 1910, when Claudie was twenty-five, they made their way to Chattanooga, Tennessee, with the hope of building a better life for themselves.

It is likely that neither Ann nor Jeremiah would see their father, Stephen Ragland, whom Meghan believes renamed himself "Wisdom," ever again, even though he lived to the relatively ripe old age of seventy-eight, breathing his last in the town of Paulding, Georgia, on October 31, 1926.

By then Jeremiah and Claudie had raised five children; one died in childbirth. Claudie, who was at the time officially designated in the census as a mulatto or of mixed race, worked as a maid at Miller Brothers department store, then the biggest store in the region. Her husband, Jeremiah, found casual jobs working in a barber shop and as a saloon porter before setting up his own tailoring business. At that time black people were barred from well-paying jobs or obtaining loans. Self-employment was the only route for self-improvement.

Just as the women in the family raised the children, they also made more of their opportunities, as they became available. Jeremiah's daughter and Meghan's great aunt Dora was the first Ragland to go to college and the first to set herself up as a professional, becoming a schoolteacher. Her younger sister Lillie did even better. She studied at the University of California as a mature student before training as a real estate agent and setting up her own business in Los Angeles. She was so successful that she was listed in the African American *Who's Who*.

Their brothers did not climb so high: one worked as a waiter, while Meghan's great-grandfather Steve found employment as a presser in a cleaner's shop in downtown Chattanooga. As Meghan's uncle Joseph admits: "Culturally, our family did not have male figures." Steve married Lois Russell, the daughter of a hotel porter, when she was fourteen or fifteen. In the census of 1930, the couple were recorded as living with their baby son, Alvin Azell, who would become Meghan's grandfather, as well as Lois's father, James Russell, and assorted nieces and roomers.

When Alvin was old enough he made his way to Cleveland, Ohio, in search of work. There he met Jeanette Johnson, the daughter of a bellboy and elevator operator at the five-star St. Regis Hotel. Soon after the end of the Second World War, Johnson had married professional roller skater Joseph Johnson, by whom she had two children, Joseph Junior and Saundra. It was not long before Johnson, who traveled from town to town to show off his skills, skated out of her life, leaving Jeanette to raise their children on her own. Enter the smooth-talking, snappily dressed Alvin Ragland, who soon had Jeanette's heart beating a little faster.

They married and moved into a basement apartment in a three-story building in downtown Cleveland. Their first child, Doria, Meghan's mother, was born in September 1956, and it was soon afterward that Alvin uprooted the family and embarked on that famous cross-country ride to begin a new life in Los Angeles, where their Ragland relations had settled. For a time, he worked for his aunt Lillie in real estate and then opened his own bric-a-brac and antique store in downtown Los Angeles. However, by then his marriage was over, and Jeanette was once again left holding the baby. He married for the second time on May 6, 1983, and his new wife, Ava Burrows, a teacher, gave birth to their only son, Joffrey, a few months later.

By this time, Doria Ragland was all grown up and with a child of her own. Two years earlier she had given birth to her daughter, Rachel Meghan Markle, at 4:46 in the morning of August 4, 1981, in West Park Hospital in Canoga Park in Los Angeles. Meghan's arrival would change the narrative of her family forever.

The blooming of Meghan's family from picking cotton under the blazing sun to seeing one of their own taking her wedding vows to a royal prince under the camera lights is an extraordinary story of upward mobility. And what a sublime contrast it makes with the not so distant past. The last American to marry a member of the British royal family was Wallis Warfield Simpson, who hailed from Baltimore, Maryland. Though she was twice divorced with two husbands living, King Edward VIII insisted on marrying her despite overwhelming opposition from the church, the government, and the empire, who objected to a divorcée becoming royal consort. As a result, he abdicated the throne, marrying Wallis at a modest ceremony in a French chateau in June 1937. Billed as the royal romance of the century, the king gave up everything for the woman he loved.

Fast-forward eighty years. While the Duke and Duchess of Windsor, as Edward and Wallis became, would have been delighted that the House of Windsor had embraced the reality of divorce, they would have been astonished that Prince Harry's bride was to be of mixed race. Wallis's family, the Warfields, had built their various fortunes on the back of slave labor.

For their part they did consider themselves benign and enlightened masters. Wallis's third cousin Edward Warfield, who was elected forty-fifth governor of Maryland in 1903, gave several speeches on the topic of "Slavery as I Knew It." However, Edwin's tolerance only went so far; in the election for governor he stood on a platform of white supremacy, believing that ill-educated blacks should be denied the franchise.

While Wallis was brought up in relative neediness—she and her mother were the poor relations of the wealthy Warfield family— she enjoyed the services of a black nanny, butler, and maids. They were part of her life, albeit as downstairs folk who never crossed a line of familiarity. Indeed, she once observed that the first time she shook the hand of a nonwhite person was when she and her husband, the Duke of Windsor, glad-handed the crowds in Nassau during his time as governor of the Bahamas during World War

Two. People of color simply did not feature in the life of Wallis or her husband except to hold out a tray of drinks. She was from a class, an age, and a region where, quite unself-consciously, Wallis and her friends were nonchalantly racist. In letters and table talk she casually used the N-word and other derogatory terms for people of color. When Wallis was born in 1896, Meghan's great-great-great-grandfather Stephen Ragland was scratching out a meager living as a sharecropper. The very idea that a biracial woman would marry a prince of the realm in the august setting of St. George's Chapel, the scene of numerous royal weddings, including that of King Edward VII and more recently the queen's third son, Prince Edward, would have been unthinkable.

Surprisingly, there are recent precedents. In 2004 the daughter of a prince, Lady Davina Windsor, married sheep shearer, surfer, and father Garry "Gazza" Lewis, a Maori, or New Zealand native, in a private ceremony at Kensington Palace. Now twenty-ninth in line to the throne, Lady Davina and her husband were invited to the wedding of Prince William and Kate Middleton and look set to be present at Harry and Meghan's betrothal. The royal family barely blinked an eyelid at this union between the daughter of the Duke and Duchess of Gloucester and a member of New Zealand's second-largest ethnic grouping. Unsurprisingly, not all members of Britain's aristocracy are quite welcoming of persons of color. When the glamorous food writer Emma McQuiston, the biracial daughter of a Nigerian oil tycoon, married Viscount Weymouth, the heir to the famous Longleat estate, in 2013 his mother's reaction was: "Are you sure about what you are doing to four hundred years of bloodline?"

Ironically, Meghan herself is not such an outsider as some may think, and her European bloodline is way older than four hundred years.

Popular interest in Meghan has inevitably largely rested on her family's history of slavery and how, through hard work and

endeavor, her ancestors made a life for themselves in an unforgiv-
ing world. What is less familiar is that Meghan has, through her
father's family, links to the royal families of Scotland, England,
and beyond. When she wrote, "Being biracial paints a blurréd
line that is equal parts staggering and illuminating," she never
realized for a moment that the blood of kings as well as slaves ran
through her veins.

For starters, it is possible to trace a direct line through twenty-
five generations to Robert I of Scotland, perhaps the most colorful
of all Scottish kings. Better known as Robert the Bruce, he is the
legendary warrior who, as he hid in a cave to avoid capture by the
English enemy, watched a spider trying to spin a web. The spider
repeatedly tried and failed to swing itself up from a long thread,
a sign of Bruce's own failure on the battlefield. He gave the spider
one last chance. If it succeeded in swinging itself up, he would
wage a final battle to liberate his country.

The spider triumphed, and so did Robert the Bruce, defeat-
ing the English at the bloody Battle of Bannockburn in 1314. He
remained king until his death in 1329, and is acknowledged as
one of the most successful and best-loved of all Scottish kings.

This fascinating connection to this distant world of kings
comes through her father's family, whose bloodline tells a story
shared by so many—ancestors whose roots were in the Old World
but who sailed west to seek a better life.

The Markles, who have their origins in Germany and Hol-
land, lived in Pennsylvania for generations working as farmers,
lime burners, carpenters, miners, soldiers, and, in the case of
Meghan's great-grandfather the giant Isaac "Ike" Markle, a fire-
man for the Pennsylvania Railroad company. Ike's son Gordon
Arnold, Meghan's grandfather, started his own filling station business, worked in the shoe industry, and wound up in an administrative position for the post office in the small town of Newport.
In March 1941, just months before the US entered the Second

World War, he married Doris Mary Rita Sanders, who hailed from New Hampshire.

It is the lineage of Meghan's grandmother that can be traced directly to the Scottish royals and more. Through her ancestor Roger Shaw, Meghan's trickle of blue blood was ultimately transported to America. The son of a wine merchant and shipper in the City of London, Shaw sailed from Plymouth in the west of England to Massachusetts around 1637.

Like many other young men, Roger Shaw saw America as the land of promise and opportunity. Thanks to his father's influence, the authorities gave him license "to sell wine, and any sorts of hard liquor, to Christians and Indians, as his judgement deemed, on just and urgent occasions, and not otherwise." In time he became a substantial landowner, a farmer, and an acknowledged pillar of the community.

It was his family, who originated from Yorkshire in the north of England, who are the critical link to royalty. Locally, they were well-respected landowners, and it was the marriage in 1490 of one of the clan, James Shaw, to Christina Bruce, the heiress daughter of Sir David Bruce, 6th Baron of Clackmannan, a direct descendant of Robert the Bruce, that sealed the royal connection.

Going back down the generations, Meghan's grandmother Doris can also boast another interesting connection to royalty, this time through her ancestor Mary Bird, who appeared in the household records for Windsor Castle in 1856 and probably worked as a maid. There is some satisfaction here in that like some latter-day Cinderella, Mary's descendant will marry her own prince.

This, though, is not the only royal bond. Meghan is also descended from the American immigrant Christopher Hussey, who lived on the whaling island of Nantucket off the coast of Massachusetts, as well as the Reverend William Skipper, who landed in New England in 1639. His royal connections and subsequent links to the Markle family ensure that, according to Boston-based

genealogist Gary Boyd Roberts, Meghan is a twenty-fourth generation descendant of the medieval King Edward III. Born at Windsor Castle, he successfully ruled England for fifty years until his
death in 1377.

Furthermore, according to Roberts, Meghan is distantly related
to most European royal families thanks to her English kinswoman
Margaret Kerdeston, who lived during the fifteenth century and
was the paternal grandmother of Anne of Foix-Candale, queen of
Hungary and Bohemia.

As Roberts observed: "Much of American and English history
is reflected in her diverse ancestry."

Of course many Europeans can claim distant links to royalty,
and Meghan has been curious about both sides of her family. During a visit to Malta, she was keen to trace her family roots. Her
ancestor Mary Bird, who worked at Windsor Castle, was married
to a soldier named Thomas. When he was stationed on the Mediterranean island, Mary joined him. Their daughter, also named
Mary, married George David Merrill and eventually emigrated to
New Hampshire in New England. It left another family branch
for Meghan to explore.

Her mixed European and African American heritage has constantly reminded her, especially when she was growing up, about
her difference and distinction. It is a difference she has learned
to embrace and acknowledge.

2

Growing Up Markle

Growing up Markle in the 1950s was like a chapter from *The Adventures of Tom Sawyer*. Young Tom Markle, Meghan's father, and his two older brothers, Mick and Fred, enjoyed an idyllic childhood in the small Pennsylvanian town of Newport, where they lived in a modest clapboard house. (Royal trivia: Newport is just 90 miles north of the birthplace of the last American to marry a royal prince, Bessie Wallis Warfield Simpson.) The boys played on monkey vines in the woods at the end of their dirt road, went fishing for catfish in the Juniata River, and in summer picked blackberries, their mother, Doris, turning their trove into delicious pies and jellies. As a teenager Tom earned his pin money literally, setting the pins in the local bowling alley. Or he would join his father, Gordon, who worked in administration for the post office, watching his beloved Philadelphia Phillies score home runs on their black and white television.

By the time Tom graduated from Newport High School, his brother Mick had joined the United States Air Force, where he worked in telecommunications, though some say he was eventually recruited into the Central Intelligence Agency. Brother Fred headed south, found religion, and eventually ended up becoming the presiding bishop of the Eastern Orthodox Catholic Church in America, located in Sanford, Florida, where he is known as Bishop Dismas.

Tom took a different attitude toward his future. After graduating, he left small-town Newport and drove to the Poconos, a mountainous resort area in northeastern Pennsylvania. There he worked at the local theater, learning the technical backstage side of the business and gaining valuable experience that gave him a step up the professional ladder. He then traveled to Chicago after getting a job as a lighting technician at WTTW, the local affiliate for the Public Broadcasting Service. He also worked at the Harper Theater alongside the new owners, Bruce and Judith Sagan, who wanted to give the Hyde Park district, also the eventual home of Barack Obama, a vibrant new cultural center. He soon became the theater's lighting director, working on the controversial musical *Hair*, dance shows, and classic Russian dramas as well as jazz and chamber music concerts.

Tom worked hard and played hard, spending downtime with his student friends from the prestigious University of Chicago. During one rowdy party at the on-campus International House in 1963, Tom, then nineteen, met eighteen-year-old Roslyn Loveless, a student who worked as a secretary in the nearby Amtrak offices. Both tall—she is five foot nine; he is six foot four—and with similar red hair, the attraction was immediate, Roslyn amused by his quirky sense of humor and "light air." They married the following year. Their only daughter, Yvonne, was born in November 1964 and their son, Tom Junior, two years later, in 1966. In those early years, life was a grind, Tom often working eighteen-hour days and Roslyn holding down a secretarial job herself while bringing up two children. It was a constant juggling act, and Roslyn's mother, Dorothy, helped out when she could.

Despite the daily pressures they still enjoyed a busy social life and had a fun circle of friends, Tom keeping everyone amused with his offbeat brand of humor. Roslyn remembers one time at a Greek restaurant when he pretended to have a parrot called Stanley and passed the imaginary parrot from one person to the next, imploring the waitresses not to stand on him. "It was hilarious," she recalls. When Yvonne and Tom Junior started to lose their milk teeth, he sent them long letters from two tooth fairies, Hector and Ethel, who described their lives and explained what would happen to their teeth. From time to time he'd take the children to work with him. It was a thrill, especially as at that time he was lighting the hugely popular puppet show *Sesame Street*. A trip to Wrigley Field to watch the Chicago Cubs baseball team, driving his dad's car in the parking lot at WTTW, being lifted into the air on the studio lighting gantry, hunting for quarters on a stage filled with foggy dry ice: these were some of the good times Tom Junior treasures.

In his eyes, Tom Senior was the fun dad, the dad who played the best games and made you laugh the hardest—when he was around. Which, sadly, was not often. Childhood expectation was invariably tinged with disappointment. He was consumed by his work, the fruits of his labor coming in local Emmy nominations—and a fat paycheck. The price he paid for such success was his marriage; the constant late nights, the boozy cast parties, and endless distraction and fatigue took their toll. One of Tom Junior's earliest memories is the sound of raised voices, slamming doors, and angry words. At some point in the early 1970s, when the children were still in elementary school, the couple decided to go their separate ways.

For a time, Tom lived in Chicago and had the children on weekends. But it didn't last long. He had a dream, and that dream was Hollywood. Sometime before their divorce in 1975, Tom left his estranged wife and children behind as he started his new life on the West Coast. The children would not see their father again for several years.

At the urging of her brother Richard, who lived in New Mexico, Roslyn and the children traveled to Albuquerque to make a new life. For a while it was a happy time. Uncle Richard was not his father, as far as Tom Junior was concerned, but at least he was around, teaching him to drive his VW Bug in a parking lot and showing him how to shoot. Plus, Richard and Roslyn got on well together. For the first time in their lives the children did not have to live with a rancorous atmosphere at home.

The downside was that as the only redhead at his new school, Tom Junior found himself bullied and picked on by his new classmates. Fellow pupils would steal his lunch money, while others started fights. He used to dread going to school, often coming home with yet another black eye. Worse was to come. One night he went to see the movie *Smokey and the Bandit* with his mother and her new boyfriend, a martial arts expert called Patrick. They arrived back home to find a full-scale robbery in progress. When Patrick tackled the thieves, he was shot in the stomach and the mouth, the bullets whistling past Tom Junior. Although Patrick survived, Tom Junior was traumatized.

Between bullying and burglary Tom Junior decided to leave Albuquerque and go live with his father, who was now enjoying life at the beachfront town of Santa Monica in Southern California. He arrived in time to enroll in high school.

Though he still idolized his father, there was one big fat fly in the ointment of his new life: his sister, Yvonne. She had moved there a few years earlier when she was fourteen. They had always fought like cats and dogs. "The sibling rivals from hell," their despairing mother called them.

When the trio moved from Santa Monica to a large home on

Providencia Street adjacent to the Woodland Hills Country Club, Tom Junior snagged the downstairs den as his bedroom. He was especially thrilled when a friend sold him a king-sized waterbed. His excitement turned to dismay when he sat on it shortly after taking delivery only to be soaked in water. Inspecting the evidence, he discovered several holes in the brand-new bed. For Tom, there was only one suspect. He recalls that his sister Yvonne immediately admitted responsibility but argued that it was retribution as she had wanted that room for herself—another episode in a bitter, resentful dance between the siblings. As her brother now recalls, "If she didn't get what she wanted out of you, she was your worst nightmare."

Enter into this bickering dynamic the figure of Doria Ragland. Small and watchful, with liquid brown eyes and a jaunty Afro, this was the woman who had turned their father Tom into gooey mush. Before he ever brought her home, the children noticed a change in their father. He was more relaxed, frequently taking time off work, cheery and lighthearted. In short, he was happy. The couple had met on the set of ABC's drama *General Hospital*, where she was training as a makeup artist and he was well established as the show's lighting director. In spite of the twelve-year age difference—Doria was closer in age to Yvonne than to her boyfriend—the couple very quickly fell for each other.

Doria's education at Fairfax High School had been badly affected by the 1971 San Fernando earthquake. The quake had destroyed nearby Los Angeles High School, so the two schools doubled up, Doria studying from seven in the morning until noon and then pupils from LAHS taking over their classroom for the afternoon. In spite of the difficulties she was a member of the Apex Club, a class for academically advanced youngsters. After graduating from Fairfax, Doria sold jewelry, helped in Alvin's antique store, called 'Twas New, and tended a bric-a-brac stall at a Sunday flea market. She also worked as a travel agent. It was a way of obtaining cut-rate air tickets so she could see the world on the cheap.

Not that Tom Junior took much notice of the new addition to the Providencia Street household. What with his skateboarding and go-karting and working for a florist, Tom Junior barely missed a beat when Doria moved in. He was too busy enjoying himself with his new circle of friends.

As for Yvonne, it appears to have been indifference, if not dislike, at first sight. Eager that Thomas use his showbiz connections to get her work as a model or an actor, she doubtless resented the fact that the new arrival was taking her father's focus away from her. During her time in Albuquerque with her mother, she had modeled jewelry and wedding gowns. Now the teenager was seeing dollar bills in the Hollywood sign. When her friends came over to the house she dismissed the presence of her father's African American girlfriend, referring to her, according to her brother, as "the maid." Her best friend, now a successful Realtor, doesn't recall Yvonne using that language, and even if she did she ascribes it to her sour Chicago sense of humor. Nonetheless, Yvonne was not, as her mother recalls, a particularly tolerant young woman.

Doria's arrival also coincided with Yvonne exploring the dark tenets of black magic, according to Tom. Even as a little girl Yvonne had had a fascination with the macabre, once bringing a moldering gravestone that she had found in the basement of their apartment block in Chicago into her bedroom. This time around, as her brother Tom recalls, she bought a copy of Anton LaVey's *Satanic Bible*, installed an altar in her bedroom, played with a Ouija board, burned black candles, and dressed in the all-black uniform of the goth. It may have been no more than a rebellious teenage obsession, and her brother never witnessed her performing any satanic rituals, but he was still disturbed by her "weird" behavior. She left the house when it was dark and rarely returned before dawn. One of Yvonne's friends recalls those years, saying that she and Yvonne would dress up and go out dancing, especially if a British band was in town. "We put on our makeup and got all decked out," she recalls. "We were out having fun." The ritual of boy meets girl, rather than anything satanic, was their aim.

Much of the back and forth between brother and sister was certainly more taunting and teasing than witchcraft. On one occasion, according to Tom Junior, she came to the flower shop where Tom Junior worked part time to borrow money from her brother. While he and his colleague Richard, a Christian Scientist, were dealing with customers she picked up Richard's Bible and drew a pentagram, the sign of the devil, on one page with her red lipstick. Before leaving she wrote "666," the mark of the beast, on another page. Young Tom had his revenge when he called the house, telling his sister that Richard was so traumatized by what she had done that he had run into the road and was hit by a bus. His ruse had her racing back to the flower store to check on Richard's condition.

Certainly Doria could be forgiven for wondering what she had got herself into when faced with this bickering, back-biting brood. It was one thing falling in love with a man twelve years her senior; it was quite another being thrown headlong into his fractious family with brother and sister continually squabbling. A strong personality with a level head on her shoulders, Doria brought a sense of family to the gloomy house.

When she arrived, everyone was used to going their own way. Tom Senior worked every hour of the day and night, Yvonne was out clubbing with her friends while Tom Junior was smoking weed with his own crowd. She brought them together as a family, Doria seen as "the cool hippie peacemaker "who liked a joint herself." She soon became friendly with their near neighbor Olga McDaniel, a former nightclub singer, Doria spending hours with her shooting the breeze and smoking a joint. "The best way I can describe

Doria is that she was like a warm hug," observed Olga's daughter. Her masterstroke was to take Tom Junior to the animal shelter and help him pick out a family dog, which he named Bo. The noisy new arrival, a golden retriever–beagle mix, soon ruled their five-bedroom home in the leafy valley suburb of Woodland Hills.

At Thanksgiving Doria invited the Markles to join the Ragland clan, including her mother, Jeanette; her father, Alvin; her half brother, Joseph; and half sister, Saundra, for a true Southern feast of sweet potato pie, gumbo, ham hocks, and beans. "Good times," recalls Tom Junior. "When I first met them, I was uneasy and nervous, but they were really warm and inclusive, the kind of family I had always wanted. They were happy assed people with a real sense of family."

That sense of family was formalized when, on December 23, 1979, Doria and Tom Senior were married at the Self-Realization Fellowship temple on Sunset Boulevard, just east of Hollywood. The venue was Doria's choice, the new bride adhering to the teachings of Yogananda, a Hindu yoga guru who arrived in Boston in 1920 and preached a philosophy of breathing and meditation as part of the yoga routine to help followers on their path to enlightenment. Hollywood stars Linda Evans and Mariel Hemingway, Apple founder Steve Jobs, and ex-Beatle George Harrison all followed his teachings. Even in such an enlightened setting, mixed marriages were still uncommon.

Less than half a century before Tom and Doria's wedding, California had repealed anti-miscegenation laws that banned marriages between black and white people. However, it was not until 1967 for anti-miscegenation laws to be declared unconstitutional throughout the nation by the United States Supreme Court, with their landmark decision in *Loving v. Virginia*.

In 1958, Richard and Mildred Loving, a white man and black woman, were married in Washington, DC. When they returned to their home in Virginia they were arrested in their bedroom under the state's Racial Integrity Act. Judge Leon Bazile suspended their sentence on the condition that the Lovings leave Virginia and not return for twenty-five years. They appealed the judgment, but Judge Bazile refused to reconsider his decision, writing, "Almighty God created the races white, black, yellow, Malay, and red, and placed them on separate continents, and but for the interference with his arrangement there would be no cause for such marriages. The fact that he separated the races shows that he did not intend the races to mix."

The Lovings, supported by the NAACP Legal Defense Fund, the Japanese American Citizens League, and a coalition of Catholic bishops, then successfully appealed to the US Supreme Court, which wrote in their decision, "Marriage is one of the 'basic civil rights of man,' fundamental to our very existence and survival... Under our Constitution, the freedom to marry, or not to marry, a person of another race resides with the individual and cannot be infringed by the State," condemning Virginia's anti-miscegenation law as "designed to maintain White supremacy." While this judgment decriminalized miscegenation, mixed race couples were still looked upon with suspicion by many, confronted by casual racism and sometimes outright hostility. Racism remains a pungent fact of daily life for many African Americans.

On their big day, Tom Senior, wearing a sportscoat and button-down shirt, and Doria, in a flowing white dress with baby's breath flowers in her hair, took their wedding vows in the presence of Brother Bhaktananda. He stressed the merging of the couple was for the "highest common good" and to achieve union with God. The children of followers of Self-Realization have a reputation as being open, inquisitive souls. So, when Doria found herself pregnant just a year after tying the knot, she and Tom couldn't wait for the new arrival. Further good news came when the news of Doria's pregnancy coincided with Tom's first nomination for a Daytime Emmy Award for his design and lighting work on *General*

Hospital; he would later be nominated for eight more—not bad for a man who was officially colorblind. If 1980 had been a good year, 1981 was going to be even better.

As the months ticked by and the summer thermometer inched upward, Doria became impatient for the waiting to be over. With the daytime temperatures often in the high nineties, she was grateful that they had an evaporative cooler and that the rambling home was dark and shady. In his spare time, Tom Senior decorated the nursery, painting the walls and hanging Disney characters and angel pictures around the white-painted crib. Finally, at 4:46 in the morning of August 4, 1981, at West Park Hospital in Canoga Park, obstetrician Malverse Martin announced that Doria and Tom were now the parents of a healthy baby girl. This latest addition to the sorority of Valley Girls was, as her mother noted, a Leo. Typical Leos are supposed to be "Warm, action-oriented and driven by the desire to be loved and admired. They have an air of royalty about them. They love to be in the limelight, which is why many of them make a career in the performing arts." Never has an astrological star sign been more accurate.

The arrival of Rachel Meghan Markle transformed her father's life. "He was just so, so happy," recalls Tom Junior. "He spent every single minute he could with her. My dad was more in love with her than anyone else in the world, and that included Doria. She became his whole life, his little princess. He was just blown away by Meghan." Her seventeen-year-old sister Yvonne was more interested in clubbing and makeup than playing with a newborn. "'Babies, yuck, no thanks,' that was our feeling," recalls one of Yvonne's friends. She was a teenager having fun, and fun was certainly not babysitting for the new arrival. Not only did Yvonne often seem indifferent to the baby now nicknamed "Flower" or "Bud," she had to have felt left out on the sidelines, her father utterly devoted to baby Rachel. Doubtless she recalled his frequent absences when she was growing up and felt somewhat jealous of the attention now focused on her baby half sister.

It became an understandable source of fiction that her father did not spend as much time as she would have liked in using his contacts to fix her up with acting or modeling jobs. That said, sometime down the road he did get her a walk-on part on *General Hospital* and an episode in the drama *Matlock*, in which she was killed off before the first commercial break. It seems that she never fully exploited these opportunities.

Not only did Tom spend every waking minute with his daughter, in his own quirky fashion he tried to impose a little discipline on the somewhat laissez-faire household in order to protect his little "Flower." Though he had always said to his son that if he and his friends wanted to smoke weed they should do so only in the house, this instruction changed with the arrival of the baby. On one occasion Tom Junior and his friends were smoking a spliff in the sitting room while Meghan was in the nursery crying. His father announced loudly that he was going upstairs to change her diaper. Shortly afterward he appeared in the sitting room carrying a full diaper. He joined the boys on the sofa, took a spoon out of his pocket and started eating the contents of the diaper. Grossed out, the boys fled the house. Only later did he reveal that he had earlier spooned chocolate pudding into a fresh diaper. It was his way of stopping the boys from smoking weed when Meghan was around.

But that was about as far as discipline went. Their house was still generally party central, Doria's friends coming over, smoking weed, playing music, practicing yoga—which Doria now taught— and barbecuing. From the outside it seemed to be one big happy family, Doria's relations, especially her mother, Jeanette, babysitting for the recently wed couple. Even Tom Junior pitched in to give Tom and Doria a break. For the most part Tom and Doria seemed happy, but then their bickering started. As much as Tom loved Meghan, he loved his job, too; he was still a workaholic and thought nothing of spending eighty or ninety hours a week on set. And in his eyes, it was paying off, Meghan proving to be his lucky charm. After two nominations, in 1982 he and his colleagues on *General Hospital* finally won a Daytime Emmy for "outstanding achievement in design excellence."

But it all came at a price. Doria had not signed up for this, dealing with his children, raising her own, kick-starting a career, and trying to run the family's cavernous house. Though it was not Tom's fault, they were living in a predominantly white neighborhood where, because of her dark skin and Meghan's light skin, people thought Doria was the nanny. They often stopped her and asked, quite innocently, where the baby's mother lived. It was a petty humiliation that she could do without.

It seemed, too, that Tom was wedded to work more than he was wedded to her. It was a feeling that had been shared by his first wife, Roslyn. Gradually, the harsh words and the fighting became the norm rather than the exception, Tom Junior and Yvonne recognizing the all too familiar sounds of a relationship breaking down. According to family friends, Tom's constant criticism of Doria over matters small and large wore her down. There came a point where Doria decided that enough was enough and went back home to her mother, Jeanette. As a family friend observed: "Doria is not a doormat, that much I know. She spoke up for herself, protected herself and her daughter fiercely. Her head was on straight. I trusted her judgment."

The couple split up when their little "Flower" was just two years old, but did not divorce for another five years. He would have custody of his daughter on weekends and drop her off on Sunday evenings. Then, as Meghan told writer Sam Kashner, the trio would sit and eat dinner off their knees as they watched *Jeopardy!* "We were so close-knit," she recalls, a memory perhaps seen through the forgiving prism of a child desperate for her parents to be united rather than accepting the bleak reality of a mother and father at odds. Others were not so sanguine, pointing to Tom's bewilderment, not to say bitterness, that Doria had given their union so little time to prove itself. By the time Meghan was old enough to appreciate *Jeopardy!* they were divorced and living separate lives.

Founded in 1945 by Ruth Pease, Little Red School House is a Hollywood institution favored for the sons and daughters of LA's showbiz elite. While parents rarely saw Johnny Depp, whose daughter attended the school, waiting outside the school gates, Flea, bassist for the Red Hot Chili Peppers, used to pick up his daughter after school in a spray-painted Mercedes-Benz. Teaching—based around the four-stage program of Swiss psychologist Jean Piaget—is eclectic, imaginative, and expensive: $18,800 for kindergarten, rising to $22,700 for grade 6. As the school chooses only the brightest and the best, older children have to take an exam before they are considered for entry. In 1983 Doria, who was now training as a social worker, and Tom enrolled two-year-old Meghan for preschool at the exclusive school.

The setup was convenient for all involved. Little Red School House was close to the ABC studios in Los Feliz, where Tom worked, and just a few minutes away from Doria's work and her new home just south of Hollywood. Meghan would stay at the school until she was eleven years old. While reading, writing, and arithmetic were at the core of the school day, children could dip into a whole range of subjects, from Spanish to quantum physics. In summer, children worked in the community garden and hiked the nature trails at Leo Carrillo Beach or nearby Griffith Park.

The school's stage shows, watched by proud parents, were another regular feature of the curriculum. When she was five,

Meghan entertained the parents with a rendition of the song "The Wheels on the Bus," and she was later featured in *Bye Bye Birdie* and *West Side Story*. One Halloween Meghan and her friend Ninaki "Nikki" Priddy played two corpses discussing the size and comfort of their respective coffins. Another time she shared the lead in an adaptation of *How the Grinch Stole Christmas*. Unfortunately, her costar, Elizabeth McCoy, came down with stomach flu just hours before the show began, leaving Meghan desperately trying to memorize both parts. "That was the worst experience of my life, trying to learn your lines," Meghan told an apologetic McCoy afterward. Ironically, no one gave a thought to asking a little girl with an unkempt mane of blond hair, thick glasses, and an awkward, clumsy manner who was lurking in the chorus. Her name was Scarlett Johansson, now one of the world's highest-paid actors.

McCoy, who these days is a renowned chef and scriptwriter, had another reason to thank Meghan. Two years Meghan's junior, Elizabeth was a self-confessed weird kid. Intense, fiercely intelligent, and overweight, she was interested in offbeat subjects like UFOs, the occult, and ghosts. Other children thought her odd. Nor did it help that she suffered from petit mal seizures, a form of epilepsy that saw her going into a trancelike state from time to time that made her unreachable. As the seizures last for only a short time, children who have them are often thought to be daydreaming or not listening.

Meghan, Elizabeth was to discover, was not like many of the other kids, who either walked on by or mocked her. The first time Meghan saw Elizabeth suffering from a seizure she came to her aid, sitting holding her hand and comforting her. Elizabeth also remembers how she provided friendship when she was being taunted by the "mean girls," as she describes them. She recalls: "I was bullied and miserable and my only salvation were the kids who liked me. I really liked Meghan a lot. She didn't turn me away if I started talking about offbeat subjects. She listened. She was cool and had cool things to say. I liked being around her."

It was clear that Meghan had inherited her mother's strong sense of right and wrong, and was prepared to stand up for herself and for others. On one occasion the so-called mean girls announced that they were starting a "White Girls Only" club and wanted Meghan to join. "Are you kidding me?' said Meghan to the gaggle of fellow pupils, dismissing them in a sentence. They went very quiet after that. That playground confrontation highlighted Meghan's own concerns about her identity. She tells the story of how, around this same time, Christmas 1988, her father bought two sets of Heart dolls containing the traditional nuclear family unit of mother, father, and two children. He bought one with black dolls and one with white and mixed them together to represent Meghan's own family. Then he wrapped them in sparkly Christmas paper and placed the box under the tree.

Her struggle to understand herself and where she was placed in the scheme of humanity instinctively made her more aware of those who had difficulties fitting in.

As Elizabeth McCoy recalls: "You never forget the people who were mean to you and who was nice. That's why I have never forgotten Meghan. She was one of the most righteous people I have ever met. If someone was being treated unfairly she stuck up for them. On one occasion I made the girl who bullied me cry. I tried to apologize, and Meghan sided with the other girl because she was the one in tears.

"Meghan called it like it was. She was going to defend those who needed it. Her attitude was: 'I can see you are hurt and I'm going to protect you.' She was a genuinely decent human being who looked out for people who needed help. She gave a damn about people other than herself."

Even Elizabeth's father, Dennys McCoy, an internationally known animation scriptwriter, singles out Meghan. He recalls:

"She stood out because she was a level-headed kid who was smart and mature for her age. We were surprised that she became an actress. We thought she would be a lawyer."

By the time she was ten, Meghan was fiercely switched on and loved to debate an issue, taking part in discussions about racism in America, most notably after the notorious beating of Rodney King, an unarmed black man, by LA cops in 1991, the Gulf War that same year, and the buildup to the 1992 presidential contest between Bill Clinton and George H. W. Bush. During one classroom discussion about the looming war in the Gulf, a fellow pupil was in tears because he didn't think his older brother, who was serving in the US military, would make it home. The issue became such a hot topic that the children, led by Meghan, staged a protest on the school grounds. They made banners and signs with antiwar slogans. Such was the interest that local TV station KTLA sent along a camera crew to film the protest.

Even nearer to home were the LA riots in late April and early May of 1992, which ignited after four Los Angeles Police Department officers, who were filmed savagely beating Rodney King, were acquitted of assault and using excessive force. As the burning and looting spread like fingers along LA's thoroughfares, Meghan and her classmates were sent home. Meghan watched with wonder as ash from burning buildings floated onto her lawn. She thought it was snowing, but her mother knew better and told her to get into the house. Even when they returned to school there was a brooding sense of anxiety; the children, including Meghan, crowded around a second-floor school window as they watched police arresting a man acting suspiciously. In total the six days of rioting left sixty-three dead and more than 2,300 injured, and led to more than 12,000 arrests.

The experience awakened the nascent activist in her, and Meghan determined to use her influence when she could. She gained something of a reputation for writing to companies, especially food giants, about damaged or faulty packages and foods. Invariably she was sent bags of chips, cookies, and the like by the food companies as compensation and regularly brought the fruits of her letter writing to share among her school friends.

Her most memorable coup was when, at age eleven, she wrote a letter to the household products company Procter & Gamble for making a sexist commercial that used the tag line "Women all over America are fighting greasy pots and pans" to sell dishwashing liquid. She and the rest of her classmates were watching the commercials as part of a social studies assignment. However, it was the reaction by two boys in her class to the dishwashing liquid ad that particularly incensed them. She recalls them saying, "Yeah, that's where women belong—in the kitchen." Meghan felt confused. She was angry and annoyed, knowing that they were wrong, but she also felt, as she later recalled, "small, too small to say anything in that moment," as she wrote later about the incident.

She went home and told her father, Tom, who suggested that she channel her feelings into handwritten letters of complaint. Not only did she write to the soap company chairman saying that the phrase should be changed to "People all over America," but also to Hillary Clinton, then the First Lady; *Nick News* anchor Linda Ellerbee; and prominent women's rights lawyer Gloria Allred, who was based in Los Angeles.

While Hillary Clinton and Linda Ellerbee wrote letters of encouragement, and Gloria Allred also offered her support, according to Meghan, she never heard from Procter & Gamble. However, when the ad aired again just a month later, she saw the fruits of her handiwork. It had been changed to say: "People all over America are fighting greasy pots and pans." Her success once again had the TV cameras arriving at the school, this time with Ellerbee interviewing Meghan and her fellow pupils about her one-schoolgirl campaign.

"I don't think it's right for kids to grow up thinking these things, that just mom does everything," Meghan told Ellerbee. "It's always, 'mom does this,' and 'mom does that.'" Sometime afterward, this and other incidents inspired her to join the Washington-based National Organization for Women. Meghan, as she proudly recalled, became one of the youngest if not the youngest member of the group, founded in 1966, which campaigns for women's rights.

More than twenty years later, in 2015, Meghan reflected on this chapter of her life while giving a speech as the newly minted UN Women Advocate for Political Participation and Leadership. "It was at that moment that I realized the magnitude of my actions. At the age of eleven, I had created my small level of impact by standing up for equality," she said at the time. While her childhood experiences were the crucible that set her on the path to activism, her mother believes that she was hardwired from birth to try to make the world a better and more equal place. In short, she had a moral compass. Doria played her own part, strict at home but also ready to show her daughter that there was more to the world than Woodland Hills. She raised her to be what she called "a global citizen," taking her to places like Oaxaca, Mexico, where Meghan recalls seeing children playing in the dirt roads and peddling Chiclets so that they could bring home a few extra pesos. When Meghan, then age ten, and her mother visited the slums of Jamaica, the schoolgirl was horrified to see such grinding poverty. "Don't look scared, Flower," her mother told her. "Be aware, but don't be afraid."

Her experience is reminiscent of the times the late Diana, Princess of Wales, privately took her boys, William and Harry, to visit the homeless and the sick in central London so that they would hopefully appreciate that life did not begin and end at the palace gates.

Meghan's letter-writing campaigns, interest in current affairs, purposeful traveling, and gender awareness were all of a piece with a young girl embarking on a journey where feminism could coexist with femininity, as well as an ethos of hard work matched by a willingness to try the new and the interesting.

By sublime irony, just as her letter-writing campaign got underway, another letter-writing campaign was kicking off, this one regarding the raunchy comedy show *Married...with Children*, for which her father was now the lighting director. Meghan often sat on the floor of the studio after school waiting for her father to finish work so he could take her home. Indeed, she thrilled her fellow classmates when she was given permission to bring several friends on set to meet the cast.

As she sat quietly reading or studying, all kinds of ribald scenes were played out, some involving various stages of undress and semi-nudity, as well as off-color jokes about sex—hardly the normal afterschool fare for a young girl. In January 1989, a Mormon from Michigan, Terry Rakolta, led a boycott of the show after the screening of an episode entitled "Her Cups Runneth Over," which involved the purchase of a bra. That episode showed the character of Al Bundy ogling a naked model in a department store.

The resulting media storm led to some sponsors withdrawing advertising and the conservative Parents Television Council describing the show as "the crudest comedy on prime time television... peppered with lewd punch lines about sex, masturbation, the gay lifestyle and the lead character's fondness for pornographic magazines and strip clubs."

Meghan later described her own misgivings about spending time around the long-running comedy when she appeared on Craig Ferguson's late night show. She told the host: "It's a very perverse place for a girl to grow up. I went to Catholic school. I'm there in my school uniform and the guests would be [former porn star] Traci Lords." While she wasn't allowed to watch the show when it aired, her mother would let her kiss the screen as her dad's name went by in the credits at the end of the program.

Perverse it may have been, but it paid the bills—and Meghan's private school fees. At this time, unbeknownst to her, her father enjoyed a slice of luck that meant he no longer had to work such a brutal schedule. In 1990 he won the California State Lottery, scooping $750,000 with five numbers, which included Meghan's birthdate. The win was ample payback for the thousands he had spent over the years buying lottery tickets.

As he still had outstanding financial matters concerning his divorce from Doria, he kept the win secret. In order to avoid registering his name with the lottery authorities, he sent an old Chicago friend to pick up his winnings. The plan, according to his son, backfired when his pal ended up swindling him out of the lion's share of his fortune in a failed jewelry business.

Before he lost his loot, Tom gave his son a substantial handout to start a flower shop and bought daughter Yvonne a second car after she wrecked the first one he had given her.

Within three years of his big win Tom had declared bankruptcy, the lottery win proving more of a curse than a blessing. At least he had kept some money aside to pay for the next stage of Meghan's education. His daughter enrolled as a freshman at Immaculate Heart, a private all-girls Catholic school just yards from his home in Los Feliz. From then on it made sense for her to live with her father during the week. It was a decision that would have far-reaching implications for the way she was seen by her new teachers and classmates.

3

A Street Called Gladys

Sixth Street in Downtown Los Angeles is not a place for the unwary, and after dark even the wary give it a wide berth. Danger lurks in the shadows; desperation loiters on the sidewalk. This is the heart of Skid Row, the mushrooming and endlessly shifting encampment of the homeless and the helpless that is a makeshift home to more than two thousand people. Los Angeles is the homeless capital of America. At the last count there were more than 57,000 men, women, and children sleeping rough in the City of Angels. Tent towns frequently spring up around the city underpasses, in empty buildings, and in other open spaces.

This particular stretch is more organized than most of the impromptu enclaves of Skid Row, with volunteers handing out water, clean socks, and food. And there is one place in particular, at the corner of Sixth and Gladys, that offers a welcome oasis of calm and tranquility amid the shouts, moans, and shrieks of those who live in the tents and cardboard sheds that line both sides of the road.

This is the Hospitality Kitchen, more popularly known as the Hippie Kitchen, which is part of the Catholic Worker community founded more than eighty years ago by Dorothy Day and Peter Maurin. Their stated goal is to "feed the hungry, shelter the homeless, care for the sick, clothe the naked, visit the prisoner." In an average day volunteers will hand out a nourishing but simple meal to around one thousand folk who line up around the block; for many it is their only food for the day. There is no prayer or proselytizing, just beans, salad, a hunk of bread, and a thick slice of goodwill.

Their uncompromising ideals have, at times, placed them in head-on conflict with the Catholic hierarchy, local police, and even other homeless charities. Catholic Worker activists are known to protest unfair treatment of the homeless, American militarism and nuclear policy, as well as the death penalty. Acts of civil disobedience have led some to suffer arrest and even jail. Former nun Catherine Morris, now eighty-three, and a stalwart of the Hippie Kitchen for more than forty years, has lost count of the number of times she and her husband, Jeff Dietrich, have been arrested for peaceful acts of civil disobedience. They like to think of themselves as the "Merry Pranksters," the name derived from the early hippie followers of counterculture author and poet Ken Kesey.

Though protest is an integral part of the Catholic Worker credo, feeding the homeless and the destitute takes priority. And it was in the garden of the Hippie Kitchen—a small outdoor haven that's filled with colorful murals, the chirping of Brazilian finches in an aviary, and water bubbling over a fountain—that Meghan Markle had what could only be described as an epiphany.

She first visited the Hippie Kitchen when she was just thirteen and found the experience "very scary." By the time Meghan enlisted as a volunteer in the early 1990s, the composition of the homeless neighborhood had drastically changed, from mainly old, white male drunks to a new, younger and more volatile community of those high on crack cocaine and other deadly drugs. "I was young, and it was rough and raw down there and, though

I was with a great volunteer group, I just felt overwhelmed," she later recalled.

She may well have chalked the visit up to experience and never ventured there again but for a classroom conversation with her Immaculate Heart High School theology teacher Maria Pollia some three years later. During class Maria, who had been a volunteer at the Hippie Kitchen for years, described her own early experience and how she faced up to her fears and doubts.

"It's one of the worst corners of Skid Row," she says. "One of the most distressed and distressing. It is heartbreaking. Driving through at night it looked like something Charles Dickens would be writing about. People huddled around blazing oil drums. It was very, very frightening. An awakening for me." Her message to the class, though, was to put your fears aside and make contact with the homeless on a human level. They are people, too, people with names, people with a past and hopefully a future.

"Life is about putting the needs of others above your own fears," she counseled. It was a message that resonated with sixteen-year-old Meghan. "That has always stayed with me," she later recalled.

After class, Meghan spoke with her teacher, who advised on the practicalities of volunteering at the Hippie Kitchen. Heartened, Meghan began to go regularly, working as a server and clearing tables, which put her directly in contact with the Hippie Kitchen's guests. Maria Pollia recalls: "What she learned was what I learned—that it is the human contact people crave. It's someone saying hello and knowing your name." Meghan earnestly absorbed all the advice and began to come back with stories from the people she had met and connected with.

"It was remarkable that once in the situation she got right in it. She wasn't just handing out stew and letting everyone go by, but she was connecting with people, she was learning their names and listening to their stories." And, as Catherine Morris observes, everyone on Skid Row has a story. It might be a hard luck story, a never catching a break story, or a wrong turn story; they would all be eye opening for Meghan, offering a new perspective on what kind of life you could be dealt. The homeless are human beings, not mere statistics.

Megan's experience was echoed by others such as schoolgirl volunteer Sophie Goldstein, who described how she, too, confronted her fears and concerns. "When I first came here, I have to admit, I was kind of nervous." she wrote on the Catholic Worker blog. "I saw the area and I was scared. Then I met the people. What the Workers told me was that a lot of the time these were people who couldn't meet up with their bills, and now they're stuck, or that they have drug problems. I got to put a face on my own prejudice.

"I realized that these are real people. They are not just crazy homeless that you hear about all the time, or that my friends talk about, or the flippant remarks that people make about the homeless." For Meghan it was a life-affirming and life-changing experience.

Up to that point, Meghan's only other experience of work was at Humphrey Yogart, a frozen yogurt shop where she worked when she was thirteen, serving customers and taking out the trash for $4 an hour, employed under a California law that permitted youngsters enrolled in school to work ten to twelve hours a week. Owner Paula Sheftel recalls that Meghan was a hard worker and popular with the customers, "who had to prove she had an outgoing personality and would work well with staff."

"A lot of the kids can't handle the pressure. It takes a special personality for somebody that young to deal with it. Meghan had that early on." Meghan had ample opportunity to practice her people skills at the often fast-paced fro-yo shop, but she also gained another valuable lesson that would later serve her well. One afternoon Meghan saw Yasmine Bleeth, one of the stars of *Baywatch* and a particular idol of hers. Finishing up with the trash bin, Meghan approached the star and blurted out, "I really like you in that Soft N Dri commercial." Bleeth smiled, asked Meghan her name, and shook her hand. Later Meghan would say, "That moment with Yasmine is exactly what I base every interaction with fans on."

A yogurt shop in Beverly Hills was a far cry from the Hippie Kitchen at Sixth and Gladys, which, like her travels with her mother to Mexico and Jamaica, honed her awareness. As she later observed: "Yes, make sure you are safe and never ever put yourself in a compromising situation, but once that is checked off the list, I think it's really important for us to remember that someone needs us, and that your act of giving/helping/doing can truly become an act of grace once you get out of your head."

If this was a practical application of her spiritual journey, her encounter with the work of Catholic theologian Thomas Merton emphasized her intellectual curiosity and emotional maturity. In a world of black and white, Merton's mercurial thinking, with its endless shape-shifting vista of gray, of muted maybes and possibilities, is hard to pin down.

The offspring of two artists, Thomas Merton is arguably the most influential American Catholic author of the twentieth century. His autobiography, *The Seven Storey Mountain*, sold more than a million copies. He wrote more than sixty other books and hundreds of poems and articles on topics ranging from monastic spirituality to civil rights, nonviolence, and the nuclear arms race. Merton lived a raucous and challenging life, fathering a child while studying at Clare College, Cambridge, in the UK, and joining the Communist Party before finally confirming to the Catholic church in 1939 when he was in his mid-twenties. In 1941, he joined the Abbey of Gethsemani in Kentucky, where he gained a reputation as a monk who was a spiritual seeker, not a settler, a man who did not recognize absolute truth but saw the grand ambivalence, the contradictions and duality of existence. In later life he explored the similarities between Buddhist and Christian monks.

For the average American sixteen-year-old weaned on an academic diet of short sentences and multiple-choice questions, Merton is a complex and demanding character.

In her 1997 theology class, titled Experiencing God, Meghan examined the teachings of Father Thomas Merton and other mystics. Her teacher, Maria Pollia, recalls that Meghan was not daunted by the intellectual challenges posed by Merton's work, embracing concepts that demand considerable maturity and considered reflection. For the first time in their school career, students were thrown into a subject without obvious answers, the course requiring more than an ability to memorize pages of a set text. Pollia recalls: "As we become more mature in the adult life, we understand that there are many inconsistencies, many dichotomies, and that life is a continuing encounter with mystery.

"For a young person to feel comfortable with that conversation is very unusual. They get there in the end, but rather than fear these concepts and backing away, Meghan was already interested in pushing deeper and deeper into these questions. She was remarkable. Someone said, would you have remembered her irrespective of Prince Harry? Absolutely. She is one of the top five outstanding students in my career, and I promise you I am not just saying that."

During this philosophy course Meghan and her classmates were faced with a real-life paradox: How could a young mother, a glamorous humanitarian in the prime of life, die in the cruel banality of a car accident. She and her friends watched the funeral of Diana, Princess of Wales, in early September 1997, tears coursing down their cheeks at the poignant moment when the cameras zoomed in on the royal coffin. Perched among the white flowers was an envelope with one word, "Mummy," containing Prince

Harry's last note to his beloved mother. Meghan was not the only one to ask how this tragedy could befall a living icon; dozens of conspiracy theories sprang up on the internet and elsewhere as millions tried to make sense of the senseless.

Nor was she the only one to feel Diana's loss in a keenly personal way. After she heard about the tragedy, she and her friend Suzy Ardakani had sat and watched old videos of the 1981 wedding between Prince Charles and Lady Diana Spencer. According to family friends, she was intrigued by Diana not just for her style but for her independent humanitarian mission, seeing her as a role model. Inspired by the princess, she and her friend Suzy collected clothes and toys for less privileged children. In fact, such was her interest in the princess that Suzy's mother Sonia even gave her a copy of my biography, *Diana, Her True Story*, which remained on her bookshelves for the next few years. As her childhood friend Ninaki Priddy observed: "She was always fascinated by the Royal family. She wants to be Princess Diana 2.0."

Diana's death was a painful reminder for the Ardakani family, who had just two years previously also experienced the life-changing force of a random act of fate. One afternoon in 1995, Matt Ardakani, Suzy's father, was working at his downtown car body shop when a deranged Vietnam veteran who had murdered his family came into the garage and started shooting at random. Mr. Ardakani was hit in the spine and lung and rushed to hospital. When Suzy was told about the shooting, it was Meghan who was the first to console the sobbing teenager and the one who accompanied her to the hospital, where they kept vigil for hours.

Suzy's mother, Sonia Ardakani, recalls: "She and Suzy sat beside Matt's bedside for many hours, praying he would pull through. We feel sure those prayers helped him survive." Though permanently paralyzed by a random act of madness, Matt did survive and is still working.

Meghan's instinctive empathy with others and her interest in giving back—a central tenet of Immaculate Heart's mission—as well as her evident maturity, thoughtfulness, and positive attitude made her the clear first choice to be a group leader at a Kairos retreat in the fall of 1998. Like hundreds of Catholic schools across America, Immaculate Heart regularly organized Kairos (Greek for critical moment) retreats for students, which were designed to help teenagers contemplate the place of God in their lives.

During the four-day retreat, which was held at the Holy Spirit Center at Encino, six girls were chosen to lead groups of eight in various discussions to encourage participation and debate. As a leader, the most daunting assignment was to make a thirty-minute presentation dealing with a challenging list of issues including self-image, trust, core values, and finding yourself.

Christine Knudsen, who has been organizing the Kairos retreat at Immaculate Heart for twenty-three years, described the qualities she watches for in the girls chosen as leaders. "You are looking for a girl who's been through something and who has a certain amount of depth to her. The kinds of insights and comments Meghan made gave her a depth because she had had to struggle with her own issues."

It was clear that her dysfunctional family background and the separation and subsequent divorce of her parents when she was still a youngster were the concerns she grappled with. "I know that was difficult for her, one parent over here and one over there and neither particularly fond of each other," recalls Mrs. Knudsen. While she was not the only girl on campus with divorced parents, what singled her out was the way she had managed them. Like many children of divorced parents, she had learned to become a skilled diplomat, mediating between her warring parents. This nihilistic parental interaction taught Meghan a valuable lesson: how to control her emotions. "She is very poised," observes a school friend. "It could be hard for her. Sometimes she felt she had to pick sides."

At the time she lived with her father, whose house was walking distance from the school in Los Feliz, and saw her mother on weekends. The older she became, the more she felt she was the one who was mothering her father. It was a source of friction, especially when she started dating. As a friend notes: "Typical teenage stuff."

There were other issues, too, that clearly troubled her, though she did not discuss them publicly at the time. Fitting in was a constant concern. As she later recalled: "My high school had cliques: the black girls and white girls, the Filipino [sic] and the Latina girls. Being biracial, I fell somewhere in between. So every day during lunch, I busied myself with meetings—French Club, student body, whatever one could possibly do between noon and one p.m.—I was there. Not so that I was more involved, but so that I wouldn't have to eat alone."

Photographer John Dlugolecki, who photographed Meghan and other students throughout high school, commented that Meghan would often talk to his wife, Vicki Conrad, about her love of drama. Vicky in turn noticed that Meghan never appeared to be part of the African American or the Asian groups of girls, or any other ethnic clique. Dlugolecki also remarked that Meghan "was not considered mixed race by her peers," adding, "We only ever saw her with Tom, never with the mom." And so it came as a mild shock to members of faculty when they finally got to meet Doria. "Everyone thought [Meghan] was Italian because she was so light skinned," recalls one former teacher. "Then we met her mother and realized she was biracial."

As poised and confident as she seemed to her classmates, at Kairos, when she discussed her own demons, at least those about her family discord, it clearly enabled her to encourage her classmates to confront their own.

Mrs. Knudsen recalls: "You have to be very honest about who you are and be willing to share all the things that you struggle with, your successes and failures. She was articulate, confident, feisty, and spunky. I remember her saying, 'Why can't we do it this way, has anybody thought about that?' She was always thinking about a better way to do something, not just complaining."

For many students the retreat is a turning moment in their young lives, a time when they face up to their own emotional issues honestly. Realizing that their classmates have their own problems is seen as a critical catalyst. "It's a time of truth telling, and the leaders are the ones who set the tone," observes Mrs. Knudsen. "The atmosphere is: 'I am willing to share my truth with you, and that makes you willing to share your truth.' So there is a lot of crying, but it is healing crying. Everything out in the open, you realize everybody has to struggle and that nobody is perfect no matter how they look."

While her fractured family background and her sense of isolation caused Meghan a great deal of heartache as she grew up, it also helped provide some of the psychological drive that would propel her toward her overarching ambition. From a young age, Meghan dreamed of becoming a famous Hollywood actor. She fantasized about winning an Oscar one day, practicing her acceptance speech in front of her bedroom mirror. As James Lipton, the venerable inquisitor for the long-running *Inside the Actors Studio*, never tires of reminding his audience, most actors come from broken homes. This often bitter experience gives them the emotional rocket fuel to power a star-making screen performance.

From day one at Immaculate Heart, Meghan threw herself whole-heartedly into the drama department. Besides being a stepping stone in following her dream, at school the drama department has a rather different function. It acts as a welcoming club, an unofficial sorority, and a close-knit family. As the winner of six Daytime Emmy awards told me: "You might be a misfit everywhere else, but here you have a sense of belonging."

As well as taking to the boards, Meghan held numerous offices, including president of the school's Genesian Players, a group devoted to the preservation of the performing arts that actively hosted or attended plays, dramatic festivals, and apprentice stage productions. However, as she didn't hold a formal office, she was always at the edge of the student council, never quite a part of it.

Immaculate Heart, which counts supermodel and TV personality Tyra Banks, beloved sitcom star Mary Tyler Moore, and Lucille Ball's actor daughter Lucie Arnaz among its alumni, was able to call on a rich roster of Hollywood luminaries to direct and produce plays and musicals.

There was leading voice coach Rachael Lawrence, choreographer and *Jersey Boys* star Joseph Leo Bwarie, and, most prominently, Gigi Perreau, a former child actor whose work is honored with a star on the Hollywood Walk of Fame. Perreau started her career in movies at the tender age of two when she played Greer Garson's daughter in the 1943 film *Madame Curie*. By the age of ten she had appeared in twenty-five films, including working on set with Nancy Reagan in the 1950 thriller *Shadow on the Wall*. When she retired from acting work, Perreau, now seventy-eight, brought her experience to staging plays and musicals at her alma mater, as well as to teaching drama classes.

Perreau remembers Meghan as a skinny kid who developed and blossomed into a beautiful and confident young woman during her time at Immaculate Heart. She recalled: "We never had a moment's problem with her, she was spot on, learned her lines when she had to, very dedicated, very focused. She was a wonderful student, a lovely girl even then, and very hardworking. She was very dedicated. I knew she would be something special."

In drama class they often discussed topics of the day, and Perreau remembers Meghan as an inquisitive youngster who loved hearing tales of Perreau's time in France and other European countries. She was keen to explore the world beyond the nearby Hollywood sign.

When she was rehearsing for a play, her father was always around. As an Emmy winner who had been nominated almost every year while working on General Hospital, he was soon roped into becoming the technical director for every school production Meghan was involved in. The majority of students were not aware that he was Meghan's dad. He was known simply as "that guy in the overalls." Those in the drama group were rather more respectful, calling him Mr. Markle. "He liked to be thought of as gruff," recalls Perreau, "but he was always very generous with the girls. If we had a late rehearsal he would go out and buy a boxful of McDonald's to feed them. Modest, too. He never asked to be credited for any work he did." He was single and shy, and Perreau admits to having a "bit of a crush" on the burly guy in overalls who was clearly trying to bring up his teenage daughter on his own. She asked him out, and they went to see a play together at the Doolittle Theatre, just south of Hollywood and Vine. Though they had a good time, nothing ever developed.

Tom's focus was on Meghan. A keen photographer, he took endless photographs of Meghan onstage, teaching her how to pose and coaching her on angles. He was proudly watching from the wings when she made her first solo singing performance, playing the secretary in the school's production of the musical Annie. Perreau recalls: "I remember her being very excited and nervous about her song," describing her performance as "delightful." Meghan went on to play an aspiring actor in the 1937 comedy Stage Door and was featured in Back Country Crimes, a black comedy by American playwright Lanie Robertson. In the March 1997 program notes for Immaculate Heart's production of Stephen Sondheim's musical Into the Woods, in which she played Little Red Riding Hood, Meghan announced her ambition to the world. In between thanking her friends and her "adorable" boyfriend, she revealed that she wished to attend Northwestern College, a prestigious university near Chicago. This, she predicted, would be her next stop on her way to Broadway. Meghan was clearly not a girl wanting in confidence.

For her junior year she appeared yet again in a school production, *Stepping Out*, but for her senior year she decided to test her ability beyond the confines of Immaculate High. It was a new challenge and offered the chance of branching out on her own without her father looking down on her from the lighting gantry. There was also the small matter of spending time alone with her then boyfriend. Thus she found herself in a room with forty other girls waiting to audition for Sophocles' Greek tragedy *Oedipus Rex* staged in the fall of 1998 by the all-boys St. Francis High School in La Cañada Flintridge.

As it was drama director Emmanuel (Manny) Eulalia's first big production at St. Francis, he wanted to make an impact, carefully choosing the girl who would play the lead role of Jocasta. It was no contest. "Meghan was a standout," he recalls. "She had that something of the 'it' about her. As a director it is what you are always looking for. She had charisma, no doubt."

After signing a formal document pledging to arrive on time, dress appropriately, and refrain from sexual and racial innuendoes—a code of behavior somewhat ahead of its time— Meghan and the rest of the cast got down to a grueling two-month schedule of rehearsals. Early on she impressed the show's director with her timekeeping, preparation, and command of the stage. In the show's musical numbers her voice packed a punch even if she quavered somewhat on the higher notes.

While she was the only girl from Immaculate Heart to audition, she already had star status at the all-boys school. She had already dated several pupils from St. Francis, including her first long-term boyfriend, Luis Segura. In time-honored fashion, it was his sister, Maria, who set them up on their first date. Describing her as "sweet and fun," doubtless Luis, now a successful Realtor in downtown Pasadena, encouraged her to enter that year's contest for homecoming queen.

This pinnacle of high school social standing came with serious competition from dozens of other girls. Hopefuls had to write an essay listing their accomplishments—Megan's regular work in the Hippie Kitchen made her an instant standout—before facing a grilling from members of the student body and faculty. The names of the finalists were read out at the fifty-yard line on a hastily erected stage during halftime at a St. Francis football game. Amid whistling and cheering, Meghan was proclaimed that year's queen and was duly crowned by the previous incumbent. The entire court then left the field in a procession of classic convertibles so that the game could continue. It was an indication of her popularity and appeal that a girl who was neither a cheerleader nor hailed from one of the closer all-girls Catholic schools was chosen.

At the dance Meghan, wearing a strapless pale blue gown and tiara, was accompanied by her date for the night, Danny Segura, her boyfriend's brother who had played Creon in the Greek tragedy. He credited Meghan, who was a familiar figure in the Segura household, with inspiring him to take to the stage, successfully auditioning for a role in the high school musical before taking on the somewhat meatier role in *Oedipus Rex*.

Even though she was now "Queen Meghan," drama director Manny Eulalia recalls that she didn't let the adulation go to her head. She remained grounded, joking around as she accepted the congratulations of her fellow cast members. Once word got out that "Queen Meghan" was the female lead in the show, tickets sold briskly for the somber tragedy. For three nights the teenage cast played to a full house in the 250-seat theater at nearby Flintridge Preparatory School. In previous years, interest in school productions had been disappointing. Not this time. When Meghan first

appeared, there was a rustle of applause despite the audience having been warned to curb their enthusiasm.

"A lot of pupils went to the show just to see Meghan," recalls
Manny with a smile. "She certainly had a fan club. Quite a few
of the boys had crushes on her." At the end of the eighty-minute
production, the audience gave Meghan and rest of the cast a standing ovation.

In the program notes she wrote, "I would like to give thanks
to Mommy, Daddy, Sushi, Aubergine, Danny boy, Brad, Gabe, all
the beautiful, amazing, gorgeous sweeties at Immaculate Heart,
the great guys at St. Francis, and the phenomenal cast and crew."

Though she was deemed a stand out in *Oedipus Rex*, Meghan
Markle's high school acting career is best remembered for her performance as the sexy South American vamp Lola in the 1955 musical comedy *Damn Yankees*. As the production was being staged by
another all-boys Catholic school, this time Loyola High School in
downtown Los Angeles, once again she had to compete against
girls from other Catholic schools. Fresh from her triumph in *Oedipus Rex*, she snagged the starring role of Lola, first played by Tony
award winner Gwen Verdon. The story, based on a modern retelling of the Faustian pact, involved the vampish Lola, her deal with
the devil, and her attempts to seduce a baseball fan turned star
player Joe Hardy, played in this production by Paul Rorie, now a
family lawyer. When Meghan, dressed in long satin gloves and a
sequined leotard, shimmied across the stage in the sassy burlesque
number "Whatever Lola Wants," she brought the house down.

"It was like *woo!*" recalls a member of the audience. "She was
extraordinary. I remember sitting there thinking, 'Oh my goodness, this is an Immaculate Heart girl.' She was wearing the little
spangly number, doing the shimmies, the whole bit. It wasn't lewd;
she was playing a character. It was sweet in a way, but it was also
like *wow*. This was a girl with star quality."

At another time in another country, something very similar happened when the normally demure student Kate Middleton sashayed down the catwalk in a sheer shift dress over a bikini at a college fashion show. Prince William, watching the parade from the front row, whispered to his companion, "She's hot." The rest is royal history. On this occasion, it was an eye opener for those teachers and classmates who were seeing a very different side to Meghan. Normally seen as fun but thoughtful, mature and controlled, Meghan's amorous song-and-dance routine was a revelation. After the show, her theology teacher Maria Pollia and her boyfriend went backstage and presented her with a bouquet of red roses. It was a touching moment. Meghan, who had been beyond excited to win the role, burst into tears. "Oh, you didn't have to do this," she sobbed, suddenly overwhelmed by the moment. As Pollia recalls: "She had appeared in many productions and she was always good. This time, though, she was a star. And that night a star was born."

An academic star, too. Her graduation ceremony in the summer of 1999, which was held at the Hollywood Bowl, was another chance to shine. She walked away with a clutch of glittering prizes that touched on her intellectual, artistic, and charitable work. She was presented with the Bank of America Fine Arts award and the Notre Dame Club of Los Angeles Achievement Award, earned a commendation in the National Achievement Scholarship program for outstanding black students, and won a service award for mentoring younger students.

The future was looking very bright. As she had predicted three years earlier, she had been accepted at Northwestern University, where she intended to study English. She was accomplished in so many fields that some expected her to eventually enter politics or the law. All felt that she would do something worthwhile with her life and at the same time give back to the community. The word *classy*, which she used to describe herself in her final yearbook, and her choice of a quote from former First Lady Eleanor Roosevelt to illustrate her senior year photograph reflected her rounded personality. It read: "Women are like teabags; they don't realize how strong they are until they're in hot water."

As her drama teacher Gigi Perreau recalled: "I wasn't sure which direction Meghan would ultimately be going in because she also had interests in humanitarian activities. She had a good heart, had absorbed the school's philosophy that there is nothing we cannot do, and she seemed to be focused on her future."

A couple of years after she graduated Meghan returned to her alma mater. She chatted to a few of her old teachers and caught up on the news. "Keep in touch, sweetheart," Perreau told her as Meghan was preparing to leave. The budding actor was still struggling to get a foothold on the greasy pole that is Hollywood and was working as a hostess in a Beverly Hills hotel restaurant to pay for acting lessons. Somewhat ruefully she told her former acting mentor: "I don't want to come back until I have really made it."

The staff and pupils of Immaculate Heart are still waiting.

4

Can You Say, "Hi?"

Summertime and the living was easy for Meghan. Freshly graduated from Immaculate Heart and with her Northwestern University future beckoning, Meghan packed her last Los Angeles summer with memories and then packed her suitcases for her first semester away from home. She would effectively be starting a new life. Not one of her classmates from Immaculate Heart or anyone she knew from LA was going to Northwestern, and she was determined to make a good impression. The orthodontics she had had during her high school years had gradually adjusted her bucked, gap-toothed grin, and now she was smiling widely without feeling self-conscious.

Once her dental work was complete she had some head shots taken to send out for auditions. As she was leaving for Chicago in the autumn, the best she could hope for was a day or two's work on one of the many music or short videos that were being shot around town. She had already earned around $600 for a couple days of work in a Tori Amos video, "1000 Oceans," which was shot in a parking lot in downtown LA. Meghan, dressed in a low-cut blue spaghetti strap top, appeared as one of a crowd curiously examining a glass box containing Amos, writhing around as she sang. It comes across as a kind of performance art—but to a melody. The four-and-a-half-minute video, directed by Erick Ifergan, climaxes with scenes of rioting kids facing police horses and hoses, a musical reprise of the LA riots. Amos's video is, for dedicated Markle watchers, the first public appearance of one of Meghan's most distinctive mannerisms, continuously brushing back her long hair from her face with her hand.

That weekend, she had another audition lined up, this time for a Shakira video. It was to be a high-energy dance fest, a world away from Amos's vision of urban alienation. Meghan's best friend Nikki Priddy was going to drive with her to the audition, then they were going to go shopping so that she could find something new to wear for the Northwestern students' reception at the Beverly Hilton hotel. The meet and greet was her first chance to scope out her fellow undergraduates and to make some first impressions herself. During the day Nikki and Meghan also planned to goof around, filming LA street scenes—and themselves—with Nikki's new video camera.

The audition for the Shakira video didn't go quite as well as Meghan had hoped. It was fun to dance crazily, but afterward she told Nikki: "I am burning up, I was really nervous I was going to fall out of my top I was just shaking around so much."

She knew her performance hadn't won her a gig as a $600-a-day featured dancer, but she was hoping for a spot as an extra. It was less money and no real camera time, but still, it would be fun. As she waited in the audition room she ran into a girl she had met at the Tori Amos video shoot. It was the last time they saw one another; Meghan did not get a call back.

After hitting the mall, the two friends drove through Los Angeles in Doria's Volvo station wagon with the personalized license plate MEGNMEE, Meghan keeping up a rolling commentary; Nikki was the camerawoman. The duo dismissed the gay majority of

West Hollywood with the jejune "We could walk down the street naked and no one would care." They zoomed in on a woman who seemed to just have had collagen injections in her lips and they marveled at the houses along Beverly Glen and other wealthy enclaves in Beverly Hills and elsewhere.

Back home at her mother's house, Meghan tried on her new outfits for the student gathering at the Beverly Hilton. She had a vision of how she wanted to project herself at Northwestern and had decided that she would focus on a monochromatic look, black and gray, a color scheme that would make her look stylish, sophisticated, and pulled together. With that in mind, she'd chosen a pencil skirt, tube top, and structured white open-front blouse that doubled as a jacket. It was a weird foreshadowing of the office wear she would don to play Rachel Zane over a decade later.

Meghan made that last summer at home count, but she was also troubled. She and her father weren't getting along, and she was deliberately avoiding him. The emotional shutters had come down—Meghan going to stay with her mother and not even visiting her father's house to pick up her mail. It was a situation that perplexed her friends as they knew that Meghan was the apple of her father's eye. Not that any of his children, Tom Junior and Yvonne included, took advantage of his laissez-faire attitude. It was Meghan's mother who was more a stickler for boundaries. Though she would join Meghan and her friends dancing to music on the radio or talking about makeup, she was stricter than her ex-husband. Meghan could twist him around her little finger. Yvonne often told the story of the time before Christmas when Meghan was looking at a jewelry catalogue and picking out a ring that Tom Senior had promised as her main festive gift. She teased her much older sister by saying that whatever her father bought Yvonne, Meghan would receive the most expensive gift as she was the most favored child. So, while the split between father and daughter was uncommon, her friends dismissed it as simply a summer storm. It was not the best send-off for her college career, as she was leaving behind her childhood home and also the girl she considered her sister, Ninaki Priddy.

Nikki had been her best friend since they could barely walk. As toddlers they were besties at the Little Red School House, spending countless sleepovers together, playing in the pool at Nikki's parents' modest three-bedroom home in North Hollywood. They remained close when they transitioned to Immaculate Heart, the duo traveling around Europe together with her parents, Dalton and Maria, and her kid sister Michelle. Nikki loved Paris so much that she studied at the Sorbonne the following summer. When they landed in London and posed in front of Buckingham Palace, they never for a moment thought that one day Meghan would be welcomed inside the black wrought iron gates. Now college and separation loomed, and they were trying to crowd every moment with laughter and fond memories.

Meghan looked around her dorm room and began unpacking. She was bunked in the freshman dorm known as North Mid-Quads and next door to the Kappa Kappa Gamma sorority house. She hadn't decided yet if she would rush—the American college ritual where student women visit all the sorority houses and find one that suits them, then hope they will be selected to join it—or just stick to friendship groups in her dorm and classes. The first few weeks at a new college are difficult enough; there is a lot of judging and sizing up as hundreds of anxious teenagers, bubbling over with hormones and excitement, try to orient themselves both physically and psychologically. Rush merely exacerbates that feeling of vulnerability, of wanting to belong. Without a friend or even an acquaintance from back home, Meghan, a naturally gregarious character, worked hard at making new friends.

But her self-esteem was about to take a most unexpected blow. She had grown up in the melting pot that is Los Angeles. Her school, Immaculate Heart, was a kaleidoscope of girls of different colors and nationalities. Now, she discovered that even though the town of Evanston, where Northwestern University is based, is just a few miles from Chicago, the college itself is overwhelmingly white. African Americans make up a third of the town, but only 5 percent of the student body. There were even fewer biracial students. At Northwestern, she stood out.

Just one week into her first semester, as Meghan sat reviewing her class schedules for her chosen major, English, a dorm mate came up and asked: "You said your mom is black and your dad is white, right?"

Meghan smiled weakly and nodded, suddenly uncomfortable. "And they're divorced?' her dorm mate continued. Meghan nodded. She gave her a knowing look. "Oh. Well that makes sense." Meghan felt a stab. The snide remark cut her deeply. *Makes sense how?* she wondered. Of course, she understood the implication: that the failure of an interracial marriage was inevitable.

Los Angeles had been a huge multicultural bubble, and now Meghan was being exposed to narrow minds and outdated, provincial thinking. This wasn't the first nor would it be the last time she would hear or be subject to a crass racial slur. As she was light-skinned, many fellow students didn't realize she was biracial, making her a fly on the wall as they made racist jokes or expressed bigoted opinions. This incident in particular stayed with her, shaping her reflections about how others around her viewed Meghan, her family, and her heritage. "My lasting memory of Meghan is her profound sense of self," remembers Professor Harvey Young of his biracial student. "She was thoughtful and understood what it means to face prejudice and discrimination."

But Meghan was just tough enough not to let it get too far under her skin—she was too busy cutting loose. Now that she wasn't under the watchful gaze of her mother, she started wearing heavier makeup and experimented with highlighting her hair.

Having made up her mind, she rushed Kappa Kappa Gamma and was initiated into the sorority, which was full of girls who were considered "intelligent hot messes." As KKG member Melania Hidalgo observed, "The thing we all have in common is that we're all very driven, ambitious, and passionate." The sorority embraced her warmly. Meghan, was eventually elected the sorority's recruitment chair, responsible for bringing in new girls into the KKG clan. As an outgoing, confident, and articulate young woman, she was well suited for the role of selling the sorority. Sometimes she was a tad too persuasive, some students, according to classmate Ann Meade, thinking her too assertive. For the most part fellow students remember her thirst for life and her "explosive personality" as a dynamic, self-possessed young woman.

As a sorority member, she also participated in the Northwestern University Dance Marathon, one of the biggest student-run charities in America. The year Meghan danced was the first time since the event's inception in 1974 that a woman, Ginger Harrald, was the emcee, though she shared the duties with a male student. While the dance marathon was no longer the grueling win-or-die dancefest of the Depression era, the thirty hours Meghan spent on her feet, day and night, certainly helped her work off her "freshman fifteen," the weight she had packed on from drinking, munching starchy dorm food, and making late-night trips to the twenty-four-hour Burger King.

Though the drinking age was twenty-one, Meghan, like so many other students, bought herself a fake ID card so that she could go enjoy the bars of Evanston. She was a regular at the Keg, a dodgy student favorite that was eventually closed down after numerous run-ins with city officials over underage drinking. Bouncers used to joke when students finally handed over a real ID once they had genuinely turned twenty-one: "Well, it's about time."

Of course, all this socializing did have a focus—the search for a boyfriend. More sophisticated and put together than most of her contemporaries, Meghan was seen as a cool catch. Normally she went for well-dressed Latin boyfriends like Luis Segura but changed gears during her time at Northwestern. Her first boyfriend was Steve Lepore, a chiseled, white, six foot five sophomore basketball player from Ohio. He made Meghan, at five foot six, feel petite. Her association with Lapore raised her stock with her KKG sorority sisters, who were "impressed she'd snared a hottie." "They made quite the pair," recalled a former classmate, but their relationship was short lived. For his junior and senior year, the high-scoring basketball star accepted a transfer offer to Wake Forest University in Winston-Salem, North Carolina. Goodbye, Meghan; hello, basketball pro prospects.

While they made a perfect-looking college couple, they had their differences. Steve's sports ambitions meant that he had to forego partying and turn in early, and the night before any game, Meghan was not welcome to stay over. Meghan, on the other hand, was a party animal who enjoyed the freedom college offered away from her parents, and drinking and staying out late.

While she may have lost her freshman-year boyfriend, Meghan did make two very close friends at Northwestern who would stay with her for life.

It was during a literature class, discussing the work of African American writer Toni Morrison, that she first met Lindsay Jill Roth, a petite blond from Lattingtown, New York, a wealthy Long Island suburb with million-dollar homes overlooking Oyster Bay. Her parents were attorneys, though her mother had retired. Unlike Meghan's friends from Immaculate Heart, Lindsay was Jewish. Smart, funny, and articulate, the two girls would study together, go out drinking and dancing, and chat long into the night, talking up a storm.

Her other best friend could not have been more different. The son of two pastors, Larnelle Quentin Foster was a flamboyant, larger-than-life African American who hid the fact that he was gay from his family and friends—although he eventually confided in Meghan. Meghan and Larnelle took classes together in the School of Communications after Meghan changed her major from English to a dual major of theater arts and international relations. The twin major reflected her indecision about whether to pursue a career in politics and the diplomatic world or strive for screen stardom. Though the latter was, as she recognized, something of an LA cliché, she was in good company—Warren Beatty, Stephen Colbert, Zach Braff, and David Schwimmer all learned their trade at the school. Larnelle, however, couldn't help but notice that her enthusiasm was more for Hollywood than the State Department. The two, who attended everything from student productions to avant-garde offerings, enjoyed discussing the theatrical structure and language of a play as much as performing. Meghan took parts in the short films made by fellow students, and she also slipped away from campus to attend auditions for TV commercials. She was doing what college students have done for years: trying the new and the difficult and seeing what fits. On weekends Meghan would often go to Larnelle's family home for meals, the two friends trying out different recipes, including Meghan's current specialty, Indian food.

The Foster family adored Meghan, attracted by her quirky sense of humor and her effervescent smile. She even accepted their invitation to join them at church. "Larnelle, you know if I had my way, you'd settle down with Meghan. I just love that girl," his mother told him. "I know, Mom," he replied. He also knew that he would break his mother's heart if she discovered that he was gay. For the time being Meghan was his cover, and he in turn provided her with companionship and an escort, a role which made him the envy of many of the straight guys on campus. "How do you go out with her?" they asked him. "Because I'm not trying anything!" laughed Larnelle.

Meghan's two closest friends represented the duality of her

heritage, the iconoclastic, eccentric and independent African American and the white professional. Their presence helped her to explore and integrate these sides of her personality, absorbing and synthesizing as she grew into her own identity.

Between semesters, it was a relief to be back in Los Angeles not only for the weather but also for the diversity, where the blond and blue-eyed are a minority. As she learned, though, the image of tolerance and acceptance was a veneer that easily scratched.

She tells a story about one night she and her mom went to a concert. As Doria was slowly backing her Volvo out of the parking space, another driver impatiently yelled at her, using the N-word. Meghan flushed, her skin prickling with frustration, feeling as well Doria's pain and rage. Meghan looked at her mother and saw her eyes welling with tears. Meghan whispered the only words she could manage: "It's okay, Mommy." But it wasn't okay. They drove home in silence, blood pounding in Meghan's ears, Doria's fingers gripping the steering wheel tightly.

The practical experience of growing up biracial was used as a jumping-off point for discussions Meghan and seven other classmates had with their history and theater professor, Harvey Young, whose seminars focused on African American plays and their meaning, impact, and history. Meghan, who had moved between two communities throughout her life, was very aware of how people responded to race, racial differences, and the idea of otherness. Young said, "She had a very sophisticated understanding of what it means to live in a racial body that gets perceived and is treated differently based upon communities in which you find yourself."

Young's class brought into focus Meghan's ambiguous place in society. She later recalled: "It was the first time I could put a name to feeling too light in the black community, too mixed in the white community."

Her experiences at Northwestern, both in and out of the

classroom, and the self-knowledge she gained would serve her well, arming her with insight and inner strength when she tried to penetrate the smooth, evasive structure that is Hollywood.

By the start of her junior year, it was clear that if Meghan continued at her current pace she would earn most of her credits for her degree way ahead of schedule. As she had time on her side and was still unsure about her path after college, she decided to go into the field to gain some practical experience in international relations. She knew that her uncle Mick Markle was employed as a specialist in communication systems for the US government—the talk in the family was that he worked for the CIA, the government's overseas spying arm. So she approached him to ask for his help in getting her an internship abroad with the State Department. "Meghan, I will help you if I can," he replied. Help he did. Uncle Mick pulled a few strings, and even though Meghan was quite late in turning in the application paperwork, that was overlooked because of her excellent academic record and her uncle's influence. Soon after, she was informed that she had secured a six-week internship as a junior press officer at the American embassy in Buenos Aires, Argentina.

It was quite the adventure for the twenty-year-old, flying from Los Angeles to Buenos Aires on her own. She joined a team of nearly thirty State Department officials and guards in the mid-sized American enclave. Before starting work, she was given an orientation to the building complex and the city, safety being the primary focus. The young student was warned about where to avoid, what to do in an emergency, and which telephone numbers to call—basic but vital information. With the anniversary of 9/11 approaching, the threat level for all American embassies around the world, including the embassy in Buenos Aires, had been raised to Code Orange security, the second highest level.

For the most part, her day-to-day life was the routine and mundane world of the office grunt, filing, answering phones, and drafting letters. As a consummate team player, she impressed her superiors with her enthusiasm and demeanor.

She was a willing worker, undertaking the tedious, run-of-the-mill jobs quickly and efficiently. Her superior, Mark Krischik, now retired, recalled her as a young woman who was good to work with and who carried out her assignments with "efficiency and ingenuity." Though memories are hazy, there was talk of a dalliance with a US Marine tasked to guard the embassy compound. But what was more certain was her love of the Spanish cuisine and the city's buzzing nightlife.

As it was her twenty-first birthday on August 4, 2002, she was given permission to travel in the convoy that was picking up the US finance secretary Paul O'Neill, who was making a whistle stop visit to South America. It was a treat. However, her opportunity to be treated like a VIP for an hour or two rapidly turned into a terrifying ordeal.

She was waiting in the motorcade when Secretary O'Neill landed at Ezeiza Airport, fifteen miles outside the center of Buenos Aires. Argentina had recently defaulted on a $141 billion debt, and neither the International Monetary Fund nor the American government were in any mood to bail them out. Before he left Washington, O'Neill had announced that South American nations should have policies in place to "ensure that aid is not diverted to Swiss bank accounts." Though his target was the corrupt political elites siphoning off billions of dollars into their own personal bank accounts, the suffering man and woman in the street blamed the United States for the economic calamity that had befallen them. After he landed at precisely five o'clock. his motorcade drove to a meeting with President Eduardo Duhalde, head of the interim government. Though O'Neill was expecting a bumpy ride, even he was perturbed when banner-waving demonstrators surrounded the convoy. "I remember the arrival because protestors banged on my limo with their placards. It was a memorable event," he later deadpanned.

The junior press officer was terrified, recalling that it was the scariest moment of her life. It was all the more concerning as the American embassy was already on orange alert not only because of the impending anniversary of 9/11 but because of intelligence reports suggesting that Islamic militants could be setting up a network in South America. Meghan would have already been wary, and it's easy to imagine how frightening she would have found an angry mob of protesters attacking her car.

However, the experience certainly didn't seem to put her off considering her future working for the government agency. "If she had stayed with the State Department she would have been an excellent addition to the US diplomatic corps. She had all that it takes to be a successful diplomat," Mark Krischik recalled.

Certainly she was sufficiently committed to a career with the State Department to take the Foreign Service Officer Test while she was still in Argentina. The three-hour exam is a mix of politics, history, general knowledge, and math, requiring an awareness of everything from the origin of be-bop to East Asian labor laws. It proved a stretch too far, and Meghan failed the exam. There were consolations, though: Meghan spent a further six weeks from school at the IES study program in Madrid, where she polished her Spanish.

When she returned to Northwestern she was able to regale her friends with tales of tapas and tango, and tried to brush off her disappointment at missing the mark on her Foreign Service Officer test. In any case, fate, it would seem, was pushing her into the world of entertainment. Her lighting director father pulled favors to put her forward for a casual role on General Hospital, just as he had done with his eldest daughter almost a decade earlier. In November 2002, Meghan auditioned for a day player role where she said around five lines. Thanks to her father's influence, she got the part. The episode aired just before Thanksgiving.

A few weeks later she was at a holiday party with friends when she was approached by a man who introduced himself as Drew. Instead of wanting to date her, he wanted to manage her. A friend had slipped him a copy of a student film in which Meghan had appeared, and he was impressed, calling Meghan to tell her, "You know what, you're going to make money, and I'll take 10 percent. I think you should stick around."

But at that time in her life Meghan couldn't stick around. She had courses to finish back at Northwestern and a graduation to attend. But she promised she'd be back. As she saw it, as one door had closed, another one opened. If the State Department didn't want her, maybe Hollywood did.

Once home from Northwestern, diploma in hand, Meghan went out and auditioned for commercials, none of which she booked, but was good for experience. By now this was a well-trodden route, Meghan having attended numerous auditions when she was still at Northwestern. Then she got a call. Her best friend from college, Lindsay Jill Roth, was working in casting for a film called *A Lot Like Love* starring comic heartthrob Ashton Kutcher. She had snagged Meghan a place for an audition with a one-word role.

"Can you say, 'Hi'?" asked the director.

"Yes, I can," replied Meghan. "But I read the script and I really respond to this other character and I would love to read for that." Naturally the other character had a bigger role.

The director and the casting staff exchanged glances. *This girl certainly has some balls,* their looks said. Meghan didn't get the role she pitched herself for, but she did get the part for which Roth had recommended her. Once on set, the director allowed her to improvise, expanding her lines from one to five. In movie terms that was a triumph.

Next she landed another small part in the futuristic law office drama *Century City*, starring Viola Davis and Nestor Carbonell, among other old hands. She played a staff member and delivered one line: "Here's to Tom Montero, who had the vision to install this amazing virtual assistant." Her scene was over in one day, and she was back to casting calls, at the mercy of the Abominable No Men. It was a scratchy hand-to-mouth existence, one experienced by thousands of Hollywood hopefuls.

On the way to an audition one day, the electric button that unlocked the doors to her Jeep Explorer failed to open. She tried the key but to no avail. Trying not to panic, she went around to the hatchback, which used a different key. By some miracle, it opened. Running short on time, she had no choice but to crawl in through the back and clamber over the seat. Thank goodness she was in shape from yoga and running, and thank goodness the car started and had a full tank of gas. When she got to the casting studio, she pulled into a deserted part of the parking lot and exited the same way.

Too broke to get her Jeep repaired, Meghan repeated this routine for months, parking far from other cars and waiting for the coast to clear before emerging from the hatch, feigning that she was searching in the back of the car for a script or photos before climbing back inside.

Of course, she knew there would be setbacks. Meghan had been around the entertainment industry for too long to believe in rags-to-riches stories. So, she stayed optimistic. Her motto was "I choose happiness," and she made it a point to stay happy, getting together with friends over pizza and wine, taking yoga classes, and going out as much as her budget permitted. One night her budget took her to a dive bar in West Hollywood that had been popularized by the young Turks in the entertainment industry (young hotshots keen on challenging the older Hollywood establishment) who liked to feel that they were slumming in an authentic beatnik environment. A loud voice tinged with a New York accent caught her attention. The owner of the voice was shooting the breeze with a couple of friends.

Over six feet tall with reddish blond hair and blue eyes, Trevor Engelson looked like a surfer or volleyball player, an archetypal California golden boy. He had the drawl and the air of a Matthew McConaughey lite, although he was born and raised in Great Neck, New York, the son of a successful orthodontist and great-grandson of Jewish immigrants.

Like Francis Ford Coppola, Trevor had attended Great Neck North High School, and like Coppola, he originally wanted to direct movies. "I realized you needed talent to do that, so that was out the window," he says self-deprecatingly. While still in high school, he managed to get himself hired as a production assistant on shoots in New York City, working tirelessly on weekends and during school breaks. The experience paid off and he was admitted to the Annenberg School of Cinematic Arts at the University of Southern California. He was on his way.

After he graduated in 1998, Trevor worked on the low-budget movie *Safe Men*, notable only for the appearance of Paul Giamatti as the strangely monikered Veal Chop. Then Engelson, who liked to think of himself as a hustler, was hired on *Deep Blue Sea*—a film that needlessly demonstrated the inevitably bloody consequences of genetically engineering super intelligent great white sharks—as a staff assistant. During his time in the office he studied how his bosses, the movie's producers, worked. He liked what he saw. It didn't seem that they were working very hard and yet they made a lot of money and got the prettiest girls. He approached one of the producers, Alan Riche, and told him earnestly: "Alan, I want to do what you do. I want to produce." Riche advised him that first he had to work as an agent. Once *Deep Blue Sea* wrapped Riche got the ambitious assistant a referral to the Endeavor Talent Agency. He started at the bottom of the ladder in the mailroom working as a driver, delivering scripts and other agency-related packages around town.

Trevor was personable and eager, and in due time he worked his way up to assistant to the motion picture literary agent Chris Donnelly. He was on the fast track to higher things. Then his ambition got in the way. While Donnelley was on vacation, Trevor sent out uncommissioned scripts, known as spec scripts, to actors and directors under the Endeavor letterhead. "I thought I was being a self-starter," Trevor admitted later. While there were no lasting hard feelings, he was fired for overstepping his remit. Never down for long, he quickly found work as an assistant to fellow USC alumni Nick Osborne and his partner Jeffrey Zarnow at O/Z Films. As Trevor put it: "They needed a hustler who could bring food to the table."

When Osborne began his own movie company, Underground Films, Trevor became his assistant, taking over the company several years later. Beneath the banter and the wisecracks, Trevor was a driven soul, a young man out to make his mark in an uncompromising industry. When Meghan first met him on that night out in West Hollywood, she liked what she saw and was attracted to his passion, drive, and ambition. He was a guy with an aphorism for every occasion. "Hope is the greatest currency we have in this business," he told the wide-eyed wannabe. True or not, it's a great pick-up line.

His favorite saying belonged to producer Neal Moritz, the man behind *The Fast and the Furious* franchise: "Don't give it five minutes if you're not gonna give it five years." Trevor said it so often that, in time, Meghan began to use it herself, presenting the phrase as though it had sprung fully formed from her head.

Her version is more refined: "Don't give it five minutes unless you can give it five years." But Trevor had aphorisms—and chutzpah—to spare. As he once told a former USC buddy: "I'm a gigantic believer that all this shit can come to an end any minute now, and you've gotta take advantage of [it]. I'm Jewish and all that, but I think you got one shot at this life, so if you have a chance to have some fun and you're not hurting anybody else and you can still take care of everything else to be taken care of and—I always find a way to have a lot of fun. That's never an issue."

He was the quintessential example of a young man who burned the candle at both ends, playing and working hard. Cuba, Palm Springs, New York: the world was his oyster—at least until he reached his credit card limit. As he said: "If I'm on a plane going somewhere, when I land I'm working, on the plane I'm working, when I'm drinking I'm working. But I'm always having a lot more fun than most other people I know." A driven producer and an ambitious actor—it was a classic Hollywood combination.

When Trevor's movie *Zoom* began production in early 2005, Meghan had recently snagged a brief appearance on the sitcom *Cuts*. It was one line, one measly line, but Meghan felt that she was on her way to the stars. Later on an anonymous blog, Working Actress, she described that feeling: "At the start of my career, I remember freaking out, and celebrating over getting one line on a shitty UPN show. At the time, that was a big success. It was phone calls of congrats, and flowers, and celebratory dinners with wine glasses clinking. It was a landmark of more work to come, and a glimmer of hope that said 'holy shit, you're really doing this.'"

While she waited for her close-up she made ends meet as a hostess in a Beverly Hills restaurant, teaching gift wrapping at a local store, and using her other skill, her impeccable handwriting, to earn decent money as a calligraphist. She had learned the skill back at Immaculate Heart, and as she later commented: "I've always had a propensity for getting the cursive down pretty well." At that time her claim to fame was writing the envelopes for the June 2005 wedding of singer Robin Thicke and actor Paula Patton.

The roles were coming, but not as quickly as she would have liked. In the summer of 2005 she was booked for a role on the show *Love, Inc.* and later in the year, around Thanksgiving, a TV movie called *Deceit.* That was followed by an appearance as an insurance salesperson on the short-lived sitcom *The War at Home.*

While Meghan was steadily but slowly chugging along, Trevor went from boom to bust. His movie *Zoom,* which was released in the summer of 2006, was an unmitigated disaster. The family action film, described as a "dull laugh-free affair," received a 3 percent rating on Rotten Tomatoes. The movie's star, Tim Allen, even received a Razzie nomination for Worst Actor.

It was not much better for Meghan. So far, 2006 had been a bust both for film and TV roles, though the couple's social life got a bit of a boost when in August they were invited to the Hamptons for the Coach Legacy Photo Exhibit. The event celebrating the American handbag manufacturer saw the couple sipping champagne and rubbing shoulders with wealthy socialites and the celebrity fringe—but it didn't help them up the Hollywood ladder.

The daily rejections would have broken someone with less grit, but Meghan knew it was a numbers game. As girls dropped out and headed home, defeated, and the more she went out for parts, the greater her chance was of booking something. As her motto said, don't give it five minutes unless you can give it five years. And her five years were not even close to being up.

Like other girls doing the rounds she had a gym bag containing the essential wardrobe for every possible part she may be called for: red for a feisty Latina, pastels for the girl next door, mustard yellow for African American. Short skirts, long skirts, blazer, bikini, and tops—everything she needed was in her trusty tote.

At the same time, as she acknowledged, being ethnically

"ambiguous" allowed her to go for virtually any role. "Sadly, it didn't matter," she later wrote for *Elle* magazine. "I wasn't black enough for the black roles and I wasn't white enough for the white ones, leaving me somewhere in the middle as the ethnic chameleon who couldn't book a job."

She was sitting in her sweats, fabric tubes covering her forearms to keep skin oil off the envelopes she was hand addressing for a calligraphy client, when her agent called.

He had secured an audition for her. There was one hitch. She had to appear in what the producers coyly described as a "body-conscious outfit," that is to say a bikini, swimsuit, short skirt, or shorts so that they could get an idea of what her body looked like. It was a cattle call for the position of briefcase girl on the popular TV game show *Deal or No Deal*, but with nothing else lined up, she agreed to go. After all, it was only a short drive from the West Hollywood home she now shared with Trevor to Culver City, where the auditions were taking place. As she picked out her shortest skirt she could have been excused for wondering: *Is this why I earned a bachelor's degree in international relations?*

5

Short Skirts, High Heels

Tameka Jacobs considers herself lucky. Then again, luck is a relative term. It was lucky she had a healthy pair of lungs when her African American mother, a prostitute addicted to meth, left her alone in her crib for two days and nights straight while she plied her trade and then got high. It was only baby Tameka's sustained screaming that alerted the neighbors to the fact that something was wrong. After the police were called little Tameka found herself in foster care, farmed out to a white woman named Mary Brown as a temporary foster parent. Ms. Brown wasn't considered suitable, and there followed a tug of war between the foster mother and social services, who wanted Tameka placed with a black family. The city won, and Tameka was raised in relative prosperity in a leafy California suburb where she learned tap, ballet, and jazz. If she had stayed with her white foster mother, Tameka is certain that she would have ended up going nowhere. Once again Lady Luck took a shine to Tameka.

Like so many teenagers, she arrived in Hollywood wide-eyed and eager to make her mark as a model or an actor. Previously she had worked for a radio station in San Francisco before trying her luck in the City of Angels. At 5 foot 10 she was a head above the competition, and striking, too. She wrote the book on multi-ethnicity, with creole, Norwegian, African American, French, and Spanish in her genes. And that's just what she knows about. She was a standout, literally, at auditions, and it was not long before she was able to leave her seedy basement apartment in gang-scarred Echo Park, which was not the hipster heaven it is today.

First, she did some modeling before auditioning for a new entertainment show, *Deal or No Deal*, hosted by Howie Mandel. The show, based on the Dutch original and replicated across the world, was predicated on the tension between greed and prudence, a sure-fire ratings winner. Contestants chose from twenty-six brief-cases that contained a cash value ranging from one cent to $1 million. During the game the contestant eliminates various briefcases in the hope of being left with the million-dollar case. Periodically the contestant is offered a deal by an unseen banker. The offer to quit the game and take modest winnings is matched by the possibility of going on and winning the big prize. The audience is always eager to see them risk it all with the briefcases.

The briefcases themselves are held by twenty-six beautiful smiling girls arranged temptingly in front of the contestant. This is where Tameka came in. She was asked to be briefcase girl 21, a position she held from the day the show opened in December 2005 to the end of its run in 2010.

When she was first asked to join, Tameka was over the moon. It was almost everything she could have asked for. She was paid $800 per episode, and they regularly recorded seven episodes a day. That was $5,600, more than $23,000 a week, when the going was good. Then there were endorsements and personal appearances thrown in. Fame and riches for standing for hours on end holding a briefcase full of pretend cash. The irony was not lost on her.

Plus it was fun being a briefcase girl. The other girls were rowdy, catty, and goofy, it was just like being in a sorority house.

They had only two enemies—the cold in the studio and the achingly high heels they were all asked to wear.

Meghan joined the gang in 2006 for season 2 after successfully passing the audition. Along with model Chrissy Teigen she began as a backup in case regular girls were ill or failed to show up. Eventually she got a full-time slot as briefcase girl 24—close to Tameka. When she first arrived, Tameka clocked her as another multiracial girl. "It was never discussed between us," she recalls. "We just looked at one another and knew." It was an unspoken code, a shared understanding of a lifetime of misunderstandings, quizzical glances, and snide comments condensed into one knowing look. They had connections in common, too—early on Tameka had been taken under the wing of model, talk show host, and all-round superstar Tyra Banks, who was, as Meghan well knew, a legend back at her old high school, Immaculate Heart. Now it was Tameka's time to return the favor, giving Meghan the lowdown on the personalities, on who and what to look out for. She briefed her on the daily routine and what to bring to set—a pair of cozy Ugg boots after a day on high heels in near-freezing temperatures was a must. As they chatted it was clear to Tameka that Meghan saw this as a stepping stone to earn some money before trying for more serious acting jobs.

The average *Deal or No Deal* day began at five thirty in the morning as Meghan and the other briefcase girls gathered for hours of hair, makeup, and final fittings for their skimpy outfits. With outfit changes every episode and multiple episodes filmed each day, they often had to endure three separate fittings. A rack of beautiful matching ball gowns would arrive to be unceremoniously hacked to pieces so the girls' legs and décolletage were on full display.

After rough fittings for length and shape there would be a final wardrobe session where the girls sucked in everything and the dresses were pinned down. Some dresses were so tight that the girls couldn't even bend down to put on their agonizingly high heels, so an assistant would be on hand to help.

The briefcase girls all wore Spanx shapewear not only to make their stomachs flatter but to keep them warm in the near-freezing studio temperatures. As a final touch they inserted what briefcase girl 13 Leyla Milani liked to call "chicken cutlets"—or it could be pads of tissues—into their bras to enhance their cleavage.

As Meghan stood there hour after hour, trying not to shiver, her feet sore from the cheap high heels, a painted smile on her face, she thought of the paycheck at the end of the week. This was not what she had in mind when she went into acting but, at only twenty-five, she was earning more money than she had ever earned in her life, and the shooting schedule was perfect: long blocks of filming followed by weeks of down time, which gave her the opportunity to attend more auditions and go traveling with the man she playfully called Trevi Trevi Trevity.

While the Hamptons had been sampled, there were other spots she wanted to visit, schedules permitting: Greece, Mexico, Thailand, anywhere in the Caribbean were all on her list. The foodie in her fantasized about going to Bangkok and sampling the menu at Chote Chitr, the restaurant that had been featured on National Public Radio and in the *New York Times*.

Of course, that was if Trevor could make the time. He was always busy, and unlike the boyfriends and husbands of her *Deal or No Deal* "sisters," Trevor never visited Meghan on set. In fact, it was so unusual that it was noted by the other girls. However, there were plenty of other celebrities, mainly sports stars, who dropped by, some clearly trying to get up close and personal with the girls. One guest caused quite the frisson: Donald Trump, then organizing the Miss Universe pageant and making a guest appearance as the banker on *Deal or No Deal* to cross-promote *The Apprentice*. The frequently bankrupt real estate mogul toured the set, giving girls his card and inviting them to play golf at one of his courses.

Tameka Jacobs recalls: "He was a creep, super creepy, but some girls were attracted to money and power and took his number."

Meghan was one of the girls who gave the future president a wide berth. Not that she was known for joining in much with any of the after-work events, occasions when a bevy of beautiful women, several minders in tow, trawled the bars of West Hollywood. As Meghan is now known as a thirsty socialite, it is surprising that she rarely, if ever, joined in these raucous nights of karaoke and chasers.

For a girl who would end up living her life on Instagram, it is remarkable, too, that she never posed for a silly picture, mugging for the cameras like the rest of her colleagues. Meghan knew her angles—after all, she had been taught by the best, her father—and always posed sweetly. If caught with a drink in her hand, it was only ever champagne, and she was never heard to swear—somewhat surprising given how well-known her eventual breakout show is for its off-color language.

Aside from promotional photos in costume on the *Deal or No Deal* set, Meghan's only promo work for the show was self-serving, appearing at a C-level gifting suite for the 2006 Emmys in casual wear, where she was duly photographed looking at yoga mats and resort wear. Meghan's lack of involvement in office gossip—she was always studying lines for an audition, recalls Leyla Milani—and after-work play was just one of the reasons she stood out. The other was her eating habits. While the other girls "sucked hard candy and ate raw vegetables" between scenes, Meghan would eat pizza or bags of chips, seemingly unconcerned about bloat or weight gain. And while many of the other girls thanked their lucky stars for this opportunity, Meghan saw the gig as a temporary berth. As Tameka recalls: "She was super sweet, adorable, a little sheltered, wholesome with a good head on her shoulders. Looking back, it was clear that she had a brand and wanted to protect that brand for a future career as a serious actor." She knew where she wanted to go, and it certainly wasn't spending her days on *Deal or No Deal.*

During the shooting break in November, she auditioned for and got the part of a Latina murder suspect on *CSI: NY.* The part once again had Meghan flashing the flesh when her character is introduced wearing a corset and suspenders. Then it was back to the cold NBC soundstage in Culver City.

During Meghan's time on *Deal or No Deal,* Trevor had a film in production, a marital comedy, *License to Wed* starring funny-man Robin Williams. Meghan secretly hoped there would be a role for her, but the bit parts that might have suited her went to more experienced actors who had worked with the director, Ken Kwapis, on the TV series *The Office.* It was to become a source of conflict between the couple; Meghan was disappointed that Trevor didn't try harder to include her in some of his productions.

No matter. She had the feeling that this could be her year. During the February round of auditions for the 2007 pilot season, she came away from a meeting with top casting agent Donna Rosenstein with a positive spring in her step. Rosenstein had been a senior vice president at ABC for many years, overseeing the casting of such series as *NYPD Blue, Roseanne,* and *Twin Peaks,* and had since set up her own company. She was Meghan's best chance yet at the big time.

She loved the part she had been asked to read for, a former stripper and streetwalker called Kelly Calhoun who had been rescued from her seedy life by a born-again Christian cop who had fallen in love with and married her.

The show, named *The Apostles,* was part police drama, part *Desperate Housewives,* complete with similar voiceover narration, and was set in a suburban Southern California cul-de-sac where all the residents were police officers and their spouses. Shortly after her reading Meghan got the news she had been longing to hear. "Meghan, you got the part," her agent excitedly told her.

When she told her father he wrote her a loving note of congratulations, the actor keeping his tender letter in a hand-carved box by the side of her bed.

Meghan's character wasn't the most feminist of women, but compared to her role as a briefcase babe, Kelly Calhoun was at least a step in the right direction. Her African American husband, played by Keith Robinson, finds himself conflicted, berating her for her immoral past but drawn to her sassy yet vulnerable personality. In the tight-knit enclave Kelly finds empowerment and friendship with the other wives. She startles them first by sharing sex tips on how to keep things hot in the bedroom and then by teaching them the tricks of the stripping trade, demonstrating how to disrobe seductively. Meghan had a good feeling about the show. It ticked all the boxes: a strong cast—Shawn Hatosy from *Alpha Dog*, who specialized in playing tightly wound, edgy characters, was one of the leads—a solid backstory, feminist themes, and plenty of room for conflict and tension in the insular cop community. It was *Desperate Housewives* in uniform.

The pilot, shot as full-length feature, was delivered in June 2007. After several viewings and much back and forth, Fox Studios decided to pass on making a full-blown series, airing it the following year as a standalone movie. It was a real blow for Meghan, who had harbored high hopes for the show. At least she could now add "stripper" to her acting résumé. Which she promptly did.

While Meghan worked on *The Apostles*, Trevor was in production on a Sandra Bullock/Bradley Cooper comedy, *All About Steve*, written by two of his clients. Bullock had taken control of the film as producer, leaving Trevor to manage his growing stable of writers and directors.

He was always hustling to get them work and to find new clients. When he went to coffee shops he handed out business cards to whoever was tapping away at their laptop. "What's the worst thing that happens? I read a shitty script?" he laughed. He read scripts nonstop, going so far as to keep a stack in their bathroom at home as well as a supply of waterproof pens so he could make notes.

As for Meghan snagging a role through her boyfriend, that had proved to be a bit of a washout. At least so far. Not so with casting agent Donna Rosenstein, who called her in to read for the role of Sadie Valencia, the spoiled daughter of a Las Vegas casino owner in this story of a crime boss's family who were struggling to go straight. There were solid expectations that the comedy, *Good Behavior*, which also starred *Chicago Fire*'s Treat Williams as her father and *Schitt's Creek*'s Catherine O'Hara as family matriarch, would be well-mannered—and funny enough—to make a series for the ABC network.

When the show, which was filmed in Las Vegas and Los Angeles and also starred the Canadian actor Patrick J. Adams, was tested to a wider audience it got a thumbs-down. In the end, it was another pilot that ended up being broadcast as a standalone TV movie.

Work did keep coming, though. Now twenty-seven, Meghan was finished with *Good Behavior*, and she was cast as the teenage vixen Wendy in *90210*, a reboot of the long-running series *Beverly Hills 90210*, which she had watched as a teenager. The new version was trying to be equally iconic but raunchier, sassier, and cooler.

In the series premiere, once again, Meghan's character has a bawdy introduction, first shown outside West Beverly Hills High performing oral sex in another student's car while pupils go back and forth. Her character lasted for just two episodes before vanishing without any plot explanation. The series, however, would run for five seasons. With various guest spots on established series like *Knight Rider*, *Without a Trace*, and the sitcom *The League*, she was almost becoming a familiar face to TV audiences. Real fame, or even just a steady paycheck—she was barely earning enough to pay for actors' health insurance—continued to elude her. She was always on the cusp of making a breakthrough.

When director J. J. Abrams, who even before his mega successes with *Star Wars* was lauded as the mastermind behind *Mission Impossible III* and *Lost*, had her playing junior FBI agent Amy Jessup in his sci-fi procedural *Fringe*, she once again had high hopes that something would come of it. She appeared in the first and second episodes of the second season, and though director Akiva Goldsman, best known for his hit *A Beautiful Mind*, hinted that audiences may be seeing more of Agent Jessup she never returned to the creepy tale of spooky shapeshifters and parallel universes. In fact, she was next seen altering her personal universe in a more conventional way, snorting a couple of lines of cocaine in the knowing TV comedy *The Boys and Girls Guide to Getting Down*. Based on the award-winning 2006 independent film, which featured her *Deal or No Deal* co-model Leyla Milani, the show charts the vagaries of the LA dating scene.

In the sex, drugs, and anything goes movie, Meghan is shown as a single girl pouring herself into a super tight black dress—shades of *Deal or No Deal*—before heading out for the night, prowling the singles scene of downtown LA, where she knocks back some blow to keep the mobile debauchery moving.

With roles where she had snorted coke, performed oral sex, and taught striptease to her name, what better credentials than to share an on-screen smooch with former junkie, funnyman, and now British movie star Russell Brand. Her "exotic" looks won her the role of Tatiana in *Get Him to the Greek*, which filmed in the spring of 2009. With no lines, she remained uncredited in the official cast list. Still she fared better than Brand's ex-wife, Katy Perry, and singer Alanis Morissette, whose scenes were deleted.

During this time, it was her partner who was getting the plaudits. Trevor was named by the *Hollywood Reporter* as one of the "Top 35 Under 35" in the Next Gen Class of 2009 for his work as a manager and producer. All those years of meetings and schmoozing were paying off—and he already had the pretty girl, as he had always dreamed of. Along with a glowing writeup in the *Hollywood Reporter*, the honor came with a party at My House, a Hollywood club notorious for its velvet ropes and bottle service, where Meghan did her best to shine as the beautiful and talented, as well as supportive, girlfriend of a bona fide mover and shaker.

Trevor could now afford to give Megan a few crumbs from his growing pile of scripts. At least it would stop her continually nagging him to give her a part in one of his productions. Two clients, Marcus Dunstan and Patrick Melton, the writers behind *Saw IV, V,* and *VI,* had put together a nineteen-minute film, *The Candidate,* based on the short story by Henry Slezar. Meghan was cast as the secretary, in one scene showing off a beautifully written, hand-addressed envelope, an in-joke about her calligraphy skills.

Trevor then found a small role for her in *Remember Me,* a 9/11-themed melodrama starring the British heartthrob Robert Pattinson. The movie, which was shot in June, was written by his client Will Fetters and turned out to be the producer's biggest hit to date, a ratings and box office success. Meghan might be proving to be his lucky charm.

Not that she thought so. Earlier that year, in January 2010, the young actor began an anonymous blog she called Working Actress, where she described in often heartbreaking detail the life of a struggling actor. In one post she wrote: "I'm not gonna lie. I've spent many days curled up in bed with a loaf of bread and some wine. A one woman pity party. It's awful and ridiculous." She described what it was like to have her minor scenes cut from a movie, the endless rejection, bitchy fellow actors at auditions, and tests shoots gone wrong. "All you are doing is setting yourself up for heartbreak," she said of this most demanding of professions. Though her blog, which abruptly ended in 2012, was anonymous, fellow bloggers and actors confirmed she was the author. "Yes, it was definitely Meghan Markle who wrote it," said actor Lancer Carter, who reproduced one of her posts on his own site.

After graduating from Fairfax High School in Los Angeles, Doria Ragland (far right, second row) worked for her father, Alvin Ragland, at his antiques business. Later she took on a job in the makeup department at ABC Studios. It was here that she met her future husband, Thomas Markle, then lighting director for the long-running drama *General Hospital. (MEGA)*

Thomas Markle, pictured in this 1962 high school portrait when he was eighteen. Shortly after graduating he headed to the Poconos, where he worked in local theaters. Later he moved to Chicago to pursue his ambition of working in stage lighting. *(MEGA)*

On December 23, 1979, African American Democrat Doria Ragland married Pennsylvania-born Republican Thomas Markle Sr. at the Self-Realization Fellowship Temple in Hollywood. Their union came just twelve years after the landmark Supreme Court ruling in *Loving v. Virginia* that allowed interracial marriage throughout the United States. *(Mail on Sunday / Solo Syndication)*

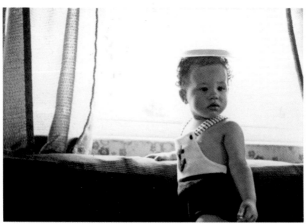

Meghan, then a two-year-old toddler, was photographed endlessly by her doting father. But soon after this picture was taken, Doria and Thomas went their separate ways. *(Mail on Sunday / Solo Syndication)*

Meghan, seen here at age five, and her mother, Doria, who worked as a travel agent, would often take trips together, visiting Mexico and Jamaica. After her parents separated, Meghan lived with her mother. Later, as a freshman, she moved in with her father, as his home and studio were close to Immaculate Heart School. *(Mail on Sunday / Solo Syndication)*

Meghan's grandfather Alvin Ragland, standing next to her Aunt Saundra, holds a smiling Meghan at a family gathering while her half-brother Tom Markle Jr. holds her ponytail. Seated are her mother, Doria, and grandmother Jeanette. *(Mail on Sunday / Solo Syndication)*

Meghan, age five, sings "The Wheels on the Bus" at her private school, the Little Red School House, in Hollywood. The budding actress appeared in numerous productions, including *West Side Story* and *How the Grinch Stole Christmas*. *(Splash News)*

Meghan at Ninaki Priddy's ninth birthday party in 1990. They were such good friends that both families considered them sisters. *(Splash News)*

Meghan, around age ten, with her Uncle Fred Markle, now presiding bishop of the Eastern Orthodox Catholic Church, with her father, Tom Markle Sr., and grandmother Doris. Meghan was devoted to her grandmother and regularly visited her at her Glendale nursing home. *(The Sun / News Licensing)*

Tom Markle Sr. worked as the lighting director for the sitcom *Married with Children*. Meghan would often bring friends, seen here with series star David Faustino, to visit the set. *(Splash News)*

Meghan in seventh grade, 1993, at the start of her first year at
Immaculate Heart, an all-girls Catholic high school in the Los Feliz
area of Los Angeles. The school was alma mater to showbiz stars Tyra
Banks, Mary Tyler Moore, and Lucie Arnaz. (© *John Dlugolecki /
Contact Press Images*)

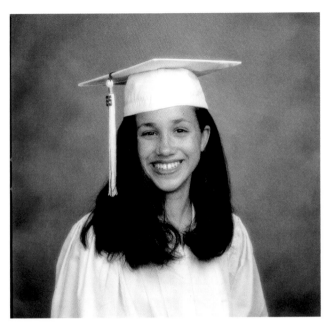

Meghan in eighth grade, August 1994. That year she first
volunteered at the Hippie Kitchen but found the experience
"very scary." She would return four years later. (© *John
Dlugolecki / Contact Press Images*)

Meghan's Immaculate Heart High School was just a few minutes walk from her
home in Los Feliz. Here she is fooling around with her school friends. (*Splash News*)

Meghan poses with her date Danny Segura for the St. Francis school prom. Meghan encouraged Danny to try his hand at acting, and he starred with her in his high school's production of *Oedipus Rex*. *(Vicki Conrad)*

Meghan and her classmate Cecilia Donnellan strike a pose at the senior year Christmas dance held in December 1998. *(© John Dlugolecki / Contact Press Images)*

During her time at Immaculate Heart, Meghan featured regularly in stage shows such as *Annie, Steppin' Out,* and *Back Country Crimes,* which were directed by former Hollywood star Gigi Perreau. In her senior year she performed at Catholic boys' schools, wowing the audience as seductress Lola in the musical *Damn Yankees* and taking the female lead in the Greek tragedy *Oedipus Rex.* Note that she is wearing the distinctive art deco-style Immaculate Heart class ring. *(© John Dlugolecki / Contact Press Images)*

A prescient photograph of Meghan and her best friend Ninaki Priddy outside Buckingham Palace during their summer trip to Europe in 1996. Neither would ever have dreamed that Meghan would one day be welcomed through the wrought-iron gates. *(Splash News)*

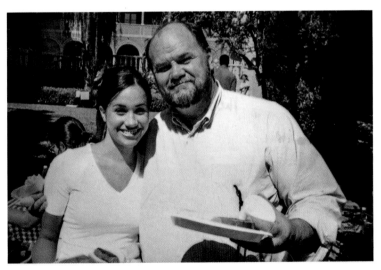

Meghan and her lighting-director father, Tom Markle, Sr., enjoying the sunshine at a school picnic. He was devoted to his daughter, spending hours setting the stage lights for her many theater performances. A keen photographer, he took hundreds of pictures of his darling daughter. *(© John Dlugolecki / Contact Press Images)*

Meghan and her fellow thespians are given a standing ovation by the appreciative audience at St. Francis High School. *(Courtesy of Emmanuel Eulalia)*

Meghan, starring as Jocasta in the Greek tragedy *Oedipus Rex*, kisses Oedipus, played by Alejandro Santiago Fresquez, in the dramatic last act. The play, which was staged at Flintridge Prepatory School in La Cañada Flintridge, was a sellout, largely because Meghan, that year's homecoming queen, was the star. Fresquez went on to study theater in college and now lives in New York. *(Courtesy of Emmanuel Eulalia)*

Meghan, as Jocasta, expresses her tearful despair when she realizes that she had committed incest with her son. She later hangs herself. *(Courtesy of Emmanuel Eulalia)*

The young actors take a break between rehearsals. Megan hitches a ride on the back of a grinning Danny Segura, kid brother of her boyfriend Luis, while Brent Giannotta, who played a shepherd, makes a mock attack with his staff. *(Courtesy of Emmanuel Eulalia)*

A delightful black-and-white portrait of Meghan. It is easy to see why she was voted homecoming queen. *(Courtesy of Emmanuel Eulalia)*

On the day of her graduation, which was held at the Hollywood Bowl in the summer of 1999, Meghan collected a raft of awards for academic ability and community service. She had proven herself an outstanding student, intellectually and socially. (© *John Dlugolecki / Contact Press Images*)

Homecoming queen Meghan is all smiles at the St. Francis High School homecoming dance. She won the honor not only because of her beauty but also her community work and her leadership ability. Here she is clearly enjoying herself, dancing cheek to cheek with Giancarlo Boccato. (© *John Dlugolecki / Contact Press Images*)

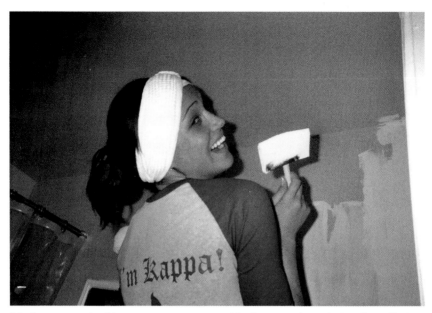

Meghan customized her room on campus at Northwestern by painting the walls in vivid colors. Before she handed back the keys she had to repaint the walls standard white. She typically turned routine decoration into a party. *(Splash News)*

Meghan celebrated her graduation from Northwestern with Ninaki Priddy and other college friends. She graduated with degrees in theater arts and international relations. Other successful Northwestern graduates include actors Warren Beatty and David Schwimmer. *(Splash News)*

After Meghan graduated college, she and her friend Ninaki Priddy took a road trip back to Los Angeles, stopping off at the Hotel Bellagio in Las Vegas, the setting for her favorite film, *Ocean's Eleven*. (*Splash News*)

Meghan backstage on *Deal or No Deal* in one of the show's less revealing and more comfortable costumes. The low-heeled saddle oxfords were a definite change from the cheap high heels the briefcase girl usually wore for tapings. (© *Tameka Jacobs*)

Meghan and her husband film producer Trevor Engelson, seen here enjoying a break on a Greek island, worked hard and played hard. Engelson boasted that even on the plane he was working. "But I'm always having a lot more fun than most other people I know." *(Splash News)*

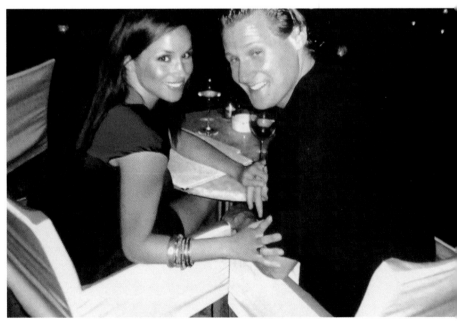

Meghan and her husband Trevor Engelson enjoy a candlelit dinner for two during a romantic vacation on the island of Santorini in the Mediterranean. *(Splash News)*

Shortly after beginning the blog, in July 2010, Meghan was again ready for her own close-up. She was cast opposite comedian Jason Sudekis in the comedy *Horrible Bosses*. In her thirty-five-second scene she played a FedEx girl whom Sudekis creepily hits on, saying that she is too "cute" for the job. Meghan was cool and polite, a professional just doing her job. That was it. Blink and you would miss her. There was, however, a major compensation. She got to work on the same set as her acting hero, Donald Sutherland, who played Jack Pellit in the movie.

"I was so excited to work with him," she enthused. "The woman in the hair department said he was a gem and that I would love him, so when I met him (and his oh-so-debonair self), I said: 'Mr. Sutherland, I hear I'm going to fall in love with you before lunch break.' He laughed, it broke the ice. And I resisted the very major urge to squeal."

Once her heart had slowed down, she had to recognize that this was yet another acting job that traded exclusively on her looks and sex appeal. Time to recalibrate. She was approaching thirty, an age in a notoriously cruel place like Hollywood when she would soon be considered over the hill. If she was not careful, her agent would be dropping hints about changing the date of birth on her résumé.

Another casting season had passed her by, and she had nothing apart from a series of auditions on her calendar. It was hard not to feel discouraged, especially when she heard of the successes of her contemporaries. Those five years were up, and she just hadn't quite made that extra leap.

Time to dip into Trevor's bran tub of aphorisms. Along with "give it five years," he had another favorite: "This is not a business for the weary. You're either gonna buy an island or be sent to one."

Meghan straightened her skirt, focused her gaze, and walked into the next casting room. She wasn't yet ready for Elba.

6

A Star Is Tailor Made

Rachel Zane was a ballbuster. A ballbuster to cast, a ballbuster to play, and a ballbuster to even name appropriately. Sexy but unapproachable, Rachel Zane was a character created as the love interest on a new show, so new they hadn't even worked out the title. Opinion was split. Some executives at the USA Network, who were developing the show in 2010, went for *A Legal Mind*. Others thought the title *Suits* was tailor-made for a snappily dressed office full of sharp lawyers. *Suits* won out. That was just one of numerous daily battles to give *Suits* a distinct identity.

Casting and chemistry were critical to give *Suits* crackle and pop. Patrick J. Adams was perfect for the part of Mike Ross, the legal genius with an eidetic memory who couldn't afford law school because he was paying to keep his sick grandma in an upscale nursing home. The actor's eyes were the key to him winning the role: piercing blue, long lashed. The rest of him was just average-looking boy next door. He combined a vibe of intelligence with just enough seediness to flesh out the part of the brilliant college dropout who made a living by taking law school entry exams for other students.

After several weeks of casting, on July 7 they had snagged *The Others* star Gabriel Macht as top lawyer Harvey Reginald Specter, and cast Rick Hoffman as the duplicitous partner Louis Litt, as well as Gina Torres, who played the sharp-tongued founding partner Jessica Lourdes Pearson.

One part remained, the role of Rachel Zane. She was a paralegal who was smart, elegantly upper class, and so highly regarded at the fictional law firm that she had her own office, while several of the fictional lawyers still labored on the main floor. She had to be sexy without being overtly so, secure in her own power as a woman, but with a certain vulnerability as shown by the fact that she was unable to pass the LSAT, the exam that determined eligibility for law school. The show's producers were looking for a woman who had "toughness and attitude while still being engaging."

"The part was just a nightmare to cast," recalls one studio executive. "Then Meghan Markle came along." Once told by famed casting director April Webster to use "less makeup, more Meghan" when auditioning, Meghan had dressed "sexy-professional-casual" to screen test for the role. Somewhat belatedly she realized that the plum colored spaghetti-strap top, black jeans, and high heels she wore were more "single lady lawyer on the prowl" than "attractive paralegal with an encyclopedic knowledge of the law."

Before her audition Meghan ran into an H&M store, picked out a simple black dress for $35 and raced back to the studio. She hadn't even time to try it on for size. The producers of the then titled *A Legal Mind* asked her to change into the new garment before taking the screen test. It was the best $35 she had ever spent. As the show's creator, Aaron Korsh, told writer Sam Kashner: "We all looked at each other after the Meghan Markle screen test like, 'Wow this is the one.' I think it's because Meghan has the ability to be smart and sharp without losing her sweetness."

With the casting of Meghan Markle, the character of Rachel Zane was made flesh. Originally the brainy and beautiful paralegal was named Rachel Lane, but the clearance department felt the name was too similar to that of a real person. So they chose the surname of the show's casting director, Bonnie Zane, an insiders' compliment to the storied Hollywood professional for her work on the show.

It was not as if Meghan was a shoo-in for the role. Now thirty, on paper she was too old to play a young paralegal, and the multiracial Gina Torres had already put a tick in the box labeled "ethnic diversity."

Her main rival was a younger, more experienced Canadian actor, blond, blue-eyed Kim Shaw. By now Meghan had learned to manage her expectations and not take rejection too personally. She was often too light, too dark, too skinny, too something or other for so many roles.

Meghan didn't feel great about her audition and called her agent, Nick Collins at the Gersh Agency, from her car. She told him that she could not get her head around the lines. It was a mouthful, the worst audition of her life. "I don't think I did a good job in that room, and I need to get back in there," she wailed. "I really want this part." Her agent had heard this before from so many of his clients, and his answer was always the same: "There's nothing I can do. Just focus on your next audition." Once again, she felt that moment of *Why am I subjecting myself to this torture?* She had a top degree, a sparkling résumé, great connections; she didn't have to put herself through the ringer every day. It was kind of inevitable, though, given her background. As she once said: "If you grow up in a coal mining town, you will probably become a coal miner. I grew up in the industry, and was always on set because of my dad, so it seems natural for me to be an actress."

In spite of her considerable misgivings, she tried to stay optimistic, going to yoga classes and meditating to stay grounded. All the while she headed out to other auditions, though none of them

inspired her as much as A *Legal Mind*. In her heart, she felt this
role would be perfect for her. It was kismet—her given first name
was Rachel, just like the part she longed to play.

While Meghan felt she had blown the audition, unbeknownst
to her, behind the scenes the executives were busy putting
together her test deal and drawing up the contract for the pilot
if the network approved. As she recalls: "We had no idea that
they loved my read. They loved my take on Rachel and they
were putting together a test deal for me. It was a really good
lesson in perspective. I think we are always going to be our own
worst critics."

The head honchos at USA Network had chosen Markle over
Shaw, formally casting her on August 24, 2010. As then USA Network copresident Jeff Wachtel explained: "Shaw was a little more
traditional blond girl next door. The decision was a tough one
because they were both really good. Meghan had a certain type
of sparkle and was a little more urbane, a little more worldly."

The deciding factor was how they wanted the relationship
between Rachel and Mike to play out. As Wachtel recalled: "One
of the things that we needed at the beginning with *Suits* was Patrick's character comes in as the hottest thing in town: he's brilliant,
has a photographic memory and fakes his way into being a lawyer
and then he comes up against this girl who turns out to be the
love of his life. We needed somebody who had a real authority to
shut him down and still be the coolest thing around. And they
had it right away. It was a lot of fun."

Meghan was still taking other auditions when her cell phone
rang with a call from her agent, telling her she had been cast in
the *Suits* series pilot and would begin filming in autumn in New
York. She was overjoyed but also wary. After all, she had gone
down this road before, especially with *The Apostles*, which, at the
time, she felt confident was going to be her big break. After eight

years going from audition to audition, had she finally caught a break? She could dream. If the pilot was a success, *Suits* could turn into a series, and then who knows. Meghan's casting garnered a short article in the *Hollywood Reporter*, noting her uncredited role in the 2010 comedy *Get Him to the Greek*.

When she began with a standard table read of the script, it was obvious that Meghan and Patrick generated chemistry, this elusive quality the showbiz equivalent of lightning in a bottle. It was vital that they had a spark between them as the ups and downs of their love story would be a narrative arc throughout the series—if the show was picked up by the network, that is.

In the fall of 2010 Meghan flew to New York to shoot the ninety-minute series pilot. Since the elation of winning the part, reality had set in. She had already shot five pilots, including one for ABC with her current costar, Patrick J. Adams, and none of them had got any further. Maybe he was her unlucky charmer. As she later observed: "A pilot is like your baby, then you wait and wait to see if it gets picked up and it's a hard thing to let go of. The one I had the most attachment to was one called *The Apostles*, which was my very first pilot. It's probably revisionist history but I look back on it now and think: "That would have been amazing. But who knows?"

On her first day of the shoot, the normally nerveless Meghan was a little edgy. Though she had grown up on film sets, it was one thing sitting in the wings watching the action, quite another to be center stage. Nonetheless, all those hours after school on professional soundstages, observing the interaction of actors and crews, overhearing the snatches of conversation and gossip between production assistants, and hanging around the craft service table, had taught her how to behave on set. She was charming to everyone, from grips to the lighting director. There was a degree of self-interest at work, having learned from her father that the placement of a light could enhance or slightly deform a pretty face, and that some of the placement depended on goodwill.

Meghan was remembered as bubbly and warm, chatty but a good listener who didn't dominate on-set conversations. She was a team player who radiated a sweet intelligence, saving her sterner, more ambitious self for those important on-set interactions with Patrick J. Adams.

In a show that became known as much for its fashion as its plotline, costume designer Jolie Andreatta's vision of Meghan's on-screen look was crucial. She later recalled: "Rachel is classic to the word with a hint of rebellion thrown in. Her style is understated and her cute figure pulls it off perfectly."

On her return from New York, Trevor took Meghan to a beach resort in Belize for a vacation. It was here amid the tropical greenery and the soothing waves that he asked his girlfriend of six years to be his bride. Meghan was thrilled—and clearly in love. "They were both googly eyed for one another," recalls a friend. "They were very much in love."

She was marrying her long-time producer boyfriend and was in a pilot where the omens looked good. There was serious talk of a TV series. At long last her Hollywood dream was coming true. As her half brother, Tom Junior, recalls: "Meg was on her way up, marrying a guy with a production company and now making good money."

All those on-set rumors turned into a joyous reality when in January 2011, USA Network gave the green light for the first series. Shooting would begin on April 25 in Toronto. Finally, after years of auditions that went nowhere, roles that ended up on the cutting room floor, and—most disheartening—pilots that never got picked up, Meghan had a series. The only downside was that she would have to take a five-hour flight if she was to see her Hollywood-based fiancé. The sacrifice was going to be worth it. As she and

Trevor caught planes like others hailed taxis, the commute was not going to be a hardship. They were both ambitious young people; if anything, Trevor was more driven than Meghan. So he was totally understanding that this was an opportunity that she could not miss.

Her joy, however, was tempered with sorrow. While she was preparing for the series, her mother phoned to tell her that Alvin Ragland, her eighty-two-year-old grandfather, had tripped and fallen as a result of getting tangled with a dog lead while out walking his dog. He had hit his head on the sidewalk, and Doria's father died of his injuries on March 12. She remembered Alvin as a real character. Meghan appreciated his knowledge of antiques, an enthusiasm that inspired her own fascination with the finer things in life. In the family reorganization following his death, Doria inherited his single-story green stucco house in what is known as the "black Beverly Hills." It was close to the University of Southern California, where, in the late spring, Doria, now a mature student, would complete her master's degree in social work. Her daughter was ecstatic, probably more effusive than her mother. She watched proudly as her mother collected her degree on a makeshift stage at one of the many graduation ceremonies taking place on the extensive campus in June. Given the difficulties of her background, the trouble at her high school following the earthquake, and the temporary jobs she had taken on to make ends meet, her achievement was a genuine personal triumph, an indication of her smarts and her determination.

The first episode of *Suits* aired on June 23, to generally favorable reviews and, more important, an enthusiastic audience. The cast, crew, and money men at the network were ecstatic, the producers thrilled that their gamble to cast Meghan opposite Patrick had paid off big time, the show's fans buzzing about the couple's on-screen chemistry.

Their off-screen chemistry was equally noticeable, almost uncomfortably so, according to guests at Meghan and Trevor's wedding which took place in Jamaica in September 2011. They had clearly developed a bond of familiarity that is invariably the corollary of working up close and personal for so long and so intensely. Patrick J. Adams has a different take on their interaction at that time. He later told writer Lesley Goldberg: "In some ways, Meghan and I were the closest because we were the youngest people in the cast and both came in with the least experience. We grew up together over the course of the show."

He might have kept his distance if he had known that she had been cast to play a calculating serial killer in an episode of the quirky crime show *Castle*, titled "Once Upon a Crime," which she filmed while *Suits* was on hiatus. As Princess Sleeping Beauty, Meghan's character plotted a complex series of murders with fairy-tale themes, and was cast for the part by her champion, Donna Rosenstein.

For Meghan, shooting her first series of *Suits* was actually more stressful than organizing her wedding. After choosing Jamaica Inn in Ocho Rios, an idyllic spot with balconies overlooking the sea, she had delegated the organization to an in-house wedding coordinator who handled every detail of this destination wedding. Given the hectic lives she and Trevor were leading, it was a life-saver. All she had to worry about was the guest list, choosing the flowers, agreeing to the menu—and packing a bikini or two. Oh, and her strappy white wedding dress.

Meghan knew a month before their nuptials that *Suits* had been picked up for a second season, a cause for celebration but also uncertainty as, once more, the newlyweds would be long-distance commuters, seeing each other every two or three weeks, depending on if Trevor had meetings or had arranged to see his family, who lived on Long Island. The couple was determined to enjoy a long weekend of parties, including beach wheelbarrow races, culminating with the wedding ceremony.

With the ocean as backdrop, the couple recited vows they had written themselves, promising to love and care for each other. One of her bridesmaids recalled, "It was such a moving wedding. I started crying the moment I saw her in her dress." Though the couple had officially married in Los Angeles in a brief civil ceremony, this was the real celebration for family and friends, complete with a rousing chorus of the traditional Jewish "Hava Nagila" sung while the bride and groom were hoisted up in chairs held above their guests' heads.

On return from their Jamaican celebration, Trevor and Meghan were able to spend more time with one another before shooting began once more in Toronto. It was just as well that she was enjoying a brief break, as her father was in need of her support. For the last few months, he had cared for his increasingly frail mother, Doris Markle, who he had flown from her home in Florida to his house in Los Feliz. As his home is close by the ABC TV studios where he worked, he was able to visit during the day to check that she was okay. Sadly, as her chronic forgetfulness slipped into dementia, that was no longer a practical option. The last straw was when she absentmindedly left a pan on the stove, causing a small kitchen fire. He arrived home to find the fire department and paramedics at the scene.

The only option was to place her in a specialist facility, moving her into Broadview Residential Care Center, an affordable nursing home in Glendale, Los Angeles. Once the first season of *Suits* wrapped, Meghan visited her as much as she could, making the twelve-mile drive from her cozy house on Hilldale in West Hollywood to see her grandmother. She read to her, brushed her hair, and did simple arts and crafts with the aging matriarch. As she slipped deeper into the gloaming of dementia, Doris did not recognize her son, Tom Senior, nor her grandson, Tom Junior. Yet her eyes would light up when she heard Meghan's voice and felt her comforting touch. "With her dementia, grandmother got weird about me and dad but was always okay with Meg," recalls Meghan's brother, Tom Junior. "I saw the private side of Meghan, a genuinely caring, loving person. She had an amazing relationship with Doris even though she didn't know her that well."

In October, she and Trevor walked the red carpet at the Anti-Defamation League Entertainment Industry Awards dinner at the Beverly Hilton hotel, the most high-level event she had ever attended. More importantly, she was master of ceremonies for the evening. She dressed the part in a simple Stella McCartney velvet cocktail dress, while Trevor, beaming with pride, looked his usual slightly rumpled self. They mingled with other celebrities, and Meghan glowed. She was on her way.

Meghan also continued to visit her ailing grandmother at the nursing home. Tom Senior and Tom Junior could only be there on weekends, but Meghan came frequently during the week as well. With Doris fading fast, Tom Senior flew in his brothers to say their last goodbyes. She died on November 25, 2011. Trevor and Meghan were present at her funeral. It was the first time that most of the Markles had met the TV producer. Meghan's brother remarked, "She was completely head over heels and seemed really happy when I saw them together, despite the sad circumstances. They seemed extremely happy together."

These family reunions were few and far between. The last time Meghan had seen her half sister Yvonne, who had rechristened herself Samantha, was when she and Tom Senior made the trip to Albuquerque for the eldest Markle daughter's college graduation. "She was lovely, very polite and sweet," recalled Tom Senior's first wife, Roselyn, about Meghan's visit. During the graduation ceremony, Meghan sat next to Samantha's preteen daughter, Noel, and made small talk with the girl, then posed for photos, smiling and trying to make everyone feel at ease.

It was the last time Meghan would see her Markle relations. The actor also left Trevor behind when she flew to Toronto to settle back into her new life, filming for nine months for the show's successful second season. Of course, the couple Skyped and Face-Timed, but it was wearing being apart, especially living through the long, gray Canadian winter. She did her best to get the Californian vibe going in her rented house in Seaton Village, lightening the wall colors and trying to convey a bright and airy feel amid the chilly gloom. Candles, leafy plants, and of course white hotel-style bedsheets with a high thread count helped to bring a touch of Hollywood to Toronto.

It might have been cold outside, but it was hot on set, the budding, but often thwarted romance between Rachel Zane and Mike Ross fueled *Suits'* growing success as much as the Machiavellian plot twists about a law firm and its clients. On screen, sparks flew between Rachel and Mike, enthralling viewers, especially after the second-season finale, which climaxed with their characters having heated sex in the fictional law firm's file room. Fans had become really invested in the fictional couple, Adams recalling a chance encounter with a Swedish hiker who had twisted his ankle on a backpacking trail in New Zealand. When Adams, who was on holiday, went to help, the young man forgot his injuries and told the actor how badly he wanted Mike and Rachel to "figure things out."

Their on-screen intimacy led to speculation that the pair had fallen into the trap of many costars: Elizabeth Taylor and Richard Burton, Angelina Jolie and Brad Pitt, Daniel Craig and Rachel Weisz. In fact, the Canadian-born Adams had fallen for an earlier female lead, Troian Bellasario, the daughter of producers Donna

Pratt and Donald P. Bellasario, who played opposite him in 2009 in the play *Equivocation*. They fell in love, but after a year they broke up, Bellasario going on to win a role in the first season of *Pretty Little Liars*. In a move that his *Suits* character Mike Ross would have approved of, Adams devised a cute way of winning back the showbiz heiress. He quietly scored a bit part on *Pretty Little Liars* and then joined his surprised ex-girlfriend on set at the table read-through. His ploy worked: the couple reunited, eventually became engaged in 2014, and married in 2016.

While the "will they, won't they" romance between Rachel and Mike gave the show its sexual tension, it was the other man in Rachel's life, her father, a powerful rival lawyer played by African American actor Wendell Pierce, who really caught the attention of the show's 4 million strong audience.

As the story develops, we learn that Rachel, much to the disappointment of her successful and wealthy father, is stuck as a paralegal because she just can't pass the law school entrance exam, the LSAT. While her character has some daddy issues, it was Rachel Zane's biracial heritage that stirred controversy, with both African American and white viewers confused that a girl who looked so white had a black father. One fan asked if she was adopted, while others were more hostile about the fictional paralegal's heritage, exposing an ugly, racist side in the show's viewership. Even though the American president himself was biracial, the decision by the show's producers to cast a woman of mixed race as a modern-day equivalent of a conventional upper-class white woman helped move the dial a little with regard to racial stereotypes and traditional images of beauty.

As the show's popularity grew, Meghan and her colleagues were asked to build a following using social media in order to help with ratings. Even though she had never heard of Instagram, she found herself opening an account and posting photographs from her private life. What began as a chore turned into an enjoyable and highly addictive daily habit, the actor building up an amazing 1.9 million followers by the time she closed the account. Her first image on May 24, 2012, showed her *Suits* script from the episode "Break Point"; a copy of *Forbes*, the American business magazine; as well as liberal TV commentator Rachel Maddow's first book, *Drift: The Unmooring of American Military Power*, about the rise of presidential authority and the diminution of Congress. With her Instagram debut Meghan was demonstrating that here was an actor with brains as well as beauty who was involved and engaged in the world around her. Subsequent posts would be less forthright, featuring favorite food, engaging selfies, travels abroad, and images of Toronto. It was a curated, very considered vision of her private world.

Her involvement in the outside world was not just through the distorting prism of Instagram. She took part in a USA Network campaign against racism, appearing on screen in *Characters Unite*, an award-winning public service program created to address the social injustices and cultural divides. Wearing a T-shirt with the words I WON'T STAND FOR RACISM, she encouraged people to stand together against prejudice while sharing her experience of being a fly on the wall while white people told black jokes or made bigoted remarks.

Closer to home the actor volunteered to help at a local Toronto soup kitchen for the homeless, the St. Felix Centre, which was founded by the Felician Sisters. She asked the show's producers if at the end of the day they would donate any leftover food from the craft service, the daily unlimited buffet of snacks designed to fuel the actors and crew through the shoots. They were happy to agree to her request, the *Suits* family also making a substantive cash donation to the homeless charity.

The cast and crew were also encouraged to bond, to be a family. It helped all round. A happy set was a productive set. They formed a tight-knit group, bicycling places and going out for drinks or dinner, playing board games and drinking whisky, as one cast member recalled, "into the wee hours." The cast vacationed together over Canadian Thanksgiving, Meghan bringing her Vitamix super-blender to whip up soups and cocktails for the group. It was during one of these group get-togethers that Meghan was inspired to take what turned out to be her favorite vacation of all time. During a casual conversation with Meghan's costar Gabriel Macht, he told her that he and his wife loved RV vacations. After listening to him wax lyrical about a trip to New Zealand, Meghan decided to follow suit. She and Trevor too rented a RV and spent two weeks driving around New Zealand's sparsely populated South Island. They went hiking over glaciers, visited wineries in Marlborough, and rented a beach house for a few days. She vividly remembers the extraordinary night they pulled up at a campsite in Akaroa, a tiny village surrounding a dead volcano. As she later recalled: "I was washing my hair and I hear something and I open the shower curtain and there is this 13-year-old boy who had crawled under the stall and was trying to steal my underwear. I grabbed my towel and I had shampoo in my hair and I yelled: 'Where is your mother?!' I found his parents and they were mortified of course. And to this day, oh my god, that kid will be sitting at home going 'that's the girl from *Suits*, I saw her naked!'" Now, of course, he will be able to boast that he saw a Hollywood princess in the buff. In spite of her encounter with this junior Peeping Tom, she voted the vacation one of the best trips of her life.

When she returned home, she discussed with Trevor the prospect of adding to their family. She wanted a dog. So just before Christmas she and Trevor found themselves gazing at a pair of six-week-old puppies at a pet adoption agency in Los Angeles. They had only recently been rescued from being put down at a dog shelter. One of the Labrador mixes was black; the other was golden. As luck would have it, David Branson Smith, the screenwriter son of a biographer of Princess Diana, Sally Bedell Smith, adopted the black puppy, whom he called Otto; Meghan took the yellow puppy, whom she named Bogart. She had talk show host and comedian Ellen DeGeneres and her wife, Portia Di Rossi, to thank for the final decision. As Meghan was communing with the tiny pooch, Ellen tapped on the glass of the viewing area and yelled: "Take the dog!" As Meghan recalls: "So I brought him home because Ellen told me to." Soon the adorable Bogart had ousted pictures of herself and her husband on her Instagram feed. She turned the pooch into a much-photographed star, the puppy bogarting the joint social media feed.

In February 2013 Meghan emailed David Smith to say that she and Trevor "always wondered if (Bogart) and his brother would recognize each other...Kind of a sweet thought." Schedules were consulted and the two brothers had a reunion on the beach at Malibu. As Sally Bedell Smith in the London *Sunday Times* recalled: "Otto bounded out of David's car straight towards Bogart. For the next hour they romped around like, well, long lost brothers." Meghan filmed and posted the reunion like a social media pro, exclaiming: "Oh my God, how sweet, they're really the same size." They never saw one another again, though two years later, in 2015, Bogart was joined by another rescue dog, a beagle mix that Meghan named Guy.

By then the other "guy" in her life was long gone. Even though Trevor opened an office in New York—only an hour's flight to Toronto—to expand his business, cracks began appearing in their marriage. What once endeared now irritated. Meghan, a self-confessed perfectionist who was as fastidious as she was controlling, had tolerated Trevor's scattered approach to life for years. He was notorious for arriving late, his clothes rumpled, his hair disheveled, and often as not a new stain on his seersucker jacket. "Sorry, bro," was a constant refrain as he hurtled from meeting to meeting, always just behind the clock.

Her home in Seaton Village was a vision of order and crisply ironed perfection. When she flew back to their Los Angeles home after Trevor had been in solo residence for a few weeks, not so much. Though Trevor would consistently visit, he often felt like an outsider, his presence an irritating distraction.

Whether she wanted to admit it to herself or not, Meghan, who once said that she couldn't imagine life without Trevor by her side, was now building a new world for herself. As Toronto was becoming more her home than Los Angeles, the dynamics in their relationship subtly altered. She was her own woman now, earning a steady income, making new friends on set and off, no longer dependent on her man's money. Or his connections.

A five-hundred-dollar Vitamix blender symbolized the growing divide. She insisted that her favorite kitchen appliance from their West Hollywood home come with her to Toronto, packing it into the backseat of her car, which was being moved by truck to Canada, even though it would have been just as easy to buy a new one. It sat on the kitchen counter in the Toronto house, a material reminder that her home was no longer in Los Angeles.

While Meghan saw her star rising, her husband's career appeared to be treading water. During this time he produced *Amber Alert,* a low-budget thriller about a pair of reality show contestants who spot a car containing a kidnapped child. Though it was an intriguing premise, the movie did little box office business and garnered fewer favorable reviews. With no new projects requiring his attention and with *Suits* on hiatus, Trevor took Meghan on a cycling vacation to Vietnam. It didn't help that he got sick with food poisoning as a result of Meghan sampling obscure local dishes like a female version of the TV globetrotter Anthony Bourdain. Their escape to exotic locales, which once provided a backdrop for their love, only served to highlight the distance between them.

He was not the only one experiencing the Meghan chill. Her

friends in Los Angeles noticed the change in her now that she was on the way up. She no longer had the time for friends she had known for years, canceling lunches on short notice or expecting them to rework their own schedules to accommodate the busy life of the rising star. A networker to her fingertips, she seemed to be carefully recalibrating her life, forging new friendships with those who could burnish and develop her career. New folk like talented fashion stylist Jessica Mulroney, who worked with Sophie Trudeau, wife of the present Canadian prime minister, and her TV personality husband Ben, the son of the former Canadian prime minister, now came into her orbit, seeing them regularly at the newly opened Soho House in Toronto. As she was expanding her social horizons, her LA circle felt they were being left behind.

Though she might be getting above herself, everyone expected Trevor to keep her feet planted on the ground. So her Californian friends were genuinely shocked when she announced the end of her two-year marriage in the summer of 2013.

As her maid of honor, Ninaki Priddy, told writer Rebecca Hardy: "I knew they fought sometimes, but it wasn't anything huge. The only obstacle was the distance because she was living in Toronto and Trevor was based in LA. I thought they were maneuvering through it. Trevor would take his work to Canada and run his office remotely."

It was such a bolt from the blue for Trevor that even at a distance of five years, he can barely contain his anger, the normally affable laid back New Yorker switching gears from his usual "Hi, bro, how's it going?" to a cold fury when her name comes into the conversation. "I have zero to say about her," he said to inquirers. Trevor went from cherishing Meghan to, as one friend observed, "feeling like he was a piece of something stuck to the bottom of her shoe." A wealthy entrepreneur pal claimed that the marriage ended so abruptly that Meghan sent Trevor her diamond wedding and engagement rings back to him by registered mail. Another confirmed that the decision to end the marriage was made by Meghan and that it had come "totally out of the blue."

There were other consequences. The breakup also fractured her thirty-odd year friendship with jewelry designer Ninaki Priddy. After listening to Trevor's side of the story, she decided she no longer wished to associate herself with Meghan. Exactly why is a close-kept secret. As she described it: "All I can say now is that I think Meghan was calculated, very calculated, in the way she handled people and relationships. She is very strategic in the way she cultivates circles of friends. Once she decides you're not part of her life, she can be very cold. It's this shutdown mechanism she has. There's nothing to negotiate, she's made her decision, and that's it. The way she handled it, Trevor definitely had the rug pulled out from under him. He was hurt."

Actor Abby Wathen, who had starred with Meghan in the low-budget movie *Random Encounters* in her pre-*Suits* days, had a different perspective on Meghan's breakup. "We both went through divorce, so we bonded on that too. I was destroyed, but she was empowered. She took her power back. It wasn't the right relationship for her, so she moved on."

Now footloose and fancy free, Meghan spent more time exploring downtown Toronto. She could be found, glass of wine in hand, at Bar Isabel, the tapas bar where the grilled octopus and garlicky roast potatoes threw her into a "carb coma." She also went into raptures about the pasta at Terroni, the local high-end Italian del chain, and also enjoyed poutine, a dish that originated in Quebec in the 1950s, comprising fries covered in gravy and cheese curds—where the squeakier the curds are, the better. On nights when she stayed at home, Meghan, who loves to cook, made vegetable soup in her beloved Vitamix or threw zucchini into the slow cooker with a little water and bouillon until it became what she called "a filthy, sexy mush" that she would toss with pasta.

It was her fascination with food that got her a gig with *Men's*

Health magazine. In 2013 they filmed an interview for their website, asking Meghan to give them the secret to a great burger and steak. It was sweet, unpolished, and very natural; as a California girl, she said, she preferred fish tacos, but for a quick meal "for her man," she would throw a steak on the grill. She also agreed to film a racier version of the same shoot. This video, which appeared two years later, showed Meghan riffing on her role on *Suits*, her hair in a bun, wearing sunglasses, a short leather skirt, and power blazer. She unbuttons her sheer black top to reveal a spotted bra. "Grilling was never so hot," screamed the film title. As the steak smoldered, so did Meghan. But there was a hesitancy in her eyes. She was playing up to the camera, but she seemed uncomfortable, conscious that she was portraying herself as a sex object to be leered at by men. She thought she had left those days behind on the game show *Deal or No Deal*. As far as she was concerned, this wasn't a part she was going to play for much longer.

During the *Suits* hiatus Meghan took the female lead in a low-budget crime thriller called *Anti-Social*. The drama, which was based on a series of real-life robberies involving graffiti gangs, was filmed in Budapest and London. While the money men on the production were looking for nude scenes between Meghan and her costar, Gregg Sulkin, who is ten years her junior, to help give the picture greater appeal, writer-director Reg Traviss stuck to his guns and refused to try to exploit his star. He later explained, "It wasn't needed for the story."

Meghan's stock and standing were rising with each season of *Suits*, which was now the highest-rated American television show in the demographic sweet spot, ages 18 to 49. She was increasingly in demand, and in November 2013 she was invited to attend the red carpet premiere of *The Hunger Games: Catching Fire*, in London's Leicester Square. Two days later Meghan and male model Oliver Cheshire were hosting the high-profile Global Gift charity gala, which benefited the Eva Longoria Foundation and

Caudwell Children charities. Not that she was a fan of the red carpet, finding the glamorous shuffle with other celebrities an ordeal. As she wrote: "I loathe walking the red carpet. It makes me nervous and itchy, and I don't know which way to look. I just revert to this nerdy child that I once was. I hate it. I get off the carpet and have to shake it off. Sounds dramatic, but it's really nerve-racking for me."

While in London, Meghan, the consummate networker, hoped to raise her public profile by discussing the last six episodes of *Suits* season 2 with members of the press. And she had another, more romantic agenda. *Daily Mail* reporter Katy Hind wasn't expecting much when she agreed to meet Meghan on a chilly night in November, just another up-and-coming actor looking for a mention or two in the press. From what she had read, Meghan's ambition was to become a politician, and she had fallen into acting during a holiday from her work at the US embassy in Buenos Aires in Argentina.

As they drank a bottle of prosecco at the rooftop bar of the Sanctum Soho hotel, the conversation turned to men, and, as Hind described, "her interest in British men of a certain, well, standing." To the reporter's surprise, Meghan took out her iPhone and showed her a picture of a handsome man on her Twitter account. "Do you know this guy Ashley Cole? He follows me and he keeps trying to talk to me on Twitter. He's trying really hard."

Katy kept her cool, replying, "I bet." Meghan continued to eagerly confide, "He wants to go out on a date while I'm over here in London. What do you think? Do you know him?"

The reporter certainly knew his reputation as both an England and Chelsea football player and the husband of Girls Aloud singer Cheryl Cole. He had cheated with several women, who had in turn sold their stories to the tabloids. Once Hind had broken the bad news, the actor seemed somewhat deflated, possibly anticipating that her visit to London may have spawned a new romance.

"Thanks, I appreciate it," Meghan told the *Mail* reporter, adding: "Some of my friends told me to stay away from him, too. I think I'll leave it."

During the next three hours, Meghan continued to down glasses of the Italian sparkling wine as she and Katy, both thirty-two, discussed the difficulties of modern romance and of finding the right guy. Meghan admitted that she was newly divorced—her decree cited "irreconcilable differences"—and was now single and ready to mingle.

The tipsy talk wound down, and the two hugged goodbye, with Katy wishing Meghan good luck. "Not that she'd need it," the reporter commented wryly as she watched Meghan, who was unwilling to call a cab, persuade the owner of the bar to drive her a few blocks through the rain to her hotel, the Dean Street Townhouse.

7

The "Aha" Moment

Feeling bloated and puffy skinned, her black leather pants a little too tight, Meghan was just a tad out of sorts as she sat alongside her *Suits* costars on the dais at the five-star Langham Hotel in Pasadena. She looked out at the sea of television critics in front of her and was rather glad that her colleagues were fielding the questions from the Television Critics Association in a long-planned January conference. So far she had sat silently watching the back and forth, the discussion moving on to the shifting time slot, *Suits* moving from ten p.m. to nine p.m. "Will that affect the cursing?" asked one critic, referring to the show's liberal use of profanity.

Meghan popped alive and grabbed the question. She looked at the show's creator and executive producer, Aaron Korsh, and play-fully rephrased the question: "Is that going to change for us being at nine o'clock—the shits and the dammits?" "Shit, no!" responded Korsh. The audience laughed. This was classic Meghan; the good sport, the slightly naughty girl next door, the guy's gal. Her inter-vention had won the crowd. But it was no longer enough. She wanted to stretch her wings; she had things to say, points to make, that went way beyond the question-and-answer format concerning all things *Suits*. She was a well-traveled young woman with an appreciation of different countries, cuisines, and cultures. Meghan had a take on everything from Middle Eastern politics to makeup. She felt her role on *Suits* was a launch pad to something more. She was not yet exploiting her full potential.

Her recent visit to London, for example, had yielded only a small mention in the *Daily Mail* and a photograph in the giveaway morning daily, *Metro UK*. She had appeared on numerous red carpets since her work on the series began, but what started out as thrilling was now routine. She was still a pretty face in the crowd.

Meghan realized that she had to do better, to expand her visibility. From the moment *Suits* became successful, she could see that her young audience, especially teenage girls, were listening to what she had to say. Her Instagram following was growing exponentially, but static pictures of her life, her food, and her dogs didn't provide an outlet for her thoughts on the world at large. She had a genuine point of view about a kaleidoscope of topics; she just needed a venue to express herself.

Just a few days later, on January 22, 2014, she attended the annual *Elle* Women in Television Celebration, her third appearance since *Suits* launched. Meghan felt that she had come home. She was inspired to be surrounded by so many creative and stimulating women like cooking and lifestyle celebrity Giada DeLaurentis and multi-award-winning actor Tracee Ellis Ross, who like Meghan was biracial. Unlike Meghan, Ross came from Hollywood royalty: her mother was Diana Ross, and her father was music manager and industry executive Robert Ellis Silberstein.

Ross's career included a stint as a model, including walking the runway for Thierry Mugler, contributing as an editor and writer for *Mirabella* and *New York* magazines, and as the star of *Girlfriends*, a long-running sitcom, for which she had won several NAACP awards. Her new comedy, *black-ish*, in which she played a biracial doctor and mother to four, was garnering rave reviews. Rubbing shoulders with Ross and others, listening to their can-do success stories, stirred the urge in Meghan to do more. She was an ambitious young woman who wanted to raise her profile but also to use her celebrity to connect with issues that genuinely caught her interest, such as gender equality. How best to integrate her multifarious interests in one coherent, well-curated platform?

The answer came indirectly and unexpectedly. In February 2014, DirecTV, the satellite television company, celebrated the Super Bowl with a huge televised pregame party the day before the big game itself. The spirited game of celebrity flag football, called DirecTV Beach Bowl, was held in a large heated tent at Pier 40 on the Hudson River in lower Manhattan. For the event they created the world's largest indoor beach, trucking in more than a million pounds of sand.

The band Paramore was scheduled to entertain the crowd, and Food Network star Andrew Zimmerman would broadcast live during half time. Ever the good sport, Meghan joined model Chrissy Teigen, a former colleague on *Deal or No Deal*, and other celebrities, including former pro quarterback Joe Montana, comedians Tracy Morgan and Tom Arnold, and the celebrity chef Guy Fieri in a beach game, which Meghan's team won.

After the show Meghan won much more: a new, influential friend, tennis legend Serena Williams. At the time, Williams held seventeen world and US tournament singles titles and almost as many for winning doubles tournaments. More important, she had parlayed her fifteen-year career as a super athlete into lucrative endorsements, including her own fashion line, and even some acting gigs.

"We hit it off immediately, taking pictures, laughing through the flag football game we were both playing in, and chatting not about tennis or acting, but about all the good old fashioned girly stuff," Meghan later wrote. "So began our friendship."

What also impressed Meghan was that she was able to say, "Check out my website." Or rather websites. She had an online clothing label as well as Instagram, Snapchat, and Reddit accounts and a regular newsletter.

That was the light bulb moment. Meghan had been mulling over a website for some time, but seeing how someone as busy and as successful as Serena controlled her own site gave her confidence that she too could follow suit—or *Suits*. Her thinking was reinforced by an approach from an e-commerce company who offered to create a site with her name front and center. At first she was excited by the idea. "It will be your name, meghanmarkle .com, and we can run it for you," they told her. Essentially her name would drive consumers to the site. While there would be some created content, the aim was to sell clothing and bric-a-brac from which Meghan would receive a percentage of sales. She pondered their offer, then she stood back for a moment and took a breath. As tempting as it sounded, the more she thought about it, it just didn't feel right. "There was so much more I wanted to share," she explained to friends. Meghan wanted a place where she could showcase her deeper self, where her voice would be heard, and where if there was e-commerce it would be thoughtful and ethical, rather than just marketing the latest fast fashion and trend. She wanted to stress the importance of giving back. Dumping a bucket of cold water over herself on the roof of golfer buddy Rory McIlroy's Manhattan apartment for the ALS Challenge and then posting an Instagram of the result wasn't quite enough, though it did raise money for a good cause, research into motor neuron disease.

She left the website idea percolating in the background. With *Suits* on hiatus, she flew to Vancouver in western Canada to appear in a Hallmark Channel TV movie called *When Sparks Fly* in which she played Amy, a plucky reporter sent back to her bucolic hometown to write a human interest piece about growing up as the daughter of fireworks manufacturers. Her old boyfriend is about to marry her high school best friend, and suddenly Amy realizes that maybe the big city life wasn't for her after all. It was a pleasing trifle and a paycheck, but that was about it. The plot about a difficult return home was the polar opposite of her next excursion, a visit to her alma mater, Northwestern University.

If she needed any more proof that she had an audience that went beyond the confines of *Suits*, she only had to look at the line snaking around the Ryan Auditorium as six hundred students shuffled forward for a coveted seat to see Meghan and the rest of the *Suits* family.

Communication studies freshman Nikita Kuekarni, who waited five hours for the event, was breathless with excitement. "I didn't think it was real when people first told me about it. I thought people were messing with me. I was excited to have Meghan come!"

Meghan basked in the attention from the Northwestern students, comparing shared college experiences and discussing her character's development. She gave her adoring audience a tour of the mind of her alter ego, Rachel Zane: "She's layered and humanized; even though she seems so confident, she really has all these insecurities and vulnerabilities, and I relate to that as a woman and I think the fans will too."

After the chat she posed for photos, signed posters, and later she and fellow star Rick Hoffman, who plays Louis Litt, recorded a promo video for the Northwestern University Dance Marathon, a charity fund-raiser in which Meghan had participated as a freshman.

This was the fourth stop of seven for the *Suits* university tour, which included the University of California at Berkeley and Los Angeles, the University of Arizona, Boston University, Harvard, and Columbia. It was a bid by the network and show's producers to reward their highly engaged collegiate audiences by treating them to a preview screening of the winter midseason premiere.

With the website now moving to the front burner, she contacted a friend, photographer Jake Rosenberg. A graduate of Ontario College of Art and Design, Rosenberg had started Coveteur.com six months after graduating with a degree in industrial design. While he loved photography, he was excited about branding and design. During a photo shoot in 2011, he and a fellow twentysomething, stylist Stephanie Mark, ended up creating a site devoted to snapshots of beautiful closets and snippets of subjects' homes. "We thought it would be fun and interesting to see what it is really like in stylish people's homes and closets," says Mark. The pair did six photos shoots and posted them on their new site, which crashed from the amount of traffic. They immediately realized they were onto something that might be profitable as well as fun.

"We would come back and talk about what we had seen, where this person we'd met was shopping, which restaurants and bars people were talking about," says Mark. "We realized we had all this content." They expanded their coverage and in 2013, redesigned the site to make space for advertising and editorial. Rosenberg listened to Meghan's concerns about her proposed site, especially when she stressed there was so much more she wanted to share. Over several glasses of wine and tapas, they discussed her vision for the site, which would essentially be an insider's guide to travel, food, fashion, and makeup with a leavening of more serious op-ed articles dealing with women's issues. Essentially it would be a dash of Gwyneth Paltrow's blog, Goop, with a soupçon of *Marie Claire* seasoned with Meghan's own style and focus.

Now with a vision for her own site, Meghan turned down the original company's offer to create a commercial "Meghan Markle" site and decided to have a go on her own. First she hired a website designer. When she showed the results to Rosenberg, his sharp and practiced eye immediately told him that this could be a problem.

"I beg you, please don't go down this path; use our graphic designer from Coveteur," he told his friend. The result was TheTig.com, which featured Meghan's own elegant handwriting, and a logo with a wine drop as the dot of the letter *i*. Meghan had chosen the name from an Italian wine called Tignanello. It is a wine born out of the vinter's desire to make his product stand out in a sea of reds. Meghan liked that idea. Standing out. She would drink to that.

For Meghan, Tignanello had a deeper meaning, representing that "aha" moment when she finally understood what components went to make a good wine, to give it length, finish, and legs. She wanted to carry that excitement of discovery into her website, writing, "The Tig is a hub for the discerning palate—those with a hunger for food, travel, fashion and beauty. I want to create a space to share all of these loves—to invite friends to share theirs as well, and to be the breeding ground for ideas and excitement—for an inspired lifestyle." Frothy, fizzy, and fun, The Tig appealed to her fan base, who appreciated her elegant style and her classy persona. At the same time, she envisaged using The Tig to draw attention to more pertinent social and political issues as they affected women.

Meghan, the aspirational girl next door, had created a site for other classy girls like her who wanted to join the party. With the help of Jake Rosenberg, fashion designer Wes Gordon, and designer Brett Heyman of the acrylic purse brand Edie Parker, who created a resin clutch labeled with "Ms. Tig" for Meghan, the stage was set. Finally, she also followed the advice of her costar Gina Torres, who had told her, using one of Meghan's longtime nicknames, "Nutmeg, just leave room for magic."

When filming started again Meghan's busy days didn't leave a lot of time for magic. She would wake up at 4:15 a.m., down a cup of hot water with fresh squeezed lemon, and eat a bowl of oatmeal with sliced bananas and agave. Then she would let the dogs out in the backyard before driving her leased Audi SUV to the set, a mazelike replica of a law office, detailed down to the pink message pads and pens on secretaries' desks, with pivoting glass walls that allowed the cameras to shoot any angle without glare. The New York skyline was a backdrop, and the location scenes were shot in Toronto, with establishing shots from the B-roll of Manhattan to give a sense of place. After early morning makeup and wardrobe, where clothes would be altered "on the inhale" to give them their tightest, sleekest fit, Meghan would wait in her trailer for her scene to be ready.

With the birth of The Tig, Meghan had her hands full, making sure that the new arrival was fed, watered, and coddled. It was a full-time occupation, staying awake until the early hours cruising Instagram for ideas about what was cool, hot, interesting, and timely; writing all the short, snappy content herself; and hustling anyone and everyone to get celebrities to answer her emailed five questions that created the format for Tig Talk. Actor and singer Emily Rossum got the ball rolling by saying that if she was down to her last $10—one of the standard questions—she would sing in the street for money. Others like fashion guru Joe Zee and blogger Jessica Stam added their thoughts, while Meghan dragooned interior designer Natasha Baradaran to talk about her favorite city, Milan. She knew that big names drove traffic and would attract other celebrities to participate. One of the first people she wanted to have for Tig Talk was model-turned-entrepreneur Heidi Klum. She emailed everyone she knew, hoping to get an email or phone number for Klum or her assistant. In the end Heidi responded, as did "the queen," who informed the actor that everything tasted better with a slug of vodka. Of course, the queen she was talking about was TV screen queen Elizabeth Hurley, who plays the conniving and occasionally cruel Queen Helena in the E! show *The Royals*, a tongue-in-cheek take on the House of Windsor.

There were profiles of cool places to visit, interesting restaurants, and innovative chefs. This feature snagged her a new love. For years she had been eating at the Harbord Room, a small restaurant in downtown Toronto that opened in 2007. It was run by handsome celebrity chef, Cory Vitiello, who boasted that he cooked the best burger in town. The foodie in Meghan was intrigued.

Over the past seven years, Vitiello had made a name for himself both in and out of kitchen. He had famously dated Canadian heiress and former politician Belinda Stronach, as well as *eTalk's* talking head Tanya Kim, before turning his attention to Canadian TV gossip reporter Mary Kitchen. Now with The Tig, Meghan had a way to get to know him better. Much better. For Meghan, love was in the air. But, as she was to discover to her horror, not online.

One evening Meghan was curled up with her laptop and a glass of wine in hand, preparing for an evening finding stories and people to populate The Tig. Her methodology was to delve into other lifestyle blogs and online news sites, follow links for inspiration, and then maybe poke around on Instagram using hashtags to guide her to potential Tig Tales. First, though, she wanted to just peek at the *Suits* pages on Facebook, Twitter, Reddit, and USANetwork.com. The latest episode had a story line featuring Rachel Zane front and center, and it was airing that night. She was curious to know the response to her character's dalliance with an old boyfriend. When Meghan took another sip of her red wine she nearly choked as she scrolled through to the comments. "You dirty bird!" "I'm unfollowing you! How could you cheat on Mike?" "Whore . . ." And it just got uglier as the episode hit different time zones and aired across the country. Meghan deleted the worst of the comments from her own page and Twitter feed and blocked the abusive users. As the night wore on she was genuinely concerned, and not a little afraid, as more and more emoji of knives and guns appeared.

Fans weren't just angry at her character, Rachel Zane, for kissing her old boyfriend, Logan Sanders, played by Brendan Hines; they were furious at Meghan Markle. They believed that the actor was responsible for the story line, not the scriptwriters. As she pondered just how fans could become so invested in a story, which was, after all, make believe, the comments kept heating up. Now there were death threats. "Meghan Markle, you slut. I wanna kill you." This was out of control.

The next morning she went to see *Suits* creator Aaron Korsh. This has to stop, she told him. "We have to scale this back." The producers and writers had always been good to her, incorporating aspects of her own personality into Rachel's character, making Rachel a foodie because Meghan enjoyed cooking and making her biracial because of Meghan's own family background. This time the lines were becoming uncomfortably blurred, with fans unable to tell the real Meghan from the fantasy of Rachel. Besides, Meghan wasn't that kind of girl. The story line going forward had Rachel more actively attempting to seduce her old boyfriend as she turned her back on Mike. That plot development didn't feel right to Meghan, not least because it presaged a possible exit for her character, something for which she wasn't yet prepared.

"I like Rachel, I like playing Rachel, I like what she stands for. And this feels really out of character," she said earnestly. It was a bold move, telling the show's creator she didn't like the direction her character was going. But she felt she owed it to the fans and to her own integrity to speak up. Plus she had been frightened by the aggressive vitriol and threats of violence.

Editor Angela Catanzaro, who had worked on the series since the beginning, agreed with Meghan, telling Korsh, "I love Rachel, but if you put that scene on the air, I would never like her again. That's not the kind of woman I would like working with my husband."

Korsh saw the wisdom in their words, and within an episode, Mike Ross and Rachel Zane's romance, much like that of their star-crossed namesakes on *Friends* a decade earlier, was correcting itself and gearing up to be back on track. Panic over. At least for the time being.

Meghan stared at her phone in disbelief. The inbox of her email was filling up almost faster than she could read the subject lines. Her site, The Tig, was proving to be more popular than she had ever imagined. At this early stage every email went directly to her mobile phone, and as Meghan quickly scrolled the ever-expanding list, one sender jumped out at her, the United Nations. It might just be a fund-raising appeal, but what the heck? Meghan opened the message and read the contents with growing surprise. The United Nations was asking her to consider becoming involved in their new gender equality program, #HeForShe. When Meghan dialed the number given in the email, the contact person at United Nations Women explained that they had read her short essay in The Tig regarding women's independence to coincide with Independence Day. She had begun by writing: "Raise a glass to yourself today—to the right to freedom, to the empowerment of the women (*and men*) who struggle to have it, and to knowing, embracing, honoring, educating and loving yourself. On this day, and beyond, celebrate your independence." She then went on to showcase the thoughts of Nigerian writer Chimamanda Ngozi Adichie.

On the back of this Tig entry, UN officials wondered if she might want to work with the international organization on a new initiative on gender equality they were promoting.

While she was honored, she also wanted to get an idea of what this project was all about, rather than blindly saying yes. "Why don't I come and intern for you for week while we're on hiatus?" she asked the staffer. "You know, answer phones, bring you coffee." Within a few weeks surprised UN officials found themselves inducting Meghan into the bustling corridors of the New York–based institution. In truth it was rather more than making the coffee. She shadowed Elizabeth Nyamayaro, head of the UN #HeForShe movement to encourage men to support women in the quest for gender equality, and Phumzile Mlambo-Ngcuka, executive director of UN Women, and sat in on meetings at the World Bank, the Clinton Foundation, and even the war room for UN secretary general Ban Ki Moon.

She was assigned a seat on the front row along with TV presenter Wolf Blitzer, NGO director Gary Barker, and actor Kiefer Sutherland, as *Harry Potter* actor and UN Goodwill Ambassador Emma Watson made a rousing speech for men as well as women to join the #HeForShe campaign. Watson noted that at the present rate of progress it would be seventy-five years before women were paid the same as men for the same work and that it would take until 2086 before all teenage girls in rural Africa would receive a secondary education.

During the launch of the campaign, Meghan experienced her very own Tig moment when she watched the interaction between the former president of Finland Tarja Halonen and a UN staffer. "Madame President, may I get you anything? Would you like you like water or a pen?" Halonen smiled and replied, "A lipstick."

It was something that Meghan connected to. She saw no contradictions between a woman running a country and still wearing lipstick—she could be feminine and a feminist at the same time. As she later wrote: "To be a breadwinner at work, and a bread baker with her kids at home."

At that time, before Donald Trump had entered the race for the presidency, one of her other feminine idols was businesswoman

Ivanka Trump, who had her own jewelry and clothing line. She was thrilled when Ivanka agreed to fill in her simple questionnaire for a Tig Talk, and more thrilled when she accepted her invitation to meet for drinks and dinner the next time Meghan was in New York.

Meghan gushed, "Don't get me started on her jewelry collection: the late night 'window shopping' I have done on my computer, snuggled up in my bed with a glass of wine, staring longingly at the beautiful designs. And there are the shoes, the home collection, the clothing, and the natural extension of her brand with a kids' collection—a smart choice given that she is now a proud mama. When we have drinks, I will make sure I order whatever she does—because this woman seems to have the formula for success (and happiness) down pat."

With well-known names like Ivanka Trump involved, her little engine that could, her nickname for her website, was gaining a head of steam. She was justifiably proud when her site was named Best of the Web in both *Elle* magazine and *InStyle*.

She was, however, in need of help to stoke the boiler. Every post on The Tig had to be cross-posted to Instagram, Pinterest, and Facebook to increase traffic; luckily there was an app for that. Even better, there was now a person, Judy Meepos. Meepos, then the deputy editor of the Tech, Yeah! section of *InStyle* magazine, had gotten a lot of internet air kisses from Meghan in August when she had written a breathless profile of Markle and The Tig. Meghan decided to hire her, Meepos joining her site in October 2014.

Meepos was not only responsible for social media but also, as she said, "wrote and edited daily postings, initiated collaborations and partnerships, and served as a market editor for posts and television." The popularity of The Tig and Meghan's account meant that after just six months her little engine was ready to earn its keep through e-commerce. She followed the lead of Jake Rosenberg and Coveteur in partnering with RewardStyle.com, an ecommerce site that, rather clumsily, billed itself as an "invitation-only end-to-end content monetization platform for top-tier digital style influencers and brands around the world"—or, in plain English, a clever way of helping upmarket blogs make money.

The site RewardStyle was founded in 2011 by Amber Venz and future husband Baxter Box as a way for Amber to monetize her fashion blog. For a while their system worked like a dream. Bloggers created clickable links from their content that lead directly to retailers and brands. If a reader clicked through and made a purchase, the blogger earned commission, creating a semi-passive income stream.

By the time Meghan had launched The Tig, Instagram was taking over as the preferred platform for influencers. While their system made it harder to buy products directly, clever web mavens worked their way around that difficulty.

With The Tig in Meepos's capable hands, Meghan boarded a plane headed to Dublin, where she had been asked to participate in the One Young World Summit, an international forum for young leaders of tomorrow. The biannual conference was the brain child of two advertising executives, David Jones and Kate Robinson, the duo aiming to "gather together the brightest young leaders from around the world, empowering them to make lasting connections to create positive change." Robinson felt that Meghan had something to say and was popular with the student-aged audience. Not only would she be discussing global issues with young people, but she would be rubbing shoulders with humanitarian celebrities like Mary Robinson, Ireland's first woman president; Sir Bob Geldof; Nobel Peace Prize winner Kofi Annan; and United Nations Goodwill Ambassador John Chau. At the event, held at Dublin Castle, she made a beeline for Ali Hewson, wife of rock star Bono, who had founded a socially conscious clothing line Edun and an ethical beauty line Nude, subjects which fascinated her.

For her forum on gender equality she was with a high-powered panel who included lawyer Sabine Chalmers, General Electric senior vice president Beth Comstock, digital pioneer Michelle Phau, and film director Maya Sanbar. In the beginning Robinson, who chaired the discussion, was worried if Meghan would cope with a question-and-answer style forum. She came away pleasantly surprised at Meghan's eloquence, saying, "It wasn't your average actress stepping up and talking about gender equality. It was the real deal—very forthright, very confident and very un-celebrity." Others in the audience were also impressed by her grasp of human rights and gender issues as well as her approachability and warmth. Human rights lawyer Phiwokuhle Nogwaza recalled: "She is really soft and gentle. She is friendly and very warm and engaging. It didn't feel like I was speaking to someone from one of the biggest shows on TV. It was like talking to a regular girl. She knew the problems in detail, which I found incredible. She is humble and really down to earth."

She also had a real knack of mixing the glamour of celebrity with commitment to her humanitarian work, she and her chef boyfriend Cory Vitiello flying to Florida in early December for Art Basel Miami, an offshoot of the Swiss original. The now annual event, started in 2002, attracts seventy-seven thousand visitors a year, and the place to see and be seen was her usual stomping ground, Soho House.

Meghan was excited. While she wasn't that into art, preferring fashion, food, and wine, she welcomed the opportunity to network with a wider range of members and guests who were arriving at the Soho Beach House, a repurposed vintage hotel on the sand. She tried not to gawk as rap mogul Russell Simmons and actor and activist Rosario Dawson strolled by or take too much interest when Goldie Hawn's daughter Kate Hudson waved at friends from a terrace. Ah, the thrill of arrival, of belonging. She had worked hard, she was on a top-rated show, and her blog was considered one of the best on the web. Miami Art Week, or at least the Soho Beach House version of it, would be hers!

Her great friend Markus Anderson, Soho House membership director, casually dressed in flip-flops and shorts, wandered over to say hello and brief them on the next few days of dancing, cocktails, and luxurious beauty treatments. This was life. A Bombay Sapphire gin gift basket awaited Meghan and Cory in their room, along with a fully stocked bar. The celebrity tent would a have full selection of tropically themed gin drinks. And then there were the sparkling wines and champagnes...

Markus Anderson is a great fixer and mixer. He has an instinct for putting strangers together who he thinks might gel. At lunch he placed Meghan next to Bahrain-born fashion designer Misha Nonoo. At the time she was an up-and-coming designer known as much for her marriage to art dealer Alexander Gilkes, friend of Princes William and Harry, as her maverick designs. Meghan and Misha got along famously, lunchtime drinks extending into evening cocktails. During the course of the afternoon they got to talking about her new collection, which was going to be unveiled at New York fashion week. Meghan would be on break from *Suits*. She would be there.

Hours later, Meghan was once again on a plane, this time headed for Spain, one of five countries she was due to visit on a whirlwind tour. This time there were no luxury hotels or smart cocktails. Instead, Meghan was taking part in the USO Holiday Tour, visiting American military bases in Spain, Italy, Turkey, Afghanistan, and England. Joining Meghan were eight-time USO tour veteran and country star Kellie Pickler and her songwriter husband, Kyle Jacobs; comedian Rob Riggle; *Glee* costar Dianna Agron; former Chicago Bears linebacker Brian Urlacher; Washington Nationals pitcher Doug Fister; and chairman of the Joint Chiefs of Staff army general Martin E. Dempsey and his wife, Deanie.

When the traveling troupe, who were joined by USO president J. D. Crouch and his wife Kristin, met at the Joint Base Andrews passenger terminal in Maryland on December 5, Deanie Dempsey told the assorted celebrities. "Embrace this experience. You will be so proud of our service members and their families." Meghan was excited and a little apprehensive. Not only would she be flying aboard *Air Force Two*, specially commissioned for this tour, she would be meeting thousands of service members and their families during the trip. While she had done fan meet and greets before, it had never been on this scale or at this intensity.

After arriving in Rota, Spain, Meghan and her USO group toured the USS *Donald K. Ross*, an Aegis missile–equipped destroyer. They performed before an audience of two thousand service personnel and their families in a hangar on the base. Meghan, in a blue hardhat, posed with servicemen before going into her routine. She knew that she, Kelly Pickler, and Dianna Agron were carrying on a time-honored tradition, following in the steps of stars like Marilyn Monroe, Bob Hope, and Jayne Mansfield who had entertained the troops, providing a sweet taste of home, a reminder of why the troops did their jobs. Now things were rather different. There were women in the military and families on the bases, so goodbye cheesecake, hello folksy and funny. On stage she did one of her routines, giving a lighthearted talk about *Suits* before showing off her five-inch heels as Pickler and her band performed the signature song "Red High Heels."

The USO tour group repeated their act in Vicenza, Italy, to soldiers of the 173rd Airborne Brigade and US Army Africa before heading to the air base at Incirlik, Turkey. Even though the base was several hundred miles from the battles raging in neighboring Syria, the atmosphere was tenser, the security tighter. Meghan smiled and tried to say more than "thank you" as she passed out cupcakes to the several hundred who gathered to watch Pickler and Jacobs perform country hits and the troupe do various comedy sketches.

The next morning the USO performers and their "chaperones" gathered on the tarmac to head to their most challenging gig, Bagram Airfield in Afghanistan. This was the most isolated outpost, home to forty thousand military personnel and service members. "Bureaucrats, administrators, logisticians and thousands of International Security Assistance Force civilian contractors live at Bagram air base," said British photographer Edmund Clark, who spent ten days there in 2013. "Unless you go out on patrol, you exist only on base."

Surrounded by fencing and barbed wire, and reinforced by sandbags, with ground penetrating radar used to make sure enemy fighters don't use tunnels to break into the coalition base, Bagram was relatively safe. Except for the occasional Taliban rocket that made it over the walls.

Meghan and her fellow performers joined service members for a holiday meal before they took to the stage. Meghan turned her back to the audience and snapped a quick selfie of the uniformed military members, then went into her inspirational speech: "I've never wanted to be a lady who lunches, I've always wanted to be a woman who works..."

Once again cupcakes were passed out, as fighter jets and C-130 transport planes taxied outside. Meghan and the others posed with groups of service members in front of a netting-draped wall. While the celebrities put on their practiced smiles for the cameras, the troops could barely muster a grin between them. Unlike the stars who had swooped in for a couple of days, they had months more of mind-numbing boredom punctuated by bursts of frenzied action to look forward to. It was a poignant interaction.

Their final stop in Cambridge, England, was a perfect way to decompress. Before their final show, airmen at the base gave the USO troupe a tour of the military hardware at their command, including F-15E Strike Eagles and CV-22 Ospreys, a helicopter-plane hybrid. Meghan spent her time chatting with families, paying special attention to the children. That evening, the Dempseys hosted a thank-you gathering for the USO performers at a Cambridge pub, the Anchor, with the performers in turn warmly thanking the Dempseys and the USO for the privilege of being able to entertain the troops. Before the evening ended, the chairman of the Joint Chiefs of Staff serenaded the group. "If only we could have gotten him to do that in Bagram!" someone joked.

That was to be Meghan's first and last USO tour. She expressed her feelings in an Instagram post where she showed a picture from the tour and then a heartfelt caption: "In gratitude to our troops, and the opportunity to thank them personally for their sacrifice and service. Such an honor and feeling very, very blessed."

8

Seeing Both Sides Now

She had her passport. Check. Her bag of homeopathic remedies. Check. Her vaccines, including hepatitis A and B,
typhoid, rabies, and tetanus, were up to date. Check. She had
super-strength mosquito repellent. Check. A bag of long-sleeved
light clothes. Check. Meghan was ready for a very grown-up journey, embarking on her first ever fact-finding mission on behalf of
the United Nations. Though her visit to Rwanda in the heart of
Africa was to focus on issues surrounding gender equality, it was
also a chance for United Nations officials to evaluate the *Suits*
star to see if she was able or willing to make the commitment as
a Goodwill Ambassador for the international organization. A UN
official pointed out that Meghan's involvement as a gender equality advocate was at the level of an informal collaboration.

In early January 2015, when she landed in Kigali, the Rwandan capital, her first stop was to be introduced to the nation's
female parliamentarians. Almost a week of meetings had been
scheduled to discuss the role of women in the nation's democ-
racy and the challenges facing Rwanda going forward. Time and
again the point was made that only when women were treated

equally in the home, at school, and in the workplace could they enjoy rich, fulfilling lives and give back to the community. The underrepresentation of women in the top jobs, a feature not just of life in developing countries but in her own nation, was an issue that always concerned her. The UN was celebrating the fact that Rwanda was the first and at the time the only country to have a female majority in the nation's parliament, with almost two-thirds of the seats taken by women.

It was a great step forward. Meghan complimented Rwandan president Paul Kagame. "We need more men like that," she said.

Though Kagame has his critics, this was a truly remarkable turnaround for a country which, just twenty years earlier, had suffered an appalling genocide. The figures were astonishing, with approximately 1 million people killed, most brutally hacked to death with machetes, and 2 million displaced into refugee camps. Meghan traveled to see the other side of Rwanda herself, the actor and her UN team traveling by van to Gihembe refugee camp, the sprawling collection of huts studded into the lush green hillside now home to seventeen thousand people who had fled the violence in the wartorn Democratic Republic of the Congo. She wanted to speak to the women at the grassroots and find out how they coped with a life that was meant to be temporary but had become permanent. Inevitably, every visit by a celebrity, even if the local population has no clue who they are, attracts a crowd, and Meghan posed happily with dozens of curious and excited local children.

As she traveled back over the bumpy dirt road, past the grazing goats and the lush green fields, she idly checked her emails, amazed that the signal was better here than in some parts of Toronto and Los Angeles. While she bounced along the road she learned that she had been invited as a guest to the BAFTAs, the British Academy film awards, which take place a few weeks before the Oscars.

Her management company told her that she would be sponsored by a high-end jewelry company that would fly her directly
from Kigali to London, where she would be whisked into hair and
makeup before being poured into a gown. "No," screamed her gut.
It had always been a dream to attend the BAFTAs, but she couldn't
shift emotional gears that quickly, from the purpose-driven work
she had been doing all week in Rwanda to the polished glamour of
an awards show. There would be other BAFTAs, other red carpets.
But for now there was only Rwanda. As she later wrote, "This type
of work is what feeds my soul."

Of course, she was not the first nor will she be the last celebrity
to struggle to reconcile the air-kissing superficiality of Hollywood
with the stark reality of life for so many in the developing world.
Oscar-winning actor and UNHCR special envoy Angelina Jolie
is a vivid example of a star who manages to straddle both worlds.
The more she became involved with her humanitarian mission,
the more she had to learn to switch off and switch on. Just like
acting, but in real life.

Shortly after her return from Rwanda Meghan was front and
center for New York Fashion Week in February. She was now
a front-row girl, watching the models at the show of her fashion mentor Wes Gordon, but she was also photographed reviewing Misha Nonoo's stylish collection. Her look was a revelation
inspired in part by the neon swirls and scribbles of British artist
Tracy Emin. The theme was Meghan's cri de coeur: the empowerment of women. Nonoo had the models do their hair themselves,
pulling it back into ponytails with a minimum of product and as
many bobby pins as they liked. Meghan appreciated the symbolism and thought Nonoo's collaboration with the orchestra Decoda
"so classy and beautiful." "It just set the tone," she enthused.

She was still raving about the collection when she appeared
on Joe Zee's streaming fashion program on Yahoo! Style. The duo
went back years, from the time they first met in 2011 drinking and

shooting the breeze until late into the night. What Joe liked about Meghan was that she was decidedly un-Hollywood; she appreciated people other than herself.

In between the glitz and the glamour her advocacy for UN Women continued, undertaking further meetings at the World Bank and the Clinton Foundation and learning more about the facts and figures of gender bias in the developing world and, for that matter, her own country. While she had always had a thoughtful side, these days her friends noticed that she seemed more considered, more seasoned, and more appreciative too of the advantages she had been given and the opportunity to make a difference. In the days when she was scrabbling to gain a foothold on the elusive ladder of success, her time was taken up not with causes but with endless auditions, simply trying to make a living. Her acting success coupled with her voice on The Tig had given her the opportunity to focus on the issues that concerned her. Gender equality had always been near the top of her priority list: witness her first letter-writing campaign regarding the advertising for dishwashing soap.

She traveled to London to support actor Emma Watson in her #HeForShe initiative, the Harry Potter actor holding a live Facebook event to engage her fans in the campaign. Then it was Meghan's turn to take center stage in front of a friendly but awe-inspiring audience. Meghan took a deep breath and focused. She was about to hit a personal milestone. Her mom and friends were there to support her in front of global luminaries like UN secretary general Ban Ki-moon, UN executive director Phumzile Mlambo-Ngcuka, actor Patricia Arquette, her UN mentor Elizabeth Nyamayaro as well as Hillary Clinton (who, ironically, the same day overshadowed Meghan's remarks with her comments about her controversial use of a private email server during her tenure as secretary of state).

On March 10, a day that she will always remember, the LA

Valley Girl was about to speak before the United Nations as the newly appointed UN Women Advocate for Leadership and Political Participation.

Understandably Meghan's voice sounded a little higher, as the normally nerveless actor opened her speech: "I am proud to be a woman and a feminist, and this evening I am extremely proud to stand before you on this significant day, which serves as a reminder to all of us of how far we've come, but also amid celebration a reminder of the road ahead..."

She told her story of the LA riots, her schoolroom, Ivory dishwashing liquid, and the chauvinist little boys at her school, of how she wrote to Procter & Gamble, women's rights lawyer Gloria Allred, journalist Linda Ellerbee, and former First Lady Hillary Clinton. The putative presidential candidate smiled at that. She spoke inspiringly of how her letter made a difference and how she felt that she had helped, in her small way, to make the change.

She took aim at the weak representation of women in the world's parliaments, citing data showing the number of women lawmakers had increased only 11 percent since 1995. "Eleven percent in twenty years. Come on. This has to change," she said to applause.

As Meghan concluded, UN secretary general Ban Ki-moon led the standing ovation. Could there be anything better? It was quite the accolade, one that would resonate as her speech was played in numerous schoolrooms around America, inspiring and provoking a new generation of young girls to make a difference.

"Meghan Markle has helped raise global attention to gender equality issues," said a spokeswoman for UN Women afterward. "UN Women trusts and hopes that in her new and important public role she will continue to use her visibility and voice to support the advancement of gender equality."

She appeared to have it all: she was a young, beautiful, articulate campaigner with a tasteful, on-trend website and a successful

TV career. Curiously, her speech to UN Women seemed to be the high-water mark of her involvement with the international organization. Once they officially appointed her an advocate, it seems that her charity work on their behalf tapered off considerably.

Nonetheless the invitations to represent the issues she cared about or to appear on chat shows now started to come in thick and fast. As a spokesperson for gender equality and a cable TV star, it was only natural for her to be asked to host the Women in Cable Telecommunications 2015 signature luncheon. Maria E. Brennan, WICT's chief executive, explained the choice, saying: "Meghan is a sterling example of someone who not only plays a strong female character, she is one in real life."

Chat show host Larry King invited her back on his show— previously she had talked *Suits* with Patrick J. Adams—to talk about her role as a women's rights advocate. Meghan was proving her skills at diplomacy, deftly deflecting Larry King's question about which country had the worst record of human rights by saying that we have to take into account cultural differences.

Hand in hand with her humanitarian work were the undoubted perks of being a glamorous TV star. As her celebrity status rose, so did her price tag. She was learning that she could charge a fee just for turning up. Turbo-charging these opportunities for her was Kruger Cowne World, a speaking, branding, and hosting agency with headquarters in Chelsea, Central London, and offices in Santa Monica.

The agency, founded in 1999, represents a whole range of celebrities such as Virgin boss Richard Branson, Cher, and Sir Bob Geldof as well as charities like One Young World, where Meghan had spoken. The skin care line Clarins and the Pakistani poet Fatima Bhutto were also clients who were frequently name-checked by the actor. Meghan's rate? Twenty thousand dollars and up per appearance.

She had entered a glorious, gilded world and was aware of the subdued hysteria of her day-to-day existence. She wrote: "I work long hours, I travel for Press, my mind memorizes. My mind spins. My days blur. My nights are restless. My hair is primped, my face is painted, my name is recognized, my star meter is rising, my life is changing."

In March, just before her speech to the United Nations, she found herself on the island of Malta in the Mediterranean. The visit, sponsored by *Elle* magazine, was a chance for her to discover her roots—and to enjoy some of the island's fabulous but oft-neglected cuisine. Malta held a special place in her heart; her paternal great-great-grandmother Mary Merrill, the daughter of Mary Bird, a former housemaid to the British royal family and a British soldier, had been born here. She was eager to know more. When she told one friend she was going to the island, they noted: "When you go to Malta, everyone will look like you." As she explored the island, it seemed her friend's prediction was spot on.

She went by ferry to the tiny island of Gozo and tasted the famous Goz cheeselet, and then after returning to the main island she explored the Casa Rocca Piccola in Valletta and viewed the Caravaggio paintings at St. John's Co-Cathedral. During a week enjoying la dolce vita, she fell in love with Maltese cuisine. Meghan threw herself into her cooking lesson with chef Pippa Mattei, Malta's equivalent of Martha Stewart, at her home in Attard. As Meghan liked to emphasize that, as a California girl, her experience with farm-to-table cuisine was hardwired, here was an opportunity to see the Maltese version. Mattei took her shopping for produce in the local farmers market, then gave her a lesson in pasta and pastizzi making, followed by a meal in Mattei's garden. Oh, if only she could bring back a suitcase full of Maltese treats.

For the girl who conjured The Tig from her favorite tipple, no visit to Malta would have been complete without a comprehensive wine tasting. The actor visited the Meridiana wine estate for a leisurely afternoon exploring fruity reds and tasty whites. As Maltese wines rarely, if ever, reach the shores of the US, this was a real treat. She didn't discover much more about her Maltese ancestry—but she did discover the delights of this bucolic island.

Her visit to Malta was a solo trip even though her chef boyfriend would have been inspired by the variety and distinctiveness of the local cuisine. Like Meghan, he was being kept busy, on the verge of starting a new venture, Flock Rotisserie and Greens, a restaurant specializing in roast chicken and salad. "I've been testing a fair bit of roast chicken on Meghan," he admitted. The chef was working virtually round the clock running three restaurants.

He was also in front of the camera too, taping episodes of *Chef in Your Ear* for Food Network Canada, which were due for broadcast in August 2015. Taking a leaf out of Meghan's philanthropy playbook, he volunteered for Kids Cook to Care, a program for youngsters who are taught how to make home-cooked meals by celebrity chefs. It would hopefully ignite their understanding of proper cooking techniques and the importance of serving the community.

With his filming and restaurant commitments, he was unable to join Meghan on her next exotic jaunt—to Istanbul, where she, together with actor Eddie Redmayne, *50 Shades* actor Jamie Dornan, and British singer Paloma Faith were on hand to celebrate the opening of the latest enclave of Soho House.

It was another glamorous interlude in her busiest and most successful year to date. Her UN speech was matched by an invitation to become the face for one of Canada's oldest and most respected retailers, Reitmans. There was more, the ninety-year-old store chain wanted her to curate her own clothing line. Not only was her face going to be on billboards and on TV all over Canada, she was going to influence how women dressed.

It was a marvelous opportunity, though when she first mentioned the overture to savvy friends they scoffed at the idea of involving herself with a retail brand that was so fuddy-duddy. "Oh, that's where my mom would buy her jeans in the eighties," they chorused. Meghan was not so sure. As an American she didn't have the same knee-jerk reaction toward this venerable retailer as her Canadian friends. At meetings with store executives, Meghan brought a fresh eye. "There are pieces here that are so cool that if you're going to reenergize it, I'd be happy to be a part of that," she said. They planned an advertising campaign starring Meghan wearing trimmer, slimmer, hipper Reitmans clothing. In one commercial, Meghan is filmed walking into an elegant restaurant where two ladies who lunch eagerly give the TV star the once over. One exclaims: "So stylish" while the other asks what she is wearing. They then try to crawl over the back of the booth to get a closer look at the label in her shirt. Catching them in the act, Meghan smiles and says, "Ladies, it's Reitmans." Another showed Meghan, all crisp business, slick high heels, and tight jeans, speaking on her cell phone as she strides out into the street. As the camera follows her down the street, she notices herself in the store's glass window. Her cute alter ego in the reflection preens and wiggles for the camera before blowing her other half a kiss. Cue her slogan for the brand: "Reitmans. Really."

Not only was she the brand ambassador, she worked hard on a capsule collection to be launched in spring 2016. Meghan was thrilled, reflecting on the days when she was a little girl and how she had sat with her mother at her clothing store, A Change of a Dress on La Brea in Los Angeles. In those far-off days, Doria had taken her daughter to fabric warehouses, where she had walked along the aisles. Now she had the opportunity to create her own fashion line. Meghan and the design team sketched out ideas, played with swatches, and examined the zippers and fit of sample pieces. As she later remarked: "I'm super involved with the design process, and I'm sure that it drives them crazy. But how could I not? It has my name on it."

First off the runway in the Meghan Markle Collection were four distinct dresses: the Soiree, Date Night, a maxi-dress named the Sunset and a Little White Dress. Once she had approved the designs, it was a fingers and toes crossed moment for the actor, anxious that her fans and the wider public appreciated her efforts. As she wrote in her blog: "I toiled over design and print, I shared my thoughts on everything and I ended up with a limited collection of pieces that reflect facets of my personal style that I think you'll love."

All the dresses sold for under $100 each, revealing the budget-conscious nature of their creator, who boasted that she shopped the sale rack. "I've always been the girl flipping through hangers looking for the best deal."

Of course, that's not quite true. When her designer friend Misha Nonoo invited her to join her at the 2015 Vogue CFDA/Vogue Fashion Fund awards in New York in early November, Meghan was thrilled to wear one of the pieces from her collection. It was a short liquid metal dress that showed off her legs combined with a plunging deep V neck. It was a showstopper, and photographers clamored for a snap of the TV star.

Not only was she a photographers' darling, a billboard pinup, and a TV regular, the ubiquitous Meghan Markle was now the central character in a chick lit novel, *What Pretty Girls Are Made Of*, written by her "bestie from the westie" Lindsay Jill Roth, who was such a frequent visitor to her Toronto home that the spare bedroom was christened Lindsay's room. It had taken Roth five years, and copious glasses of wine, to craft the jaunty novel based on the exploits of her heroine, Alison Kraft. Since Alison was a little girl, all she has ever dreamed of is being an actor. Too bad that after years of auditions she doesn't have the stellar career she envisioned. After some soul searching, she looks for other jobs and ends up working for a makeup guru.

It was of course a thinly disguised portrait of Meghan during

her lean years in the noughties. Lindsay had all the research material she needed, not just from Meghan's lips but from the blog
Working Actress, about the ups and downs of life for a struggling
wannabe, which Meghan is now credited with writing. Meghan
loved it, posting effusive Instagrams touting the fluffy tome. Naturally she was at the summer launch party, afterward taking her pal
to an ice hockey game. Not only did Lindsay give her actor friend
a shout-out for helping her explore "what pretty is," she sent a copy
of her amusing trifle to Kate Middleton at Kensington Palace, her
accompanying card informing the duchess that in her eyes she was
the definition of "prettiness."

Lindsay then proudly posted the pro forma thank-you note
from the Duchess of Cambridge's office online. She never for a
second contemplated meeting the future queen at Windsor Castle
after her best friend married Prince Harry. If she had suggested
that plot to her publisher, they would have laughed her out of their
New York offices.

In fact, Meghan *was* about to get married, but neither to Prince
Harry nor her boyfriend Cory Vitiello. She was due to walk down
the aisle with badass lawyer Mike Ross in the climax to *Suits* season 5. Filming was scheduled for November 13 before the show
wrapped for the Christmas break. As she read the script, Meghan
thought that if she was getting married, at the very least she—or
Rachel—wanted a say in the style of the wedding dress. She contacted *Suits* costumer Jolie Andreatta and her friend, wedding
stylist Jessica Mulroney, for inspiration. The three women met at
the Toronto outpost of New York–based bridal store Kleinfeld. The
store, which boasts thirty thousand square feet of bridal wear in
Manhattan, has a much smaller outlet at the Bay. "I need something that will be comfortable and won't wrinkle, that's classic and
sort of fairy tale," explained Meghan. Jessica pulled out an Anne
Barge full-skirted V-neck with Swiss dot netting. Meghan tried it
on. "It screams Rachel!" she exclaimed.

"We need the dress in two days," said Jolie. "Can we do this?" In the original script Mike and Rachel were finally going to get hitched. However, after producer Gabriel Macht and series creator Aaron Korsh reviewed the scenario, they decided it would be more plausible if Mike went to jail and told Meghan's character, a sobbing Rachel Zane, that he cannot marry her—at least not yet. Maybe later.... This was the cliffhanger for the series 5 finale, which was broadcast in March 2016.

After filming her emotional scenes with Mike Ross, Meghan flew to a place about as cold as, if not colder than, Toronto. The California girl headed to Iceland to see the northern lights, along the way discovering the Town of Elves, Álfabærinn, where she couldn't resist posting a photograph on her Instagram site. From admittedly knowing little about the inner workings of the internet, Meghan was now a social media junkie, posting cute selfies, wry observations—New Year's resolutions were to "run a marathon, stop biting my nails, stop swearing and relearn French"—and intelligent essays on her burgeoning accounts.

In the eighteen months since it had launched, Meghan had assiduously used The Tig to promote what she felt was important and beautiful: a charming photograph of her mom on Mother's Day, a recipe for beet pasta with arugula pesto, suggested reading lists, her favorite picture by Australian artist Gray Malin, or a shot of her eating a raw urchin as she stood in the warm Caribbean surf. Meghan was relentless, diligent, and disciplined about creating daily content. She brought in guest writers like PR guru Lucy Meadmore to write about a trip to Costa Rica, her yoga coach Duncan Parviainen, and her *Suits* costar Abigail Spencer. However, there was a serious underpinning to all this gauze. In an essay titled "Champions of Change," Meghan wrote passionately about race relations, retelling the family story about the segregation they suffered during a road trip from Ohio to California. "It reminds me of how young our country is," she told her readers.

"How far we've come and how far we still have to come. It makes me think of the countless black jokes people have shared in front of me, not realizing I am mixed, unaware that I am the ethnically ambiguous fly on the wall." With its mix of serious and frivolous, girly and gritty, The Tig had the feel of an upmarket women's magazine but in Meghan's distinctive voice. As she said about her baby: "It's my outlet to say my own words and to share all these things that I find inspiring and exciting, but also attainable." The baby was bringing home a little bacon, too. Through her shopping program and the promotion of brands such as Birchbox, a subscription beauty box brand, she was now making a little money off the venture. "I would never take ads," she said. "Or sell a $100 candle. Obnoxious."

There were times she had to remind herself not to give in to the compulsion to photograph and share every last detail of her life. She had to remember to surrender to the moment, to enjoy real life. As Warren Beatty, the then boyfriend of Madonna, said of the star when she was making the documentary Truth or Dare, "she doesn't want to live off camera much less talk." He made that withering remark in the days before social media ran rampant. Now Meghan was one of a generation who, if they were not careful, would only define their existence through social media. As I write, a young boy, now known as the #selfiekid, became an overnight sensation after taking a selfie with singer Justin Timberlake during the 2018 Super Bowl halftime show. After taking the shot, rather than joining in the singing and dancing, being in the present, the young man went back to his phone to review his pictures and thus validate his real experience. Somehow it was a moment that defines the age we live in.

The real world kept intruding, though. In February 2016 the actor flew to Kigale once again to undertake charity work. First, she celebrated Valentine's Day—not with Cory but with friends in New York's West Village. It had become a pattern, both ambitious people who were neither willing to give the time or effort to nurture a meaningful relationship. He was immersed in his restaurant chain and television career as a celebrity chef, Meghan in her world as an actor, humanitarian, and fashion personality. It was clear that the writing was on the wall for their two-year relationship, neither being willing to relinquish any part of their professional lives to sustain their romance.

So much of their relationship had been spent in going their separate ways, Meghan in particular spending much of her free time traveling. This time her visit to Africa was arranged not by the United Nations but by World Vision Canada, an Evangelical Christian humanitarian aid charity. Their sister organization, World Vision US, had hit the headlines the previous year with their United States office's decision not to hire Christians in same-sex marriages. It was a policy position quickly disavowed by their independent Canadian neighbor. The charity's mission statement reads: "Motivated by our faith in Jesus Christ, World Vision serves alongside the poor and oppressed as a demonstration of God's unconditional love for all people. World Vision serves all people, regardless of religion, race, ethnicity, or gender."

On the surface it was an odd choice, especially as Meghan seemed to have stalled with United Nations Women and had nothing on her schedule in relation to her role as UN advocate. However, World Vision Canada was eager to harness her celebrity to promote their work in the developing world, notably, bringing clean water to rural villages. Whatever misgivings she may have had, she accepted their invitation to see their work in Rwanda. It was an enthusiastic meeting of minds, recalled Laura Dewar, WVC chief marketing officer. "She's remarkably approachable. She was very open to a conversation about the kinds of causes that moved her and that she would like to learn more about."

This was a very different kind of visit than her UN-sponsored trip, where she met female parliamentarians and discussed how they could best promote women's issues in a mainly rural nation. Her tour this time was much more traditional, top-down benevolence, Meghan watching a well being completed in a village and then helping turn on the mechanism that drew the water to the surface. All the while her friend Gabor Jurina, a fashion photographer, captured the scenes.

Though her visit did not directly focus on gender equality, Meghan quickly grasped the concept that a community's access to clean water keeps young girls in school because they aren't walking hours each day to find water for their families. Traditionally, in many rural communities in Rwanda and elsewhere, girls find wood and water, and boys tend the animals.

Later, after taking part in a dance lesson, she visited a school in the Gasabo District and met twenty-five students whose access to a clean water pipeline, installed by World Vision Canada, had transformed their lives. She sat with the children as they painted with watercolors using water drawn from the well, their paint-dipped fingers creating images of their dreams and futures.

When she returned to Toronto she staged a charity art sale, using the children's art as a basis for the Watercolor Project. The invitation-only function, held on March 22 at the LUMAS gallery in downtown Toronto, was hosted by Meghan and raised more than $15,000, enough to bring clean water to an entire rural community. Applauded as World Vision's newly minted global ambassador, she told the sixty-strong audience: "Access to clean water allows women to invest in their own businesses and community. It promotes grassroots leadership, and, of course, it reinforces the health and wellness of children and adults. Every single piece of it is so interconnected, and clean water, this one life source, is the key to it all."

Meghan was now the official face of the organization, short snappy videos of her appearing on the charity's website, financial statements, and promotional material. Unlike the United Nations, where Meghan was one of many celebrities working to promote important issues within the organization, here Meghan was the figurehead of this Christian charity, one of Canada's largest.

In charity and commerce Meghan was now the representative for two storied Canadian organizations, World Vision Canada and Reitmans.

Meghan spun and posed in front of the white backdrop as her friend Gabor Jurina snapped away. Video was also rolling, capturing behind the scenes action as Meghan modeled the four dresses in her first capsule collection for Reitmans. Then she dashed home to write copy about the collection for The Tig.

She waxed rapturous over the Los Angeles–inspired maxi-dress, trilled over the Rachel Zane–esque "little black dress," and gushed about the white flouncy dress with an asymmetrical hem. The maroon date night dress made Meghan feel "fashion-y and Frenchie." The day before the April 27 launch of her collection, Meghan hastened to New York to the taping of the finale of *The Fashion Fund*, a Vogue-sponsored event where designers battle it out to win sponsorship and funding for their line. She was mixing and matching with fashion luminaries, the perfect lead in into the launch of her collection. Meghan was also traveling alone.

In news that shocked none of her friends, she and Cory decided to go their separate ways—as they had been doing in effect for most of their relationship. Nonetheless the breakup still had an effect, a friend of Meghan's remarking that she felt "down, vulnerable and hurt" by the split. Though there were hints that Cory was seeing other women, the root of the issue was the plain fact that neither side was prepared to make any commitment.

She put on a brave face, grabbed a glass of champagne, and enjoyed the launch of her first fashion collection. It was an immediate hit.

Thanks to Meghan's dedicated selling and her star power, the

Meghan Markle Collection virtually sold out on day one. Eat your heart out, Kate Moss. Meghan was thrilled especially as the company were so enthused about sales that her second capsule collection, to be released in the fall of 2016, was a done deal.

The actor barely had time to finish her glass of bubbly before she was one of the celebrity guests at luncheon to honor ten game-changing women under the age of twenty-five. Meghan along with Olympic athletes and successful internet startup founders were designated mentors of the finalists at the fifty-ninth anniversary of the Glamour College Women of the Year. Now a grizzled veteran, Meghan was asked about the most common misconception about college girls. "You realize there is so much depth, there is so much incredible inspiration, and that young women are thinking outside of the box in a way that we haven't seen before. It is the biggest sign that we are in good hands, that our world is going to be just fine, and that these are the women who are going to be the players changing the game."

She wasn't so confident of the future a couple of weeks later when she agreed to appear on Comedy Central and join a panel discussion on Larry Wilmore's *The Nightly Show*.

With the presidential election just six months away and Republican candidates dropping like flies, Donald Trump looked like the front-runner. On the night she appeared, his endless attacks on Fox News anchor Megyn Kelly, calling her "sick" and "overrated," had finally engendered a response from the Republican-leaning channel. In a statement backing Kelly, they said: "Donald Trump's vitriolic attacks against Megyn Kelly and his extreme, sick obsession with her is beneath the dignity of a presidential candidate who wants to occupy the highest office in the land."

Wilmore asked his guests: "Do you think the momentum surrounding Mr. Trump could be stopped?" Meghan joined in the banter with the host and his correspondents, laughing wryly, "It's really the moment that I go, we film *Suits* in Toronto and I might just stay in Canada. I mean, come on, if that's reality we are talking about, come on, that is a game changer in terms of how we move in the world here."

A few minutes later she jumped in to make other points, "Yes, of course Trump is divisive. Think about just female voters alone. I think it was in 2012, the Republican Party lost the female vote by twelve points. That's a huge number." She went on to label Trump a "misogynist" and suggested that voting for Hillary Clinton was made easier because of the moral fiber of the man she was up against. "Trump has made it easy to see that you don't really want that kind of world that he's painting," she argued.

It would not be long before Trump's long shadow would affect her life in ways that she could never have contemplated even in her wildest dreams.

9

When Harry Met Meghan

Sometimes timing is everything. If Meghan Markle had met the man standing before her, casually dressed, hand outstretched in greeting, a couple of years earlier, she would have smiled, made friendly small talk, and moved on. Prince Harry would not have impressed—except as an anecdote to tell her friends.

Of course she would have noticed his ginger hair and beard—her father, half brother, and former husband, Trevor Engelson, are all strawberry blonds—and that at 6 foot 1 he is not far off her father's height, although skinnier and fitter, with the rangy, loping gait of a young man who's spent a lot of time in the great outdoors. But Meghan would have found the early Harry hard work, something of a lost soul.

Looking back, Harry would be the first to admit that during his twenties, his life had descended in to "total chaos," the prince struggling to process the black cloud of grief that had enveloped his life since the moment he had been awakened from his bed in Balmoral in the summer of 1997 and was told that his mother, Diana, Princess of Wales, had died in a car accident.

Though millions of tears had been shed as people around the

globe watched the prince, then only twelve, walk behind his mother's coffin in the televised funeral, only he had been left to pick up the pieces of his life. Not even his brother, Prince William—sober, pragmatic and sensible—had been able to reach him at times.

Without a mother, without a steadying, nurturing influence in his life, Harry had gone off the rails. He became notorious as an angry drunk who lurched out of London nightclubs, ready to throw a punch at the loathsome paparazzi who dogged his every footstep. For years he was carefully protected by highly paid public relations professionals who smoothed over his public escapades. So when, in February 2004, Harry was branded a "horrible young man" by influential columnist Carol Sarler over his late-night escapades, Prince Charles's communications director, Paddy Harverson, swung into action, defending the prince's behavior during this gap year.

Harry flew to Lesotho and was photographed with an orphan named Mutsu Potsane, Harry speaking of his deep shock about the impact of AIDS on the country. The trip was followed up by royal aides helpfully releasing a letter he wrote to patients in a hospital unit dealing with the victims of rape and abuse. It was a classic public relations exercise, using Harry's evident personal qualities—an easygoing manner, fundamental decency, and sense of fun—together with his mother's humanitarian legacy to project a different narrative about a young man best known for his nightclubbing.

For many years this was the go-to template for the prince, any nighttime indiscretions more than compensated for by his charity work and his life as a professional soldier, serving for a time in Afghanistan before training to fly Apache helicopters. In Prince Harry's world there has always been someone to do the sweeping up. When he dressed up in a Nazi uniform for a Colonials and Natives fancy dress party shortly before Holocaust Memorial Day in 2005, his minders accepted that it was a "poor choice of costume" but that there was no malice in his decision. Similarly, when he was caught on video referring to a fellow officer cadet at Sandhurst as "our dear little Paki friend" and another as looking like a "raghead," a pejorative term for an Arab, once again his PR minder Paddy Harverson came to the rescue.

If Meghan had been in his life at that time, she would not have been impressed by his casual racism. Nor were others. "He was a very lost young man," a former royal official told me. "Harry was deeply troubled, unhappy, and immature, imbued with the slanted, quietly racist views of those from his class and background."

Perhaps the low point in Harry's party lifestyle came in 2012, when he was pictured cavorting naked in a Las Vegas hotel room during a game of strip billiards with a bunch of strangers, some of whom had camera phones and uploaded his antics for the startled world to watch. "Too much army not enough prince," was his rueful response.

In spite of the uproar, by and large the prince retained the affection of the public, who instinctively sympathized with the emotional difficulties he and his brother had gone through with their parents' bitter divorce and their mother's untimely death. The difference was that William's more grounded temperament and later on having the support of a sensible and stable wife helped to see him through the dark nights of the soul. The younger brother found a curious respite from his demons and a sense of purpose during his time in the Army. He is not the first nor will he be the last person who has been given direction and discipline by the military.

One episode in particular has had a profound impact on the course of his life. At the end of his first tour of duty in 2008, on a flight home from Afghanistan, he traveled with the coffin of a dead Danish soldier, which had been loaded on board by his friends, and with three British troops all in induced comas who were being transported with their missing limbs, wrapped in plastic.

"The way I viewed service and sacrifice changed forever," he recalled. "I knew it was my responsibility to use the great platform that I have to help the world understand and be inspired by the spirit of those who wear the uniform." That flight set him on the trajectory that would culminate in the Invictus Games. His mother would have been proud.

The prince's idea was to combine his royal connections, his lifelong interest in the Armed Forces, and his passion for humanitarian causes into one focused event. The Invictus Games are an international multisport jamboree in which sick, wounded, or injured servicemen and women compete in a variety of sports, such as indoor rowing and wheelchair basketball. In September 2014, after a year of planning and meetings, the first games, which involved three hundred army personnel from around the world, were held in London. The games were a triumph, giving the prince, who was due to leave the army in 2015, new focus and impetus. He was fully committed to using his unique position to help and encourage those who were at the sharp end of modern warfare, veterans who had been damaged and injured but who were prepared to fight on, albeit on a basketball or tennis court. The Invictus Games were the making of Harry. "Since then he has become the man he is today," observes a former royal courtier. "It has not been an easy process. He has become more open and developed into someone who genuinely cares about social issues."

The experience opened up something in Harry, and increasingly, he became happy to talk about his personal hopes and dreams, too. His conversations, public and private, were peppered with talk of the princely problem of finding a partner, of settling down and raising a family. It was clear that he had reached a crossroads in his life and that his days of sowing wild oats were coming to an end. As the rest of his friends were settling down and starting families, it seemed that Prince Harry was in danger of becoming the last man standing. He had seen his brother enjoying the simple joys of family life and wanted that experience for himself.

At a birthday party in February 2016, he told TV presenter Denise Van Outen: "I'm not dating and for the first time ever I want to find a wife." It became a familiar refrain. Three months later when he was in Orlando, Florida, for the Invictus Games, he again brought up the subject of love and marriage. "At the moment my focus is very much on work, but if someone slips into my life then that's absolutely fantastic. I am not putting work before the idea of family and marriage. I just haven't had that many opportunities to get out there and meet people."

The difficulty of finding someone "willing to take me on" was an issue that was always at the back of his mind every time he met someone new. Were they attracted to him for his personality or his title? As one of his friends pointed out: "You have to be a very special girl to want to be a princess."

As Meghan Markle nestled back in her seat in preparation for landing at Heathrow Airport, she had love and marriage on her mind. The actor was returning from a long weekend on the Greek island of Hydra, once home to the lugubrious poet and singer Leonard Cohen. It had been several days of wine, red mullet, hummus, and incredible yoga moves as Meghan; her best friend from college, Lindsay Jill Roth; and Lindsay's bridesmaids discussed wedding dresses, veils, flowers, the past, and the future. Her relationship with celebrity chef Cory Vitiello had ended recently, withered on the vine as both their lives became busier and busier, and Meghan relished time away from Toronto and the house they had shared there.

As matron of honor to Lindsay, who since leaving Northwestern had embarked on a career as a TV producer and novelist, Meghan had taken her role very seriously, considerately organizing the bachelorette party on this beautiful Greek resort island rather than some raucous downtown club. "There is something wholly cathartic about being able to turn it all off—to sunbathe with no one watching, swim, eat copious amounts and toast to the day," she wrote in her blog, The Tig. The mini vacation was a triumph, as was her earlier surprise invitation asking Lindsay to Toronto, where she had arranged a wedding dress fitting at the upmarket Kleinfeld Hudson's Bay bridal boutique (its New York sister store was made famous by the TV show *Say Yes to the Dress*) with the help of another of her great friends, Jessica Mulroney, who worked in public relations for the bridal shop. Lindsay, who was marrying a British actuary, viewed a selection of dresses and fell in love with a wedding gown from fashionable Lebanese designer Zuhair Murad, who has dressed many of the Hollywood's elite, including Taylor Swift, Beyoncé, and Katy Perry.

Having executed her duties as the impeccable bridesmaid, once she arrived in London Meghan now went looking for her own prince charming.

With more than 300,000 Twitter followers, a morning breakfast show, and a friendship with then Republican presidential nominee Donald Trump and Simon Cowell, media royalty Piers Morgan was a favorable catch for an up-and-coming actor seeking her name in headlines. After all, her week-long visit to London was mainly to promote the upcoming season of *Suits* and to dress to impress at Wimbledon, where her sponsor Ralph Lauren held (center) court.

Already Twitter buddies who had enjoyed an energetic back-and-forth online, she contacted Piers on June 29 while she was sitting in the stands watching her friend, tennis legend Serena Williams, at Wimbledon. She suggested they meet. They arranged an early evening drink at his local pub, the Scarsdale Tavern in Kensington. Piers was a *Suits* aficionado, but this was the first time he had met "Rachel Zane" in the flesh. He recalled: "She looked every inch the Hollywood superstar—very slim, very leggy, very elegant, and impossibly glamorous." Or as the landlord put it, "a stunner."

As she sipped a dirty martini they chatted about *Suits*, her background, her days as a briefcase girl, gun control in America, her passion for calligraphy, women's rights, and her one-time ambition to be a TV presenter. Piers was duly flattered and impressed; "Fabulous, warm, funny, intelligent, and highly entertaining," he later recalled. "She seemed real, too. Not one of those phony actress types so prevalent in California."

At eight o'clock, she left for her dinner date at the private members' club 5 Hertford Street amid a flurry of texts, observing that she was recently single, "out of practice" with the dating scene and trying to fend off "persistent men."

Was Meghan leaving a media prince to meet the real thing? Though Piers has a track record as a celebrity Cupid—I was at the lunch where he first introduced Paul McCartney to Heather Mills, whom he later married—it is doubtful a woman as socially careful and perkily camera ready as Meghan would have downed a couple of stiff martinis before meeting the queen's grandson.

Professionally, the reason for her visit to London in the first place was to promote the new season of *Suits* and designer Ralph Lauren. Her big day was June 30, so she had to be bright eyed, bushy tailed, and ready for another afternoon of dazzling smiles— and the odd glass of champagne.

With her networking hat on, Meghan was working closely with Violet von Westenholz, a Ralph Lauren PR executive, who had organized her "Suits Day" and her marketing efforts on behalf of the RL fashion brand. "How much more can I adore this gem," an effusive Meghan wrote of her new bestie. It's worth noting that not only is Violet a well-connected fashion maven but her father, Baron Piers von Westenholz, an upmarket interior designer, is a friend of Prince Charles while her sister, Victoria, was once seen as a possible match for Prince Harry.

For years Violet and Victoria had joined Princes Charles, William, and Harry on their annual skiing trips to Switzerland. While she has been modest about her matchmaking skills—"I might leave that for other people to say," she told the *Daily Telegraph*—it seems likely that she set up Meghan and Harry on their famous blind date timed to coincide with his return from a World War One commemoration in France.

Meghan has always been very careful to emphasize that they met in July, insisting that *Vanity Fair* magazine, which had published a flattering article about her, print a correction when they indicated that the couple first met in May 2016 in Toronto. If Violet had the royal connections, then Meghan's friend Canadian-born Markus Anderson, the brand ambassador for the exclusive Soho House, who had just returned from a holiday in Madrid with Meghan, was on hand to rustle up a private room at the members' only club for an intimate evening away from prying eyes.

The scene was set, Cupid's arrow was aquiver, and the stars, as Harry observed during his engagement interview, were aligned. Not that Meghan had much of an opinion about the man she was about to meet. When she was asked during a TV quiz to choose between William and Harry, she appeared nonplussed and the presenter had to encourage her to choose the prince who was still single. Meghan, it appeared, preferred the actor Dennis Quaid, in any case.

Harry had his work cut out. That said, Meghan was meeting a very different Harry from the young man who made a profession of falling out of bars. On July 1, he had just returned from France, where he had joined the then prime minister David Cameron, Prince Charles, the Duke and Duchess of Cambridge, and other dignitaries at a service to commemorate the one hundredth anniversary of the start of the Battle of the Somme, the bloodiest day of warfare in British history. At an evening vigil for the fallen, Harry had read "Before Action," a poem penned by Lieutenant W. N. Hodgson, who died in action the following day. The event had been a somber and moving reminder of the enormity of that day. And Harry returned in sober spirits.

Meghan was meeting a grown-up, a man with focus and resolve, a sense of who he was and what he could achieve. She had asked her friends before their meeting if he was kind and nice, and the answer lay in his blue eyes. As they say in the movies, they had each other at "hello." She was immediately sensitive to him, aware that this was a man who, beneath the banter and the surface chatter, was looking for a safe harbor. The question she asked herself after that first intoxicating meeting was could she provide it—and all that entailed.

They were mesmerized by one another, Harry enthralled by her beauty, sophistication, and perceptiveness. She understood him as a man, not a title. In that subtle one-upmanship of a first date, he realized that while his grandmother might be the queen, Meghan had given a speech at a UN forum. As he subsequently confessed, he realized that he would have to up his game.

At the end of the evening, they said their goodnights and went their separate ways, he to Nottingham Cottage at Kensington Palace, she to a room at the Dean Street townhouse in Soho. Both were buzzing. As she relived that fateful evening in her mind, she perhaps wondered if she had been too eager to accept his invitation to meet again the following day.

As Harry later confirmed, the couple enjoyed back-to-back dates, making every minute matter before she had to fly back to Toronto on July 5 to continue promoting the new season of *Suits*. The normally self-contained actor was smitten. Unable to keep her feelings contained, her Instagram account gave away just a little; on July 3 she posted a picture of two Love Hearts candies that bore a simple message: KISS ME. Next to the photograph Meghan posted "Love Hearts in London."

She had even taken herself by surprise. When Harry asked if she would be interested in joining him on safari for a few days in August—mere weeks after their first meeting—she found herself saying, "Yes, please." Schedules were consulted, days were agreed upon, plans were made. She had to pinch herself. Here she was about to travel halfway around the world to spend five days in a tented camp in the middle of nowhere with a man she had met twice. It was a side to herself that she was just discovering.

The last full day she had in London she spent at Wimbledon, where she sat in the players' box along with *Vogue* editor Anna Wintour and her niece. As she was watching her friend Serena Williams thrash Russian Svetlana Kuznetsova, it began to rain. Meghan was wearing a simple but expensive black suede Ralph Lauren dress, so Anna, ever the fashionista, offered the actor her wool cardigan so that the suede would not be stained by the water while they waited for the roof to be installed. Once play resumed, Anna recovered her cardigan and Serena eased her way through to the last eight.

Though she was nursing the biggest secret of her life, Meghan was focused on the action, standing to applaud her friend's out-standing play. However, courtside photographers were more focused on Wintour and on Kate Middleton's sister Pippa than on Meghan. She was placed under the heading "incidental people" by one photographic agency. Not for much longer.

"Gutted to be leaving London," Meghan told her 1.9 million Instagram followers before she boarded her flight to Toronto. It would be some months before even her close friends realized exactly why the parting was so bittersweet. As she sipped a glass of champagne on board the flight, she would have had time to ponder the preposterous course her life had taken. But not that long. Hours after she had landed, her life continued its dizzying pace. She barely had time to make a fuss of her rescue dogs, Bogart and Guy, and check in with the design team at Reitmans about her upcoming winter capsule collection before this one-woman perpetual motion machine was on her travels again, flying to New York and Boston to continue the promotional tour for *Suits*.

In Boston she posed for pictures and made a video for *Good*

Housekeeping magazine, while for NBC's *Today* show she discussed her recipe for a grilled Caesar salad before talking about the plot developments in the new series.

During her publicity tour she realized how little she knew of her boyfriend's home country. On July 12 she took part in a lighthearted quiz on the Dave TV channel. She had gamely tried, and failed, a series of questions about Britain, looking perplexed when asked what "apples and pears" meant in Cockney rhyming slang. (Answer: Stairs.)

Meghan was also amazed by the national animals of England, Scotland, and Wales, complaining: "Am I supposed to know that?" She pointed out that even the British camerawoman did not know that a lion was the national animal of England. "Am I supposed to know that? You don't know that," she said.

She was delighted to discover that the national animal of Scotland is a unicorn, saying: "No! Really? It's a unicorn! We're all moving to Scotland." When she realized that a dragon is the national animal of Wales, she said: "Are these real right now? It's a dragon. Lions and unicorns and dragons, oh my."

On August 4, she was in New York for her thirty-fifth birthday and stayed in the five-star St. Regis hotel in midtown in preparation for her friend Lindsay's big day. "Happy birthday to the most kind, generous, wickedly smart and gorgeous inside and out maid of honor a girl could want," Lindsay told her via social media. Intriguingly, on her birthday a bouquet of peonies, her favorite flowers, were delivered to her hotel suite. A princely offering perhaps?

Certainly something was going on in Meghan's heart. "I am feeling so incredibly joyful right now," she wrote on The Tig. "So grateful and content that all I could wish for is more of the same. More surprises, more adventure."

She was certainly not short of adventures. In mid-August, after the Roth wedding, she left behind the elegant butler service at the storied St. Regis in New York and flew to Rome, where she joined her style guru friend Jessica Mulroney. They planned to embrace la dolce vita in some style, checking into the equally civilized Le Sirenuse hotel on the Amalfi coast in Italy.

With breathtaking views of the Bay of Positano, it is hard not to feel that this is but an ante room to paradise. Typically, Meghan publicized every detail of their four-day stay, even giving the holiday the hashtag #MJxItaly. They lounged around the pool, strolled into the market square, and took pictures of their breakfast under the heading "Eat Pray Love." Meghan, who had had a couple of weeks to ponder the impending safari with Prince Harry, gave an indication of her romantic feelings when she held up a red leather-bound volume titled *Amore Etern'* (Eternal Love) and photographed it under the light of a full moon. It was, she said, given to her by friends as a good omen.

At the end of their stay she kissed Jessica goodbye, who was one of only a handful of friends who knew the secret of her next destination, and prepared for her thirteen-hour flight to Johannesburg.

There may have been a slight raising of eyebrows inside the royal palaces when the news percolated through that Prince Harry was taking yet another girlfriend on a safari holiday to Botswana.

Those who monitor these things would have noted that this was his seventh holiday in Botswana with the fourth female companion to join him for a few romantic nights under the stars in a southern African hideaway. The young man certainly had style.

And he was not the only prince of the realm to fall headlong in love with the delights of the African continent. Another Harry, his great uncle, the Duke of Gloucester, enjoyed a torrid affair with the famous and married aviatrix Beryl Markham during a visit to Kenya in 1928. The duke's elder brother, the Prince of Wales, later and briefly King Edward VIII, took his mistress, Lady Thelma Furness, on safari while her husband camped nearby. "This was our Eden and we were alone in it," she wrote breathlessly. "His arms about me were the only reality, his words of love my only bridge to life."

There is something about the vast plains, the never-ending skies, the daily struggle for existence that seems to bring out the passionate and the spiritual in a prince. Prince Charles has passed on his more mystical appreciation of southern Africa to both of his sons. His message to William and Harry was that the exploration of the outer world allowed a deeper engagement with the inner world, a chance to seek truth in their surroundings.

Charles's own guide was the South African philosopher Laurens van der Post, who encouraged the future king to find peace in the vast featureless wilderness of the Kalahari Desert. During a visit in March 1987 Charles and van der Post traveled to the desert by Land Rover, slept under canvas, and chatted around a campfire, listening to the sounds of the desert while marveling at the brilliant night sky. On the third day they came across a herd of zebra that stretched across the flat horizon. It was such a magnificent and imposing natural wonder that Charles found himself moved to tears. Nowhere else on the planet gives such a vivid reminder of the ineluctable rhythm of life—and of death—than the African plains.

Perhaps with these thoughts and reflections in mind, Prince Charles invited Prince Harry to join him on a five-day visit to South Africa, Swaziland, and Lesotho just two months after Harry's mother had died in a Parisian underpass. Harry was still struggling to come to terms with her loss, and his father thought that time away from England would help the healing process.

Accompanying Harry, who was then thirteen, was his "surrogate mum," Tiggy Legge Bourke, who had been an official companion to the young boy during his parents' separation; his school friend Charlie Henderson; and Mark Dyer, a former equerry to the Prince of Wales. While Harry's father undertook official

engagements, the young prince was taken on his first South African safari. It was the beginning of a lifelong love affair.

After touring some of the famous battlegrounds, such as Rorke's
Drift from the famous Zulu war of 1879, the prince met South
Africa's first president, Nelson Mandela, and the Spice Girls, who
were then at the height of their popularity and had traveled to
South Africa to perform at a charity concert.

It was six years before he enjoyed a return visit. The prince,
then nineteen, spent two months of his school gap year in the
impoverished kingdom of Lesotho, the landlocked country that
suffered from one of the highest HIV-AIDS infection rates in the
world. Initially it was seen by many as a cynical public relations
exercise to restore the prince's stained reputation. But not as far
as Harry was concerned. Moved by the plight of the children and
with his mother's memory clearly in mind, Harry joined forces
with the country's Prince Seeiso, who had lost his own mother.
In 2006 they set up the Sentebale charity to help children suffering from AIDS to lead fulfilled and productive lives. The Sentebale charity—the name means "forget me not"—was so popular
and, thanks to the prince's involvement, became so well known
outside the nation's boundaries that it expanded into neighboring Botswana. He has energetically supported it ever since. In
2008 he recruited his brother to take part in a one-thousand-mile
cross country motorbike trek along South Africa's eastern cape to
raise money for Sentebale and other charities supporting disad-
vantaged children. "It's not just a bimble across the countryside,
we're expected to fall off many a time," noted Harry.

Alongside his visits to help conservation projects as well as his
charity work for Sentebale and official duties, Harry made Africa
his favorite holiday destination—especially when trying to impress
a girlfriend. Before Meghan, he had taken TV sports presenter
Natalie Pinkham, Zimbabwean-born Chelsy Davy, and actor Cressida Bonas on safari. Botswana was the preferred destination. As

his biographer Penny Junor observed: "Africa is the one place on earth where Prince Harry can be truly himself. It is his 'second home.' Under African skies, he is not a prince he is just Harry."

The problem with these romances was that once he arrived back in Britain, the HRH tag got in the way of building an honest, workable commitment. Harry's previous serious relationships with Chelsy Davy and Cressida Bonas foundered because the women couldn't cope with being in the spotlight. As Harry's first serious girlfriend, Chelsy bore the unwelcome media attention for seven years. During their on-off relationship that lasted from 2004 to 2011, the feisty blonde was often described as the love of his life.

She became part of the royal set and was invited to the weddings of Prince William and Kate Middleton, and Princess Anne's daughter, Zara Phillips, and rugby player Mike Tindall. The trainee lawyer admitted that she found it difficult to cope with the pressure. "It was so full on—crazy, scary and uncomfortable," she later confessed. "It was tough being chased down the road by photographers. I was trying to be a normal kid and it was horrible." These days, she enjoys a "calm" life making jewelry.

Cressida told a similar story. She put her acting career on hold during her two-year romance with the prince. Though nervous of the paparazzi, she agreed to join him in public at a charity event at Wembley Arena in north London. In a telling exchange, she felt that as an actor she was being defined by a "famous man" rather than what she had achieved herself. "Yeah, I think it's that thing of being pigeonholed," she complained. "Especially in this country [Britain] I find people are very quick to put you in a box or put you in a corner."

Other girlfriends, such as lingerie model Florence "Flee" Brudenell-Bruce, a former girlfriend of Formula One racing champion Jensen Button, seemed to enjoy the limelight—but not Harry's roving eye. For his part he complained, as have princes down the ages, about the difficulty of finding a partner who wanted him for himself. As one of his friends observed: "He's always wary in case women throw themselves at him to make a name for themselves. And often the sincere ones who love him for who he is don't want to live in the goldfish bowl that is the royal family for the next fifty years."

But despite the obstacles, it doesn't appear to have been too much of a hardship, the prince enjoying romances, confirmed or suspected, with a veritable galaxy of beautiful, successful women, among them, actors Sienna Miller and Margot Robbie, TV presenter Poppy James, Brazilian socialite Antonia Packard, and German model Anastasia Guseva. The list is by no means exhaustive. Just a few weeks before he met Meghan for the first time, he was seen "dirty dancing" with a pair of brunettes and downing shots at Jak's bar in West London. Though his headline antics had been curbed, his newfound maturity remains tempered with a healthy dose of mischief.

10

Into Africa

In August 2016, as far as the public and media were concerned, Harry was taking yet another trip to Africa. The prince was scheduled to spend several weeks in Malawi helping to protect elephants from poaching before traveling to Botswana to work on measures to save the dwindling rhino population. He had taken part in a similar effort the previous year in Namibia. As well as his charity work, he was to be a guest at the August 6 wedding of his cousin George McCorquodale to Bianca Moore at Netherwood, a wedding venue, in KwaZulu-Natal, South Africa. Unfortunately, the social occasion ended up eclipsing his good works. *The Sun* newspaper lasciviously described how the prince and his friends, all the worse for wear, were said to have stripped a younger cousin naked during a drunken late night session of high jinks. Under the headline JAGER LOUT HARRY STRIPS WED GUEST, a fellow reveler was quoted as saying: "Harry was on his best behavior during the wedding but afterwards he went pretty wild. Everyone was laughing having a good time."

For all the banter and horseplay, Harry had something more meaningful on his mind. Later that month, after working with herds of elephants in Botswana, he was scheduled to meet Meghan at Johannesburg airport in South Africa to join her on the flight to Maun Airport in northern Botswana. The final leg of their journey was a bouncy ride along a series of dirt roads in a rugged 4×4 off-roader. At a roadblock the couple had to get out of their vehicle and walk across a disinfectant mat, a precaution to prevent diseases from the outside world getting into the vast game reserve. When the couple arrived at the exclusive tented camp known as Meno a Kwena, or "teeth of the crocodile," they were greeted by breathtaking views across the dark blue waters of the nearby Boteti River, meandering along the valley below them. It was a magnificent natural paradise, with herds of elephants, zebra, and wildebeest cooling off in the waters. A casual visitor would never know that for nearly twenty years the river had been dry and had only come back to life in 2008 when millions of gallons of water came gushing through from the Okavango Delta due to a shift in tectonic plates.

Situated halfway between the delta and the spectacular Central Kalahari Game Reserve, the camp has nine luxurious guest tents, all with en suite bathrooms equipped with solar-powered hot and cold running showers.

It is run by conservationist David Dugmore, an old friend not just of Harry but also his brother and father. He and his brother Roger, who organizes mobile safaris, were guests at William and Kate's wedding in 2011. At the forefront of dealing with the conflict between wildlife and cattle farming, Dugmore's views have helped shape the thinking of the princes about conservation. He has a radical plan to make Botswana the biggest conservation project in the world by creating a transfrontier park in which animals can freely migrate between the Okavango and the Kalahari.

Doubtless he discussed the latest developments with the prince, while giving a conservation primer to Harry's American girlfriend.

However, they had not come thousands of miles to learn about conservation, interested though they both were in the topic. Their days and nights under canvas in the middle of nowhere were a chance to get to know one another without any distractions. That meant, for once, the chattily effusive Meghan Markle maintained radio silence on her social media accounts, the normally prolific web maven going dark between August 21 and 28.

Conversationally, Harry, who has spoken about his ambition to be a safari guide, was on home turf, the old Africa hand well able to impress Meghan with his local knowledge of the bush and the dynamic relationship between indigenous tribes and the native flora and fauna. After all, what is there not to love about a guy who spends his holidays saving elephants and rhinos?

Though Meghan had been to Rwanda on behalf of World Vision Canada, she had never experienced anything so remote and primitive. Sipping a glass of decent red wine by the pool at Le Sirenuse in Positano simply did not compare with watching the vast herds roaming the plains, a sundowner cocktail in hand.

When the sun finally did go down, after a meal of chicken or game stew, they drank in the shimmering carapace of the stars above them. And when they retired for the night, they were lulled to sleep by the chirping of the yellow-throated sand grouse and the melancholy call of zebra at the water's edge. At dawn they were awoken by a chattering chorus of birds, noisier than usual, as it was their mating season.

During the days, the couple was able to choose from walking tours and day-long safaris deep into the Kalahari Desert. Along the banks of the river, crocodiles are a common sight, while sharp-eyed visitors can occasionally see lions and cheetahs. After a dusty safari the couple could relax in the natural rock swimming pool overlooking the river—crocodiles excluded.

It was here, in this natural idyll, where the couple cemented their relationship, both of them realizing that they had found something special. As Harry later described: "It was absolutely amazing to get to know her as quickly as I did."

In spite of the difficulties of distance and busy schedules, by the end of those magical six days they knew that their blossoming love affair was too precious to waste. As Meghan later told the BBC: "I think that very early on when we realized we were going to commit to each other, we knew we had to invest the time and energy and whatever it took to make that happen."

Luckily, they had a template in Meghan's friend, the recently married Lindsay Roth, who had managed to juggle executive producing *The Real Girl's Kitchen* for the Cooking Channel in New York while dating London-based Gavin Jordan, an actuary for Ernst & Young. Their long-distance relationship had thrived and even ended in marriage—as had many others in Harry's circle.

However, with due respect to Harry's male friends, none of them would qualify for the position of the world's most eligible bachelor. Harry had taken that gig—together with all that entails in terms of media, and public, fascination with his life. And as tricky as a long-distance relationship was, they had other considerations to bear in mind. Of paramount importance was secrecy. Meghan and Harry needed their romance to be private, at least long enough for the time to honestly decide if their relationship was going to succeed in the long run—or whether it was a feverish summer fling that would not endure the winter chills and inevitable absences.

They faced obstacles that just don't occur in most relationships; Meghan had to ask herself if she was in love with the man or the position, and if she loved the man, could she cope with the position? She might be a popular actor and used to being recognized in public, but that was nothing compared to the scrutiny she would be under should she choose to go the distance with Harry. Midrange celebrity boyfriends like chef Cory Vitiello were one thing, but royalty was quite another. Could she take it? And for that matter, could her family and friends?

For his part, Harry had fallen for a (slightly) older, biracial divorcée from California. He didn't need any reminding of the chaos and bitterness caused by the last American to marry a member of the royal family. When King Edward VIII fell for Wallis Simpson, the twice-divorced woman from Baltimore, he abdicated the throne rather than give her up.

Long after Edward VIII had gone into self-imposed exile, divorce remained the great no-no inside the royal family. In the 1950s Harry's great aunt, Princess Margaret, the queen's sister, had agreed, after much pressure from the church and politicians, to walk away from her relationship with another divorcé, the late king's equerry, Group Captain Peter Townsend. Her life was never really the same again.

Of course, his father, Prince Charles, had married his mistress, Camilla Parker Bowles, at Windsor in 2005 after leaving a decent interval following the death of Diana and that of his disapproving grandmother, the queen mother, who died in 2002. That union signaled a permanent retreat from the moral position the royal family had clung to during the bitter run-up to the abdication.

There was much history for Meghan to learn and absorb—much more than dragons, unicorns, and lions! Though he was instinctively protective toward her, Harry wanted Meghan to clearly understand what she was getting into and make her own choices, hopefully in his favor. He was much more the anxious supplicant, worried that the price of fame could be his future happiness. Like clambering into the unheated plunge pool at the Meno a Kweno camp, it was best if her introduction into his world was "pole, pole" (slowly, slowly).

The trick was in planning and timing. Many long-distance couples apply the twenty-one-day survival rule—to make sure that they see one another at least every three weeks. Harry and Meghan managed every fourteen days. Jet lag—not the paparazzi—became their main enemy. Meghan would often arrive in Toronto and go straight to the set of *Suits* and start filming. As she later recalled: "I think we were able to really have so much time just to connect and we never went longer than two weeks without seeing each other, even though we were obviously doing a long-distance relationship...we made it work."

When they compared schedules before they parted, it was clear that if anything Meghan was the busier of the pair that fall, what with her TV filming commitments, promoting her new fashion collection on behalf of Reitmans, her blog, and humanitarian work. Even before Harry came into her life she was often up until the wee hours scouring the internet for inspiration for The Tig. Now she was going to be stretched even further.

Upon his return to London, Harry was soon back in the royal routine. After celebrating his thirty-second birthday on September 15 on the queen's estate at Balmoral in the Scottish Highlands, he undertook engagements in Aberdeen on behalf of the Diana, Princess of Wales Memorial Fund, the charity set up in his mother's name that recognizes young people who have made a difference to their communities.

Meanwhile, on the last weekend in September, Meghan traveled to Ottawa, the Canadian capital, to attend her second One Young World Summit. The nonprofit had Meghan's resounding endorsement: "They are delegates who are speaking out against human rights violations, environmental crises, gender equality issues, discrimination and injustice. They are the change." Meghan, who had already spoken at the Dublin conference in 2014, joined other inspirational counselors, notably Mary Robinson, the former Irish president; Canadian prime minister Justin Trudeau; as well as actor Emma Watson; and fellow Kruger Cowne clients including former UN secretary general Kofi Annan, poet and activist Fatima Bhutto, and singer Cher. As a sign of her standing, she was asked by *Vanity Fair* photographer Jason Schmidt to pose alongside Mary Robinson, Fatima Bhutto, and

Saudi activist Loujain al-Hathloul with the Ottawa Parliament building as a backdrop.

Inside the conference center, Meghan, speaking without notes, told a women's equality forum about the time she had confronted the creator of *Suits* concerning the fact that the scriptwriters were sketching too many scenes that opened with her character, Rachel Zane, emerging naked from a shower dressed only in a towel. It was sexist, it was unnecessary, and it was stopped. Her complaint came years before the rebellion about the way women were treated by Hollywood, in the light of the Harvey Weinstein scandal, and the subsequent #MeToo campaign. For all her own professional difficulties, she admitted to feeling humbled, nervous, and rather emotional when she introduced activist Luwam Estifanos, who had bravely escaped a life of slavery in Eritrea and now works to end that government-sponsored practice in her home country.

Meghan's exposure at the conference was a reminder to Harry, if any were needed, that he was dating a very special woman. A keeper, as they say. She arrived in London shortly afterward for a reunion with the prince. As the watchword was privacy, they stayed at his modest grace and favor home on the grounds of Kensington Palace. Best remembered now as the place where thousands of people laid flowers in the summer of 1997 in memory of Diana, Princess of Wales, the palace is probably the most exclusive village in Britain, home to an assortment of royals, including the Duke and Duchess of Cambridge and their children, courtiers, and retired staff. Like any village, it feeds on a diet of gossip and rumor, but for the most part what happens inside Kensington Palace stays inside Kensington Palace.

If Meghan was expecting to be sleeping in a palace, she was sadly disappointed. Harry's home of Nottingham Cottage was smaller than her own place in Toronto—and with lower ceilings. It had been the home of Prince William and Kate while the capacious apartment 1a Clock Court, the former residence of the late Princess

Margaret, was being renovated. Cozy and neat, the cottage, known as Notts Cott by residents, boasts two bedrooms, two bathrooms, two reception rooms, and a small garden. In summer it has the feel of being in the heart of an English country village, which perhaps explains why the first thing Harry did when he moved in was to install a hammock in the garden to laze away sunny afternoons.

It had the virtue, though, of being private and secure, the exits and entrances watched 24 hours a day by armed police. It is here, as schedules permitted, where they began living together, quietly, secretly, unobtrusively. Meghan recalled, "I don't think that I would call it a whirlwind in terms of our relationship. Obviously there have been layers attached to how public it has become after we had a good five, six months almost with just privacy, which was amazing."

Fortunately for Meghan, the palace also has a high walking score—places available on foot—which meant the actor was able to go jogging—mobile meditation, as she calls it—around the park or stroll on Kensington High Street to go shopping. It will doubtless have given her a kick to know that when she went into Whole Foods, the American-owned supermarket, which shares a building with journalists from the *Mail* newspaper group, she was operating in "enemy territory."

Not that Kensington Palace was a home away from home. It was a culture shock. Not just the security but the rather utilitarian way the royals lived. Take, for example, food. As a rule, the royal family eat to live rather than live to eat, watching their diets so that they remain the same shape and weight. "Bloody organic," said Prince Philip to palace chef Darren O'Grady one day when confronted with a basket of his eldest son's homegrown produce.

When Harry was growing up a treat was to be taken to McDonald's for a hamburger by his mother. For the most part, he was brought up on institutional food at his boarding schools and then, during his Army career, fed with whatever was available, especially when he was based in Afghanistan. Even on formal occasions, when palace chefs pull out the culinary stops, he was raised in a family where traditionally everyone stopped eating once the Queen finished. When she put down her cutlery it was a signal for all the plates to be cleared away. Hardly the recipe for a calm digestion.

Though all members of the royal family have their dietary quirks, none seemingly enjoy the act of cooking—though Prince Philip does like to barbecue when in Balmoral. Meghan, though, comes from the other end of the foodie chain: she loves cooking, exploring new foods, and experimenting with fresh flavors. During the first few months of their romance, Meghan's blog, The Tig, enthused over recipes for pumpkin fondue, spiced broccoli and hempseed stew, poached pear in orange, spelt Anzac biscuits, and red wine hot chocolate. As she likes to sample her recommendations, Harry will have been the royal guinea pig.

Meghan extolled the virtues of a "holistic plant-based food delivery service" complete with brand ambassadors who were "experts, influencers and leaders in the wellness world." Maybe it was wise to have kept Prince Philip out of the loop on that one.

Just as Meghan encouraged a helping of culinary adventure, so she dramatically changed the contents of his fridge. Meghan never leaves home unless she has hummus, carrots, green juice, almonds, and chia seed pudding in the fridge. When California met Kensington, there was only going to be one victor in the dietary smackdown. As one observer noted: "Americans like to change their men in many small ways."

They were, however, hardly prisoners of the palace. As Harry doubtless told himself, if his mother could keep her longtime romance with heart surgeon Hasnat Khan a secret, then he could do the same with Meghan. They enjoyed a quiet trip to see the musical The Lion King and visited Princess Eugenie, the Duchess of York's daughter, and her soon-to-be fiancé Jack Brookbank at her apartment at St. James's Palace.

"Eugenie and Meghan have become firm friends, bonding over a shared love of art, dogs, and late-night macaroni suppers," one friend of the couple later revealed. "Eugenie loves Meghan to bits and believes she is perfect for Harry." The prince also carefully introduced her to his closest friends, notably Hugh van Cutsem and Rose Astor, and his school friend Tom "Skippy" Inskip and his wife, flame-haired literary agent Lara Hughes-Young. One of the first to run the rule over his brother's latest was Prince William, the couple frequently visiting the Duke and Duchess and their children, Prince George and Princess Charlotte, at their Kensington Palace home.

They also visited the gastropub Sands End in South West London, which is owned by Harry's "second dad" and mentor Mark Dyer. Dyer was utterly delighted that Harry had found a "good sort" after so many years of drifting and occasional debauchery. It helped that Mark is married to Texan heiress Amanda Kline, who was able to give Meghan recommendations for mundane but vital matters, such as hairdressers, nail bars, and beauty salons.

"Meghan loved her from the start," observed a friend of the Dyers. "She is a compatriot and terribly kind and jolly—and Harry trusts the Dyers implicitly."

One weekend they headed to the Cotswolds, staying at the Oxfordshire farmhouse run by Soho House. It is a seriously stylish hang out for metropolitan hipsters who want to road test their designer wellies. Every night a cocktail cart visits the various rooms and wooden cabins, dispensing martinis and, in Harry's case, aged Scotch whiskey. While staying at Soho Farmhouse, the club's founder, Nick Jones, introduced Meghan to musician Richard Jones, husband of singer Sophie Ellis-Bextor, whom Meghan had met at the opening of Soho House in Istanbul in 2015. A keen amateur pilot, he said to Meghan, "Let me show you how to fly a plane." As he later recalled, "She jumped at it. I took her up with me and she loved it. She was great, a natural, and we flew over the Cotswolds."

On October 11 she boarded a rather larger conveyance than Richard Jones's single prop and flew from London to Atlanta, Georgia, where she was a guest speaker at a blogging conference aimed specifically at millennial women who want to network and learn how best to use digital space. In a thirty-five-minute discussion on stage with Create and Cultivate founder Jaclyn Johnson, she passed on her own pearls of internet wisdom and made it clear that she planned to expand The Tig. By now her baby had grown into a toddler that needed constant feeding. Her brand, which she described as "aspirational girl next door," needed help, someone who could instinctively know how to channel Meghan and continue to feed The Tig. She clearly wanted to be able to balance her site with her private life, but she had not yet given serious attention or thought to how her royal romance could impact the life of her social media baby. During the taped conversation she also gave her adoring audience a window into the whirlwind that was her world, admitting that she had arrived from London the previous night and after the conference was flying to Toronto to film three episodes of *Suits* for the show's sixth season. Her talk left the audience impressed by her candor and smarts. "Charming, intelligent and unafraid to let her guard down, Meghan is the definition of the modern woman," noted Jaclyn Johnson.

Once Megan had finished filming it was Harry's turn to join her in Toronto. Unlike Meghan, who's normally the camera-ready girl sitting in business class in her jeans, chinos, and black tailored blazer, a cashmere scarf on her shoulders, quietly reading *The Economist* while listening to Petit Biscuit or Christine and the Queens on her designer headphones, Harry is the boy in a beanie, traveling head down, avoiding eye contact. Fortunately, unlike in London, Paris, and New York, there is no paparazzi culture in the Ontario capital, so life was more relaxed for the couple, and once again they were able to continue with their relationship outside of public or media scrutiny.

Apart from an SUV containing plainclothes police that was parked unobtrusively on her tree-lined street in the affluent neighborhood of Seaton Village, there was no obvious sign that a member of the royal family had come to visit.

With its wooden floors and light-painted walls, Meghan's open-plan property has the feel of Southern California, a trick that is hard to pull off on a dull October afternoon in Toronto. Unlike Nottingham Cottage's relatively utilitarian interior, the rented property is suitably luxurious, with a cinema room, a high-end eat-in kitchen, three bedrooms, and two bathrooms. Her rescue dogs, Bogart and Guy, had the run of the house and despite having a kennel outside the pair often slept on Meghan's king-sized bed. When Harry came to stay, doubtless she dressed them in the Union Jack jumpers she bought to amuse her royal boyfriend.

Meghan would also throw barbecue parties for friends who were "in the know," such as Jessica and Ben Mulroney, on a small deck, or they went to Soho House for drinks.

Housed in an elegant Georgian building in the west of the city on Adelaide Street, the club provided the cozy corners and intimate bars where the couple could escape with Meghan's closest friends. Here they could enjoy the Italian-style cuisine or venture onto the rooftop terrace for panoramic views of the downtown skyline.

For much of the time they just hung out, Meghan cooking dishes fit for a prince, mainly pasta and her signature roast chicken. At Halloween, the eve of Meghan's collection for Reitmans hitting the stores, they met at Princess Eugenie and Jack Brooksbank, who were in Canada on holiday, at Soho House for supper before Harry donned a mask and went trick-or-treating with his girlfriend.

It was a fun and carefree evening, but their days of secrecy and privacy were coming to an end.

Meghan and Harry were about to be unmasked.

11

A Very Public Romance

On a briskly chilly but blue-skied day at the end of October 2016, Camilla Tominey, the royal editor of the *Sunday Express*, was cheering on her young son in a Sunday league soccer match. Much to his mother's delight, the six-year-old was on the score sheet.

Some hours earlier his mother had scored, too, breaking the biggest royal story of her career. Under the headline HARRY'S SECRET ROMANCE WITH A TV STAR, and billed as a "Royal World Exclusive," she told her readers that Prince Harry was "secretly dating a stunning US actress, model and human rights campaigner." Her story went on to detail the romance between the queen's grandson and *Suits* actor Meghan Markle. It quoted a source as saying that Harry is the happiest he has been in years.

Her editor, Martin Townsend, was equally happy, so thrilled with the royal exclusive that he shared it with the *Sunday Star*, sister paper to the *Sunday Express*.

The story was gold dust. And Camilla was absolutely confident of her source. For once the newspaper decided against placing a courtesy call into the press office at Kensington Palace. The fear was that the palace would put out a statement, thus spoiling their scoop.

It was just like the old days of Fleet Street, the one-time newspaper capital of Britain. Normally Sunday newspapers have a gentleman's agreement where they swap their first editions so that if a rival has missed a story, they have a chance to catch up for later editions. Not this night. Townsend decided to deliberately delay printing the first edition of the paper so that none of his rivals were in a position to match their scoop. Late on Saturday night frantic calls from journalists were being made to Kensington Palace when word spread that the *Express* had landed "a big one." Camilla's agitated competitors were met with "No comment" by the duty press officer. Off the record, Prince Harry's communications director, Jason Knauf, an aggressive American, was reluctantly admitting that the article "had a ring of truth about it."

Within minutes of the *Sunday Express* story breaking, social media went into meltdown as bloggers, royal enthusiasts, *Suits* fans, and online newspapers worldwide spread the news. Overnight Meghan Markle went from being a moderately well-known actor to one of the most famous people on the planet.

When the story became public, Harry was staying with Meghan in Toronto. After he took a call from Jason Knauf to tell him their cover had been blown, he and Meghan poured themselves a glass of wine and toasted each other. But the celebration came with a sober warning, Harry telling Meghan: "Our lives will never be the same again."

At least they no longer had to hide from the world. Nor was the actor going to lose her mischievous sense of humor over this dramatic development in her life. Just hours after the story broke, she posted a cryptic photo on her Instagram site of two bananas cuddling, with the caption "Sleep tight xx." The photograph which showed the bananas spooning—lying next to each other like a pair of spoons—attracted thousands of likes from her followers, who realized what she was alluding to. One user posted "Princess Meghan Markle," while another wrote, "Is this a message for your red-haired Prince?"

Equally tongue in check was another photo she posted showing a cup of English breakfast tea and a jigsaw, perhaps indicating how the couple was spending their time indoors. But their lighthearted attitude did not last long.

There is a famous scene in the movie *Notting Hill* where Julia Roberts, who plays a glamorous American actor, opens the front door of the home of her bookseller boyfriend, played by Hugh Grant, to be confronted by a baying pack of photographers and reporters. Roberts promptly slams the door and heads inside. That's probably how Meghan felt when, dressed in a long coat, a beanie hat, and dark glasses, she ventured out of her front door and made her way through the mob of media into a waiting Dodge van which then whisked her to work on the set of *Suits*. Harry somehow had managed to make his escape earlier and had caught a flight back to London.

Meghan might have been a veteran of promotional panels, forums, and podiums, but nothing could prepare her for the sonic boom, the shock wave of publicity that hit her.

Within the space of a few days, the print and digital media had painted her as a "gold digger," whose "torrid sex scenes" from *Suits* were featured on porn sites. One story suggested that Prince Harry was responsible for breaking up Meghan's relationship with chef Cory Vitiello, another that the prince had inundated her with texts until she agreed to meet for a date.

Under the headline HARRY GIRL'S ON PORNHUB, *The Sun* helpfully reported that she was featured on the adult site, where she could be seen "stripping off and groaning," straddling her costar Patrick J. Adams in an office, as well as mounting him on a sofa. "It also includes close-ups of her crotch and her lacy bra—and has been viewed more than 40,600 times." Another porn site superimposed Meghan's head onto the body of a glamour model.

Commentators had a field day. Columnist Rachel Johnson, sister of British foreign secretary Boris Johnson, described Meghan's mother, Doria, as a "dreadlocked African-American lady from the wrong side of the tracks." She continued, "If there is an issue from her alleged union with Prince Harry, the Windsors will thicken their watery, thin blue blood and Spencer pale skin and ginger hair with some rich and exotic DNA."

Her remarks acted as the call of the hunting horn for a torrent of racist abuse from online trolls. "Prince Harry could marry into gangster royalty—his new love is from a crime ridden Los Angeles neighbourhood," claimed the online *Daily Star*. The story suggested that Meghan's mother lived in a high-crime neighborhood surrounded by "bloodbath murders and drug-induced violence."

In a matter of days, Meghan experienced racism and sexism on a level beyond any she had come across before. While she had been discussing and writing about such issues for the last few years, nothing came close to this onslaught. It was neither pleasant nor accurate, Meghan the campaigner, the humanitarian, and the woman reduced to a two-dimensional caricature. As biographer Sam Kashner wrote: "Criticism of Markle has been snob ridden, racist and uninformed."

It was reminiscent of the gleeful horror that greeted Prince Andrew's romance with American actor Kathleen "Koo" Stark when it was revealed that she had starred in an erotic film which involved a tender lesbian shower scene. But back then there was no internet. This time around Twitter, Facebook, online forums, and comment sections gave the whole world and its worst side the platform to "join the conversation."

While Meghan was sympathizing with her mother who found herself accosted by photographers every time she went out as well as confused friends wondering what they should say to the media, other members of her own family added to the tumult.

Her half sister Yvonne, who was now calling herself Samantha, appeared particularly keen to share the limelight. Describing Meghan, whom she had not seen for years, as "princess pushy," Samantha accused her of being a shallow social climber with a "soft spot for gingers." Samantha, who suffers from multiple sclerosis and uses a wheelchair, went on to say that her half sister's behavior was "not befitting of a Royal Family member," berating her for shunning her family after she became famous. Then Meghan's young half nephew Tyler Dooley weighed in, announcing that Meghan, whom he had also not spoken to for years, was "blissfully happy" and that the actor was "hurt and stung" by his aunt's accusations. If nothing else these scattered comments gave a sense of the dysfunction at the heart of Meghan's family.

The coverage was Harry's worst nightmare come true. Meghan had made the mistake of falling in love with him. Now she, her family, and her friends were destined to suffer because she made him happy. Through it all, neither Harry nor Meghan had made any statement. Kensington Palace also remained tight-lipped. But the media bedlam could not continue for much longer. Perhaps the deciding story was the one that appeared in the *Sun*. Under the lascivious headline FANCY QUICK PUCK MEG, it was suggested that Meghan's marriage to Trevor Engelson had collapsed because she had become close to Canadian ice hockey star Michael Del Zotto. While Del Zotto and his agent categorically denied the suggestion, Harry decided to act. He contacted his brother, who had faced similar hysterical coverage during his courtship with Kate Middleton. They chewed over the problem, and though William was cautious about issuing a statement, especially as it would confirm Meghan was Harry's girlfriend, he felt that matters had gone too far to remain silent. Unlike their father, William and Harry are not of the old royal school whose motto was "Never complain, never explain." They have a track record of aggressively using the law to seek redress against intrusive photographers and other media outlets that invade their privacy. Harry went so far as to suggest hiring a retired Scotland Yard protection officer to watch over her. Meghan thought the idea "charming but unnecessary." That didn't stop the *Suits* producers from hiring their own heavies to protect their valuable asset, increasing security on set and accompanying her to and from work.

Amid these media histrionics their communications secretary Jason Knauf drafted a lengthy statement that addressed Harry's concerns and complaints. There was no hiding the anger and distress that suffused the bulletin, the voice of a young man trying to protect the woman he loved—and preserve their future together. On November 8, Kensington Palace formally released the extraordinary statement. It acknowledged that there would be curiosity about his private life, but the past week "has seen a line crossed."

"His girlfriend, Meghan Markle, has been subject to a wave of abuse and harassment. Some of this has been very public—the smear on the front page of a national newspaper; the racial undertones of comment pieces; and the outright sexism and racism of social media trolls and web article comments. Some of it has been hidden from the public—the nightly legal battles to keep defamatory stories out of papers; her mother having to struggle past photographers in order to get to her front door; the attempts of reporters and photographers to gain illegal entry to her home and the calls to police that followed; the substantial bribes offered by papers to her ex-boyfriend; the bombardment of nearly every friend, co-worker, and loved one in her life.

"Prince Harry is worried about Ms. Markle's safety and is deeply disappointed that he has not been able to protect her. It is not right that a few months into a relationship with him that Ms. Markle should be subjected to such a storm. He knows commentators will say this is 'the price she has to pay' and that 'this is all part of the game.' He strongly disagrees. This is not a game—it is her life and his."

While the prince's statement helped calm the hysteria, his formal confirmation that Meghan was indeed his girlfriend meant that all media outlets, not just the British tabloids, now saw Meghan as a possible royal bride. Picture editors around the world scoured their back catalogues for shots of the latest royal-in-waiting. A photograph of her modeling a wedding dress for a scene from *Suits* was manna from heaven.

Her now official proximity to the royal family became the new agenda, several newspapers wrongly reporting that Meghan had helped Harry celebrate his thirty-second birthday at Balmoral, and that during her time in the Scottish Highlands she had even met with Prince Charles, who found her "charming."

Though the story was incorrect, they were on the right scent. Meghan was indeed now an accepted part of the royal furniture—as senior journalist Richard Kay, who had been a close friend of Diana, Princess of Wales, discovered when, on November 10, 2016, he popped out of his office to buy a sandwich for his lunch.

As he strolled down busy Kensington High Street he could scarcely believe his eyes when he spotted Meghan walking along the road, holding two bags filled with produce from the Whole Foods Market store.

He followed her back to Kensington Palace and saw her waved through security into the grounds. It was an obvious sign that the relationship between the actor and the fifth in line to the throne was "serious." Kay observed: "The timing of Miss Markle's visit is hugely significant, not least because it appears she was in the UK when Harry publicly declared his love for her."

What was even more telling was the fact that Meghan had spent only two days with Harry before flying back to Toronto to resume filming of *Suits*. Now that was commitment, the actor taking the trouble to see her boyfriend before he embarked on an official two-week tour of the Caribbean.

On the tour he would be representing the Queen at independence anniversary celebrations in Barbados, Guyana, and Antigua. It was a test of his mettle—and he knew full well that his grandmother would be monitoring his progress, as it was one of his first overseas tours to represent Her Majesty. It would prove to be an official tour of more import than he realized at the time.

Among many other activities he took an AIDS test with superstar Rihanna in Barbados, observed a minute's silence for Fidel Castro in St. Vincent, and played cricket in St. Lucia.

Harry managed to remain cool when, at a reception for three hundred guests, Antiguan prime minister Gaston Browne suggested he and Meghan should return to the island for their honeymoon. "I believe we are expecting a new princess soon. I want you to know that you are very welcome to come on your honeymoon here," he was reported to have said. Harry was later introduced to a group of scantily clad models with the words: "Whatever is done here, stays here. So don't worry." The prince said nothing but afterward told aides he found the incident "pretty distasteful."

Not that Meghan was worried. He was in constant touch with her via Skype, reporting back on the progress of his solo visit. He was given full marks by the trailing media, royal editor Camilla Tominey commenting: "With his American girlfriend Meghan Markle putting a spring in his step, it's fair to say Prince Harry has rarely been on better form. Comfortable in his own skin and completely at ease with the spotlight being shone on his official duties as the queen's representative overseas, he has truly come of age."

Though the attendant media were assured that the prince was heading back to London, it was a red herring. Harry took a 1,700-mile detour to spend a few precious hours holed up in Meghan's rented house in Toronto. Her followers had the first clue that Harry was on his way when Meghan posted a picture of herself wearing a necklace with M and H as well as a snap of her beagle, Guy, in his Union Jack jumper. For the first time, a grand royal passion was being played out before the eyes on social media. Not that such access would last long. Within forty-eight hours the prince was flying back to London. He had just time enough to take a shower before he was on parade in the City of London answering phones and joking with callers for an annual charity fund-raiser where his charity Sentebale was a recipient.

Harry then joined his friends for a shooting weekend at Oettingen Castle in Bavaria, Germany, before he was reunited with Meghan, who came for a weeklong stay at Nottingham Cottage in early December.

They bought their first Christmas tree together, and the staff at the Battersea garden center Pines and Needles gave them a bunch of mistletoe for good luck. For the most part they managed to elude the watchful paparazzi, the couple wearing matching blue beanie hats to obscure their faces. They walked through the theater district, where they saw the slapstick comedy *Peter Pan Goes Wrong* and later the brilliantly staged *The Curious Incident of the Dog in the Night-time*, based on Mark Haddon's novel.

Much as they would have liked to spend Christmas together, royal tradition threw a wrench in their plans. Every year the extended royal family gather at Sandringham, the queen's twenty-thousand-acre estate in Norfolk. Girlfriends and boyfriends are excluded.

They did, however, see in the New Year together at Nottingham Cottage before flying on January 2 to the remote town of Tromsø in northern Norway on the edge of the Arctic Circle to see the dazzling and awe-inspiring aurora borealis, or northern lights.

Even if the happy couple were not quite ready to make a formal commitment to one another, they and others had to anticipate the future. In his mind *Suits* creator Aaron Korsh decided that Meghan's private life now overshadowed her character, Rachel Zane. For her sake it was best to write her out of the hit series. As he said later: "I had a decision to make. I didn't want to intrude and ask her: 'Hey what's going on and what are you going to do?' So collectively with the writers we decided to take a gamble that these two people were in love and it would work out." As Harry's previous actor girlfriend Cressida Bonas had discovered, there was a high professional price to pay for dating a prince. If the Harry and Meghan romance had petered out, Meghan would have been out of work. It was a high-stakes romance with consequences for her career with every passing week.

Indeed, for how much longer could a potential princess be seen cuddling up to her screen lover, Patrick J. Adams, her hand placed suggestively on his knee? When Adams was asked by a fan what it was like "making out on screen with a potential future English princess," he replied deadpan: "The same as it was before she was a potential future princess."

That said, both Meghan and her romantic costar Patrick J. Adams had by now appeared in more than one hundred episodes of the hit show. As far as he was concerned, it was time to hang up his role in *Suits*. Even if Meghan had felt the same way, her personal life took this professional decision out of her hands.

As he later told the *Hollywood Reporter*: "There was this natural sense that we both knew that the time had come for both of us. It went unspoken and we just enjoyed the hell out of the last few episodes that we got to shoot. We both knew that we wouldn't be coming back. It made every one of our scenes that much more special. We had a great time. We could laugh through it. Even the things that might have frustrated us about the show, they became things that we could have a good laugh about and compare notes on just how crazy this thing had become."

For as long as she was on the show, the producers were ready and willing to use her royal connections and newfound celebrity—that February she was ranked fourth among the most eligible dinner guests by *Tatler* magazine—to boost ratings. One trailer promoted the characters as "almost royalty," while another featured a scene from a previous season of Meghan in a wedding dress.

Others had the same idea. The gritty British crime movie *Anti-Social*, originally released in 2015, was repackaged as a "special edition" and featured Meghan's name prominently in the publicity. In the movie she played a fashion model named Kirsten and was seen emerging from a shower dressed in a towel, drinking champagne, and kissing an on-screen lover. A number of Trevor Engelson's friends, who knew that he had always been reluctant to cast Meghan in his productions, now teased him mercilessly telling the Hollywood producer that he could have made a fortune repackaging his movies if Meghan had been featured in the original. "He got a lot of flak," a friend told me.

Meghan herself had some serious commercial decisions to make. It wasn't about money or self-promotion. Her blog, The Tig, had meant the world to her. It was her baby. She had watched it grow from a modest one-woman show to a brand that represented her very civilized, refined, yet adventurous view of life. It was aspirational and frothily feminine but always with a serious point, be it about gender equality or human rights. The Tig was, as she always said, the little engine that could. Now she realized that her blog couldn't go on as it had in the past as long as she remained within the royal orbit. Her pictures, comments, recommendations, and thoughts would be taken out of context and associated with Prince Harry or the royal family or both. She was no longer Meghan the blogger; she was one half of a partnership in which the man she wanted to spend the rest of her life with was fifth (now sixth) in line to the throne. Different rules applied. For all her protestations and doubts, she conceded that if she was going to go forward with her prince, at some point she would have to severely modify the contents of The Tig.

This was to be her first major reality check, running a blog and dating a royal. If matters became more formal, in the shape of an engagement ring, then she would have to rethink the entire existence of her social media platforms. A friend said: "She's trying to figure out how to scale back what she puts out there about her life, including her social media and website. If she had to leave all that she's doing for the relationship to work, she would without hesitation."

But it was much harder than it sounded. In January 2017, for instance, with her Global Ambassador hat on, she flew to India on behalf of World Vision Canada. The five-day visit was intended to focus on child poverty and specifically on why teenage girls from "slum communities" dropped out of school. The answer partly lay in the fact that when girls at school begin menstruating there are no facilities in the local schools to help them cope with this perfectly natural change in their bodies. Ashamed, they stay away from school. It is a hidden issue, one that Meghan felt could be easily solved with the proper use of resources. She felt comfortable taking on these issues, telling an audience in Atlanta before she left that humanitarian work made her life feel more "balanced." Her newfound international celebrity enabled her views to find a wider audience, and her essay on her visit to Delhi and Mumbai to discover why periods affected the potential of millions of teenage girls appeared in the March edition of Time magazine.

Her humanitarian work was a ticklish issue, though. While the palace may not have objected in principle to the causes she espoused, they were not undertaken under the umbrella of the royal family. In short, she was acting as a freelance operation within the corporate royal "firm."

There was bound to be a conflict at some point. In her own mind Meghan had to square the intellectual and emotional circle.

The Tig was designed to empower women and encourage gender equality. Yet she accepted that the mushrooming interest in her blog and Instagram had little to do with her work on *Suits* and more with the fact that she was dating a man who was in his position of authority and influence simply by dint of birth. The irony was not lost on Meghan. She is no fool, realizing that in the long run her association with Prince Harry would ultimately give her a megaphone with which to articulate the issues that she held dear. The price was giving up her baby. In early March 2017 she said a sad farewell to her thousands of Tig followers:

"After close to three beautiful years on this adventure with you, it's time to say goodbye to The Tig," she wrote. "What began as a passion project (my little engine that could) evolved into an amazing community of inspiration, support, fun and frivolity. Keep finding those Tig moments of discovery, keep laughing and taking risks, and keep being 'the change you wish to see in the world.'"

Her Instagram, which had 1.9 million followers, went the same way. One fan, Jennifer Oakes, wrote: "Never mind the people who would see you remain single forever, with marriage comes sacrifice (both sides)."

Not everyone was so understanding. Shortly before she closed down her popular and influential website, her half sister Samantha launched another broadside: "There is so much more to focus on in the world than shoes and handbags," she tweeted. "Meghan Markle needs to practice what she preaches or change her speeches." Samantha's belated criticism, just as the site was about to close, indicated how out of the family loop she was.

Within days of kissing a fond farewell to her online community, Meghan was given a classic lesson about life in the royal goldfish bowl. In early March, Harry and Meghan made their separate ways to Jamaica for the three-day wedding festivities of his close friend Tom "Skippy" Inskip and literary agent Laura Hughes-Young.

Harry met Meghan at the airport and drove her to the exclusive Round Hill Hotel at Montego Bay, where they were booked into a $7,000-a-night villa. They changed into their swimwear, Harry sporting a pair of green swim trunks, Meghan a dark blue bikini topped off with her trademark white fedora. They kissed and cuddled as they paddled in the warm Caribbean water. Suddenly Harry's mood turned dark. It was nothing to do with Meghan. It was the presence of paparazzi, their long lenses focused on the couple. Even Meghan's consoling arm around his shoulders did little to calm him down. Although the British media did not publish the offending pictures, several European magazines and websites had no such qualms.

The prince complained first to the *Daily Mail* online for using the pictures and then, when they did not delete them from their website, made a formal complaint to the Independent Press Standards Organisation. In May the committee found in the prince's favor, stating: "The Committee found that the complainant had been photographed in circumstances in which he had a reasonable expectation of privacy. He had not consented to the images' publication, and Mail Online had not sought to justify their publication in the public interest." They ordered the online newspaper to prominently display the ruling for at least twenty-four hours.

Following his media spat, the next day Harry was one of fourteen ushers for the wedding in the Hopewell Baptist Church. He was in a jauntier mood, and Meghan, who wore a patterned floral $2,000 Erdem dress, was noticeably affectionate and loving throughout the ceremony.

Pastor Conrad Thomas, who conducted the service, said afterward: "Harry and Meghan held hands and I will never forget their radiant smiles. They looked so happy together. I told him 'It's your turn next, sir.'"

At the evening reception, guests including the Duchess of York and her daughter Princess Eugenie, feasted on jerk chicken and

lobster washed down by rum cocktails and champagne. Unfortunately, Harry knocked over a tray of drinks as he did a "Michael
Jackson moonwalk" on the dance floor.

"He was going backwards as 'Billie Jean' blared out when he
banged into a waitress carrying a tray of drinks and sent them flying" said an onlooker. "Harry gasped, looked shocked and put his
hands on the waitress's shoulders and apologized."

It was a temporary blip in an evening of drinking, dancing,
and jollity. Meghan and Harry were on the dance floor or in each
other's arms—or both. Love was definitely in the air.

After the raucous party, Harry took Meghan to the exclusive
Caves Hotel in Negril for three precious days alone. Afterward,
their long-distance commute continued, Meghan flying back to
Toronto but returning to London a week later. Her absences from
Canada were now so frequent that she had to hire a dog sitter to
look after Bogart and Guy.

That said, soon it was Harry's turn to arrive on her doorstep,
spending Easter at her home. He had other reasons for being in
the city—in September the Invictus Games were due to take place,
and he had many meetings to attend and numerous agendas to
go through. Top of the list on his personal agenda was a firm
decision for Meghan to be by his side at some point during the
games. Veteran reporter Phil Dampier quoted a royal source as
saying: "Harry wants everything out in the open and for the days
of skulking around avoiding photographers to be over. He wants
to show Meghan off as his future wife and the Games, which he
has put his heart and soul into, will be the perfect platform to do
that." Dampler was on the money.

At long last, after nearly two unconventional years of courtship, four months in private, the rest in public, the romance
between Harry and Meghan hit a traditional groove. Meghan
drove to Coworth Park near Berkshire on May 6 to watch her
boyfriend play polo. It is something of a royal rite of passage.

Some of the best—and most affectionate—photographs ever taken of Princess Diana were when she attended polo matches involving Prince Charles. Kate Middleton, too, was always keenly on point when Prince William got in the saddle. It was no different when Meghan, who was accompanied by Mark Dyer and his wife, Amanda, arrived at the ground. She dutifully clapped and smiled as she followed the back and forth of this most unspectator-friendly of sports. Fellow attendees at the charity match, which raised funds for Sentebale and another of Harry's charities, WellChild, included Oscar-winning actor Eddie Redmayne, former ballerina Darcey Bussell, and actor Matt Smith, who plays Prince Philip in the hit Netflix series *The Crown*.

Harry made them all wait. But it would be worth it. The following day, after playing in a match with Prince William, Harry gave the cameramen what they wanted—he kissed Meghan in the parking lot. Game on.

Once again Meghan flew home, only to return just a week later to attend Pippa Middleton's wedding to financier James Matthews on May 20. So as not to overshadow the bride's big day, Meghan stayed away from the wedding ceremony at St. Mark's Church in the village of Englefield, Berkshire. After the service, Harry drove back to London to pick her up and then took her to the reception at the Middleton family home in the nearby village of Bucklebury.

The evidence had been piling up all year, and by now it was clear that it was only a matter of time before she was walking down the aisle herself to marry her royal prince. An informal strategy was emerging to clear the way for their own announcement. It had started with the closure Meghan's various social media sites, including The Tig and her Instagram account, continued with the decision to involve Meghan with the Invictus Games and, of course, followed by that kiss at the polo match. These days when she arrived at Heathrow Airport, often as not Harry was waiting on the tarmac and was able to whisk her through the VIP mini terminal. So when Meghan attended a *Suits* convention in Austin, Texas, though she dodged questions about her future, most of her fans reluctantly concluded that this season would probably be her last. When Meghan admitted that the sex scenes she had done in the past seemed "weird now," it appeared as if the writing was on the wall for her character, Rachel Zane.

A couple of weeks later, in mid-July, Meghan opened the door of her Toronto home and greeted Sam Kashner, the best-selling biographer of *Furious Love*, his dissection of another power couple, actors Richard Burton and Elizabeth Taylor. From that moment he arrived at her front door, bookies no longer needed to take bets on a royal marriage. The bespectacled scribe was there on behalf of *Vanity Fair* magazine not only to savor the pasta she had bought specially from the fashionable Italian deli Terroni, but to imbibe her life.

It was an extraordinary development. Traditionally royal brides-to-be are Sphinxlike, blushing furiously, ducking away from photographers, smiling politely but not saying a word. It is the uniting thread that links Lady Diana Spencer, Sarah Ferguson, Sophie Rhys-Jones, and Catherine Middleton. They know the consequences. In the days when Diana's sister Sarah was dating Prince Charles, she was cast into the outer darkness the moment she chatted to royal correspondent James Whitaker about her relationship.

For Meghan to be giving an interview before any engagement announcement was a royal first, all the more so as she would not have gone ahead without the agreement of Prince Harry; his private secretary, Edward Lane Fox; and their communications director, Jason Knauf. Nor was she making anodyne remarks about fashion and *Suits* with the odd aside about her royal romance. No, Meghan was telling her true story—in her own words. She was emphatic, no dithering around the issue.

"We're a couple," she told Kashner. "We're in love. I'm sure that there will be a time when we will have to come forward and present ourselves and have stories to tell, but I hope what people will understand is that this is our time. This is for us. It's part of what makes it so special, that it's just ours. But we're happy. Personally, I love a great love story."

Just so he got the point she emphasized: "We're two people who are really happy and in love."

There was one troubling sentence amid the startlingly open declaration of love and commitment: "I'm still the same person that I am, and I've never defined myself by my relationship." Perhaps not in the past. But certainly, in her future. *Vanity Fair* would not have given her a prized cover with the boldface headline SHE'S JUST WILD ABOUT HARRY if she had been simply an actor on a mid-range TV drama. The clue was in the title. His title. Whether or not she wanted to embrace the idea, in the future her considerable influence, her ability to make the change, will rest on something she has keenly fought against, namely women gaining power not through their own endeavors but because of whom they marry.

That was a conundrum to ponder another day. For the moment she was going to Botswana, where the internet signal was weak, as she and Harry celebrated her thirty-sixth birthday. The prince was so happy to be returning to his second home that he even gave a thumbs-up to waiting photographers when he was reunited with Meghan at the airport. His gesture sent the media rumor mill churning. Journalists did not know that Meghan and Harry had already visited Botswana, and as William had proposed to Kate in Kenya in 2010, the obvious conclusion was that, during this trip, Harry would get down on one knee. The vacation was romantic enough. The couple once again stayed at the Meno a Kwena camp before driving their rental car on the eight-hour journey to Victoria Falls, one of the natural wonders of the world.

During their visit they stayed at the privately owned Tongabezi Lodge by the Zambesi River, where they were enticed with sunset cruises, romantic sampan (a type of flat-bottomed boat) dinners, and early morning game drives. They even had their own valet to cater for their every whim.

At the end of the holiday, though speculation was at fever pitch about a royal engagement, Meghan made herself scarce when Princes William and Harry together with the Duchess of Cambridge marked the twentieth anniversary of Diana's death with a visit to the White Garden at Kensington Palace, which had been specially planted with her favorite flowers. They then met representatives of charities supported by the late princess.

The drumbeat of marital speculation grew ever louder, especially when it was learned that in early September Meghan had returned the Audi she leased while living in Toronto, innocently stating that she was "moving to London in November."

The critical test was the Invictus Games, which began in her adopted city, Toronto, on September 23. Harry's own baby had grown into a mini-Olympics featuring 550 competitors from seventeen countries taking part in twelve sports. It was hardly surprising when he chose that week for Meghan to make her debut on the world stage as a potential royal bride. Just before the Games began, Harry visited the set of *Suits* with Meghan, who introduced him to her costars, the scriptwriters, and the crew.

"Meghan showed him around and everyone was so excited. He's incredibly supportive of her work," a member of the cast was quoted as saying.

At the opening ceremony in the Air Canada Centre, Harry sat with First Lady Melania Trump, Canadian prime minister Justin Trudeau, and Ukraine's president Petro Poroshenko. As was widely anticipated, Meghan was in the crowd accompanied by her Canadian-born friend Markus Anderson, who had previously been so instrumental in helping arrange Meghan and Harry's first date. Wearing a purple dress and matching leather jacket slung over her shoulders, Meghan seemed comfortable and relaxed. Though she was not in the VIP section, the presence of a Scotland Yard bodyguard sitting near her was a sign that her days on the outside were numbered.

She listened intently as Harry told the audience of competitors, their friends and families: "You are all winners, and don't forget that you are proving to the world that anything is possible."

As Toronto sweltered in a heat wave with temperatures nudging 35°C (95°F), the burning question was when would they be seen together. It was hot topic number one.

Two days after the opening ceremony, a posse of photographers who were snapping the wheelchair tennis match between Australia and New Zealand were approached by a Kensington Palace press officer.

Without naming Harry or Meghan, she whispered to them: "When they arrive, stay in your seats and don't move out of them. If you do, they will leave."

A few minutes later the waiting press pack watched in disbelief as, hand in hand, Meghan and Harry walked in to Nathan Phillips Square and sat down at the side of the court. In the choreography of their romance, this was a showstopper. They laughed and joked, stroked each other's arms, whispered sweet nothings and chatted to the families and friends of the competitors. When Meghan was handed a bottle of water, Harry advised her to put it on the floor and not drink it in view of the cameras. Pictures of celebrities drinking can look awkward and clumsy.

Meghan had her own agenda. Instinctively attuned to the semiology of fashion, it was entirely deliberate that she teamed her ripped blue jeans with a loose-fitting shirt designed by her great friend Misha Nonoo and called "the husband shirt." Naturally, the white shirt, which Meghan had once described on her blog as "my very favorite button down" sold out within minutes. That her handbag was made by the ethical brand Everlane also sent out a message: what she wore mattered.

One of the few sour notes was when Meghan's half sister

Samantha tweeted: "It's a shame that Prince Harry's girlfriend Meghan Markle is embarrassed by her sister in a wheelchair."

Though Meghan's half sister may not have agreed, no one was going to rain on this parade.

The enthusiastic crowd enjoyed another sideshow with the arrival of former president Barack Obama along with former vice president Joe Biden and his wife, Jill. The former world leaders were mobbed by cheering spectators as word spread of their arrival. Harry and his American guests looked totally relaxed as they cracked jokes and posed for selfies with members of the crowd.

During his whistle-stop visit to the city, former president Obama joined Harry at a city center hotel, where a suite of rooms had been rigged up into a makeshift radio studio. The prince conducted a twenty-minute interview with the former president about life after the White House, and their relaxed chat became the centerpiece of Harry's debut as a guest presenter on BBC Radio Four's *Today* program in late December.

As the games came to an end, Harry told the cheering crowd, "You have delivered the biggest Invictus Games yet, with the most incredible atmosphere, making our competitors feel like the stars they are."

At the closing ceremony, Harry gave Meghan a kiss on the cheek as they watched Kelly Clarkson, Bryan Adams, and legendary rocker Bruce Springsteen play the games out. Standing beside them in the VIP enclosure was Meghan's mother, Doria Ragland, who had flown from Los Angeles to see her daughter and, it was now universally assumed, to inspect her future son-in-law.

It was time to dust off the morning suit.

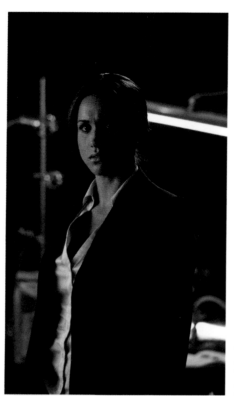

In 2008, when Meghan appeared as junior FBI agent Amy Jessup in director J. J. Abrams's sci-fi drama *Fringe*, she hoped that she would last the series. That she lasted only two episodes came as a disappointment, one of many she faced as an aspiring actor. *(Moviestore / REX / Shutterstock)*

Suits producers cast Gina Torres (left) as a founding partner of the fictional law firm; Rick Hoffman as her devious colleague, Louis Litt; Meghan Markle as the sophisticated paralegal Rachel Zane; Gabriel Macht as hot-shot lawyer Harvey Specter; and Patrick J. Adams as brilliant lawyer Mike Ross, Rachel's love interest. *(Frank Ockenfels / Dutch Oven / Kobal / REX / Shutterstock)*

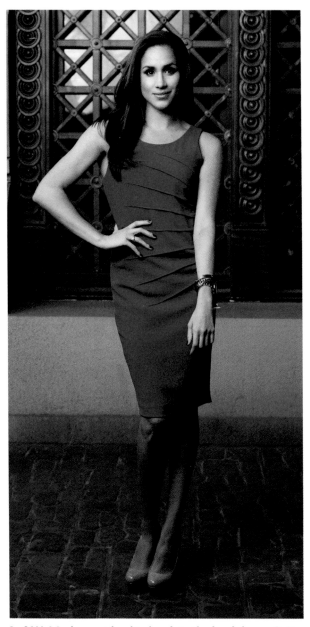

In 2011 Meghan got her big break in the legal drama *Suits*, a TV series in which the designer clothes were as important as the script. Meghan's sleek, sophisticated look attracted a huge fan following. Her hair was so important to her character, Rachel Zane, that she was contractually obligated to wear it down on camera. (*Dutch Oven / Kobal / REX / Shutterstock*)

Meghan visited New Mexico with her father when her older half sister, Samantha Markle Grant, graduated from the University of New Mexico with a degree in criminology. During the trip she met her father's first wife, Roslyn Loveless, and Samantha's daughter Noel Rasmussen. Their meeting, in 2008, was one of the last times Meghan would see her half sister. (*Mail on Sunday / Solo Syndication*)

Meghan and her mother, Doria, in Jamaica during Meghan's destination wedding weekend in 2011. Meghan's love of travel began as a child when Doria, then a travel agent, took her to the Caribbean and Mexico. While Meghan's love of travel is lifelong, her first marriage lasted only two years before she abruptly divorced her husband Trevor Engelson. (*Splash News*)

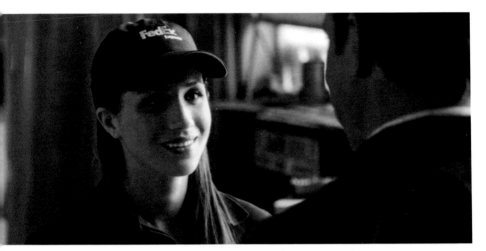

Meghan's last small role before she was hired for *Suits* was playing an attractive FedEx delivery girl, opposite the leering comedian Jason Sudeikis, in the comedy *Horrible Bosses*. During filming she met her dream actor Donald Sutherland. (*Alpha Press*)

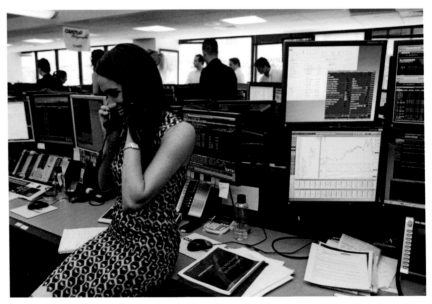

Meghan mans the phone at a fund-raiser for the 2013 annual Charity Day, hosted by brokers Cantor Fitzgerald and held each year to commemorate their friends and colleagues who perished in the September 11 terrorist attack. (*Mike McGregor / Getty Images for Cantor Fitzgerald*)

Meghan at the sprawling Bagram Airfield in Afghanistan during her 2014 goodwill tour. Meghan and her fellow performers ate and took photos with service members, passed out cupcakes, and performed onstage. From left to right: Washington Nationals pitcher Doug Fister, Meghan Markle, comedian Rob Riggle, country music performer Kelly Pickler, actor Dianna Agron, and retired Chicago Bears linebacker Brian Urlacher (far right). (DOD Photo / Alamy)

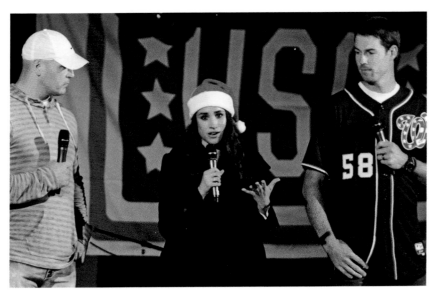

Meghan on board the USS Ross on December 6, 2014, with former Chicago Bears linebacker Brian Urlacher (left) and Washington Nationals pitcher Doug Fister as part of a USO holiday tour. Later she would post on her Instagram account: "In gratitude to our troops, and the opportunity to thank them personally for their sacrifice and service. Such an honor and feeling very, very blessed." (DOD Photo / Alamy)

Meghan co-starred with Christopher Jacot in the 2014 Hallmark Channel movie *When Sparks Fly* during a break from filming *Suits*. She played a big-city reporter returning home to her small town, where she learns her best friend is marrying her ex-boyfriend. The feel-good movie was a departure from Meghan's sassy role on *Suits*. *(Pictorial Press Ltd / Alamy)*

At the 2014 One Young World Summit, held in Dublin, Ireland, Meghan was invited to speak on gender equality and human rights. Here she and the panel applaud a point made by a member of the audience. During the weekend, intended to encourage young leaders of tomorrow, Meghan met former UN secretary-general Kofi Annan and writer Fatima Bhutto. *(Clodagh Kilcoyne / Getty Images)*

On March 10, 2015, Meghan delivered a highly regarded speech before the United Nations Women organization as the newly appointed UN Women Advocate for Women's Leadership and Political Participation. Her mother, Doria, and Hillary Clinton were in the audience as Meghan recounted taking on Proctor & Gamble over a sexist advertising campaign when she was just eleven. *(WENN Ltd / Alamy)*

Meghan and her boyfriend celebrity chef Cory Vitiello attending a fashion event during the glitzy Miami Art Basel show, which was held in December 2014. The couple were guests of the exclusive members' club Soho House. *(Ben Rosser / BFAnyc. com / REX / Shutterstock)*

Meghan with Misha Nonoo at the Twelfth Annual CDFA/Vogue Fashion Fund awards, November 2, 2015, in New York. Meghan is wearing a showstopping metallic dress from the designer's collection. *(Nicholas Hunt / Getty Images)*

On their second trip to Botswana in 2017, Prince Harry and Meghan celebrated her thirty-sixth birthday when they briefly stayed at the Meno a Kwena camp before driving their hired car on an eight-hour journey to Victoria Falls, one of the natural wonders of the world. (*The Sun / News Licensing*)

During a visit to Wimbledon in 2016, Meghan wore an expensive black suede Ralph Lauren dress when she watched her friend Serena Williams on court. When a brief rain shower disrupted the match, fashion guru Anna Wintour, who was also in the players' box, loaned Meghan a sweater to protect her dress. (*Karwai Tang / WireImage / Getty Images*)

Chic and stylish, Meghan arrives at an AOL Build forum in downtown New York to discuss her role as a paralegal in the hugely popular legal drama *Suits*. *(Evan Agostini / Invision / AP / REX / Shutterstock)*

Meghan, with Prince Harry's mentor Mark Dyer and wife, Amanda, watch the prince play polo at the Audi Challenge on June 5, 2017. A former equerry to the Prince of Wales, Dyer arranged Harry's gap-year trip to Lesotho and was instrumental in assisting the prince to establish Sentebale, an HIV/AIDS charity focusing on children who suffer from the deadly disease. *(Photograph by Mark Stewart, Camera Press London)*

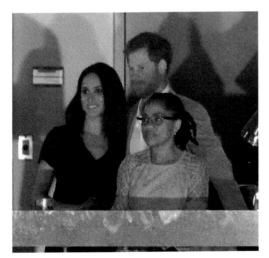

Meghan's mother, Doria Ragland, joined her daughter and Prince Harry at the closing of the Invictus Games in Toronto. With her arrival, it meant that the engagement announcement was only a matter of weeks away. *(Karwai Tang / WireImage / Getty Images)*

When Meghan and Prince Harry officially attended the Invictus Games together on September 25, 2017, they caused a media frenzy. Photographers were instructed not to move when the couple, who walked hand in hand, arrived at the Toronto stadium. They put on quite a show, stroking each other's arms, whispering to each other, and chatting with families of competitors. (*Chris Jackson / Getty Images for the Invictus Games Foundation*)

Meghan's last trip for World Vision Canada was to India, in January 2017, where she promoted education for young women, stressing the importance of menstrual supplies and separate toilet facilities to encourage school attendance. She later wrote a frank essay in *Time* magazine about the issue. One of her stops was the Myna Mahila Foundation, a charity employing women to make sanitary supplies that are sold locally. (*World Vision / Splash*)

(*Opposite*) Prince Harry and Meghan pose for photographers in the Sunken Garden at Kensington Palace after their engagement was announced on November 27, 2017. The Sunken Garden was one of Princess Diana's favorite spots. (*Facundo Arrizabalaga / EPA-EFE / REX / Shutterstock*)

Prince Harry and Meghan Markle visit Nottingham on their first official joint royal engagement on December 1, 2017. She appeared relaxed, if a little nervous, as she went into the royal handshaking mode and made conversation about the weather. *(WENN Ltd / Alamy)*

On Christmas Day, Meghan attended St. Mary Magdalene Church in Sandringham with her future in-laws. This was a break with tradition, as only couples who were married or single family members attended the royal family's holiday gathering. As the Queen left the church to return to Sandringham House, the royal ladies, including Meghan, dropped a brief curtsy. While her future sister-in-law Catherine Middleton dropped a perfectly relaxed curtsy, Meghan's was much more wobbly, a sign that practice was needed. *(Chris Jackson / Getty Images)*

The next royal generation: Catherine and William, the Duke and Duchess of Cambridge, with Meghan Markle and Prince Harry after church on Christmas Day, 2017. The royal quartet are now known as the Fab Four, the nickname used for the pop group the Beatles. *(Photograph by Paul John Bayfield, Camera Press London)*

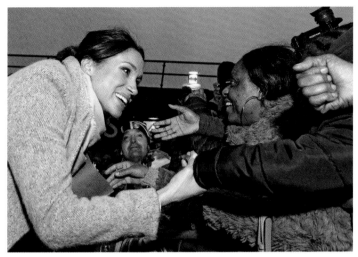

Meghan greets a crowd of well-wishers in Brixton, in south London, while visiting community radio station Reprezent 107.3 FM on January 9, 2017. After wearing an expensive designer gown for her official engagement photographs, Meghan stuck to a simple and inexpensive black sweater from the mid-market food and clothing store Marks & Spencer for this event. *(Dominic Lipinski / AFP / Getty Images)*

As part of Meghan's lessons in all things British, Harry took her on visits to Scotland, England, and Wales, where she visited Cardiff, the latter's capital. Meghan wore jeans made in Wales, carried a bag made by a small British manufacturer, and wore velvet boots by a British designer. Her Prince of Wales check jacket was made by a British company that aims to make the most sustainable and least polluting wool clothing in the world. *(Andrew Bartlett / Alamy)*

Prince Harry, Meghan Markle, and Catherine Middleton, then six months pregnant, at "Making a Difference Together," the first annual Royal Foundation Forum in London in February 2018. Since Meghan joined the royal family in November, more than a million fans had clicked on royal social media sites. (*Chris Jackson / AP / REX / Shutterstock*)

12

Tea with Her Majesty

It was the most important audition of her life. No rehearsal, no script, no second takes. This was live and improvised. When she was driven through the gates of Buckingham Palace on an overcast, drizzly Thursday in October in a black Ford Galaxy with darkened windows, she was about to give the performance of her career. Even though she has often said that she is not a woman who gets nervous, she could be forgiven for being a tad dry mouthed. She was about to meet the Queen for afternoon tea. Gulp. Of course, she had Prince Harry by her side, holding her hand, telling her it would be fine, just be yourself. Still, it was tea with the Queen of England.

There was a touch of cloak and dagger about the affair, which did little to quell the nerves. The Ford Galaxy nosed in so close to the sovereign's entrance that Harry, Meghan, and their Scotland Yard bodyguard were able to slip inside unnoticed.

They were then escorted along the seeming miles of red carpet to the queen's private sitting room, which overlooks the palace gardens by Constitution Hill. So discreetly did they arrive and depart that even senior palace servants were unaware of their visit until a few days later.

If truth be told, Meghan had quietly anticipated this moment. A few months before, she had taken a secret excursion to Rose Tree Cottage, a little slice of England nestled in Pasadena in the suburbs of Los Angeles. It sells a plethora of British goodies, but the centerpiece of owner Edmund Fry's emporium is the serving of afternoon tea. Meghan has visited several times, not only to buy English gifts but to take afternoon tea. Perhaps there had been just a little rehearsing, after all.

In a city dominated by coffee and to-go cups, Rose Tree Cottage brings a soupçon of English refinement. It is where Meghan learned to crook her finger as she sipped her Earl Grey from her cup and saucer, necessary skills to remember after she dropped a curtsy to her future mother-in-law. However, the offering of thinly sliced sandwiches of cucumber and egg mayonnaise, the selection of small scones and cakes, and Her Majesty's own Queen Mary blend of tea, with the option of coffee for the American visitor, tell only part of the story.

Afternoon tea is a chance for the Queen to catch up on the Upstairs gossip from her ladies-in-waiting, the Downstairs chatter from her senior servants, and to see members of her family. In times past, Princess Diana—when she hadn't brought the boys with her, which was often—used these informal occasions to tackle the Queen over her eldest son's affair with Camilla Parker Bowles. As she sipped her tea, the princess was looking for sympathy— vainly, as it turned out. The topic was much too emotionally unsavory for her regal mother-in-law, so the matter was dropped.

Though the encounter with Meghan Markle and Prince Harry was much less fraught, there was still an air of tension about the occasion. This was perhaps inevitable. As the fifth in line to the throne, the prince had to obtain his grandmother's formal permission to marry. It was by no means a foregone conclusion. She could say no. She'd done it before. Then what?

For centuries the royal houses of Europe have been defined by bloodline and breeding. In Queen Victoria's day, English princes and princesses could only marry their German counterparts. That changed during World War One, when in 1917 George V not only changed the family name to Windsor but allowed his offspring to marry English aristocrats. Down the decades, even this edict has been considerably diluted.

For the most part, the queen's brood have married common-ers, though not divorced commoners. An Olympic horseman, an equerry, a photographer, the daughter of the royal polo manager, and a public relations executive have all joined the royal family without a title between them. Only Lady Diana Spencer was from a traditionally aristocratic family—and look where that got them. The House of Windsor has been sustained by commoners, not by bluebloods. In fact, the same could be said of most of the royal houses of Europe. Meghan's divorce was no longer a concern, as it had been for the previous American to marry a royal, and neither was her biracial heritage.

Any possible uncertainty about the outcome of this meeting lay not with Meghan, but with the man she wanted to marry. He is the one who has been if not on trial then under close scrutiny.

If he had come to see Grannie a few years earlier, when he had an unenviable reputation as an angry drunk with poor judgment, it would have been doubtful that the Queen would have agreed to him marrying a divorced mixed-race American actor. "It would have been a grim, unhappy confrontation," observed a former senior royal official, just as it was when she had to put her foot down in 1955 over her sister, Margaret, marrying Group Captain Peter Townsend, who was divorced. If anything, Harry's transfor-mation over the last few years has, together with the popular union between Prince William and Kate Middleton, secured the future of the monarchy. Harry's impeccable behavior when representing the Queen abroad and his commitment to the Invictus Games have been shrewdly watched and assessed by the sovereign. As a courtier told me: "The queen trusts her grandsons. She has confidence in them in a way that she never has had with her eldest son. They have really established themselves as being in touch with the public. William and Harry have star quality, believable and authentic heirs to the monarchy."

The final seal of approval came from the queen's corgis. This normally irascible breed were friendly and welcoming when Meghan entered the queen's sitting room. As Prince Harry said, somewhat ruefully: "I've spent the last thirty-three years being barked at; this one walks in, absolutely nothing." They lay at her feet and wagged their tails. "Very sweet," Meghan later told interviewer Mishal Husain.

During their one-hour meeting, Meghan witnessed at firsthand the genuine respect and love Harry feels for his grandmother. "She's an incredible woman," she said afterward.

With a flurry of barks and a final curtsy, Harry and Meghan bade their farewells, swiftly leaving the palace before the royal gossip factory was able to get into gear. Job done.

Not quite. Meghan still had to speak to her elusive father and bring him up to speed. Since his retirement, Tom Senior had become more reclusive, heading to Mexico, where he had bought an apartment in the popular beach town of Rosarito, ten miles south of the American border. He changed his mobile phones frequently and even moved on from one apartment because the widow of the recently deceased owner was becoming "too friendly."

When she finally reached her father, she told him her news, warning him that the media would try to speak with him when the engagement was announced. Of course, he had already spoken with Prince Harry, so he knew what was coming down the pike.

At some point Harry had asked the voice at the other end of the mobile phone for permission to marry his daughter. Not quite as traditional as tea with the Queen had been, but then there was not much about this romance that conformed to the conventional royal playbook.

But now that the ring was on the finger, there were other more delicate family matters Meghan needed to raise with her father. She made it clear that she wanted him to walk her down the aisle and give her away. It was a big ask. Meghan realized just how shy and self-effacing he was and knew that appearing in such a public setting would be an excruciating ordeal for him.

Furthermore, it was by no means certain that, even if he wanted, he could walk the length of St. George's Chapel. Memories of the day Lady Diana Spencer painstakingly walked down the aisle of St. Paul's Cathedral with her father, Earl Spencer, who had suffered a severe stroke, struggling manfully to stay by her side, came flooding back. Physically Tom Senior was not in good shape, suffering from high blood pressure and a dodgy knee. Not only did he walk with a pronounced limp, but he was also in constant pain. Doctors had told him that he needed a full knee replacement. Not only was he considerably overweight, but he was a heavy smoker. His surgeon would not operate before he had quit smoking and lost a few pounds.

From his home in Grants Pass, Oregon, Tom Junior could feel his father's agonizing dilemma. "My father worships the ground Meghan walks on. I know how proud he will be to take her arm and walk her down the aisle. But I also know how terrified he will be. If he doesn't go, he will regret it for the rest of his life. He has to know that he is not representing his family he is representing America."

If the walking down the aisle was a concern, the very thought of making a speech at the wedding breakfast in front of the Queen, Prince Philip, Prince Charles, and the rest of the royal family made him half-faint in trepidation. Meghan told him that if he felt unable to speak, she had no problem giving the speech herself. In any case, the bride's speech is becoming an accepted fixture at regular weddings; why not make it a tradition at royal weddings?

There was also the tricky subject of her wider family. During a difficult phone conversation with her father, she told him that she didn't want her half brother or half sister, Tom Junior and Samantha (formerly Yvonne) Grant, attending the wedding.

While her father may have felt that Meghan was placing him in a difficult position, it should not have come as any surprise. Ever since her romance with Prince Harry was revealed, Samantha had been sniping from the sidelines, doubtless jealous that her sister was enjoying the spotlight and wanting to garner attention for herself. She even used Tom Senior's health to criticize her half sister, arguing that Meghan should pay back the money he had spent on her college education so that her father could afford the best possible health care.

Samantha and Meghan had never gelled as children; as adults they could have been living on different planets. Meghan wanted nothing to do with her. Several months before, for example, Meghan had given her father her new cell number, which he quite innocently had passed on to Samantha. In turn she sent Meghan a text saying that it had been years since they had spoken but if she wanted to resume the connection she would be happy to advise and guide her. Meghan was furious. Samantha was the last person she wanted advice from. Meghan's mother, Doria, called her ex-husband and tore into him, telling him never to give out Meghan's private telephone number again. "Well, she is her sister," replied Tom Senior sheepishly.

With both families alerted, it was time for the happy couple to take a public bow. Their engagement was announced at ten a.m. on Monday, November 27, 2017. The news was released from

Clarence House, the home of Prince Charles and the Duchess of Cornwall. Harry's father expressed his "delight" at the engagement. The bulletin continued: "His Royal Highness and Ms. Markle became engaged in London earlier this month. Prince Harry has informed Her Majesty The Queen and other close members of his family. Prince Harry has also sought and received the blessing of Ms. Markle's parents."

Within minutes, dozens of reporters, photographers, and TV crews assembled outside Kensington Palace for a photo call at the Sunken Garden. At two in the afternoon, on a bitterly cold, windy day, the happy couple emerged and walked arm in arm down to the side of the pond. Harry looked more nervous than his bride, and Meghan stroked his arm reassuringly. They answered a couple of shouted questions, and the prince told the throng that he knew she was the one the first time they met and described himself as "thrilled, over the moon." Meghan smiled and said they were "so very happy."

As they walked away, Meghan rubbed his back as if to say, "well done." The couple walked arm in arm back to the palace for a twenty-minute interview with BBC reporter and campaigner Mishal Husain. The forty-four-year-old mother of three, who had been named Broadcaster of the Year at the 2015 London Press Club Awards, first caught Meghan's eye for her campaign to win equal pay for women working at the BBC, and she and Harry handpicked her to undertake their engagement interview.

The televised conversation began with the couple describing the moment the prince proposed, saying that they were in Nottingham Cottage, roasting a chicken, when he got on one knee and asked her to marry him. "Just an amazing surprise, it was so sweet and natural and very romantic," said Meghan, who confessed that she said yes before he had finished the proposal. They recalled that they had met one another through a mutual friend on a blind date in July 2016, and after two back-to-back meetings Meghan had agreed to join him on a safari holiday in Botswana. At the time Harry had never heard of *Suits* or the California actor, and she admitted that she didn't have much of an idea about Harry.

This had helped rather than hindered the development of their love affair. As Meghan observed: "Everything that I've learned about him I learned through him as opposed to having grown up around different news stories, or tabloids, or whatever else. Anything I learned about him and his family was what he would share with me and vice versa. So for both of us it was just a really authentic and organic way to get to know each other." It helped to cushion the shock they both experienced with the level of media interest once the romance became public.

Nurturing their relationship had been their priority, and the couple described how they had made a promise from the start to make their long-distance relationship work. "It was just a choice, right," said Meghan. "I think that very early on when we realized we were going to commit to each other; we knew we had to invest the time and the energy and whatever it took to make that happen."

It helped to navigate the bumps in the road that virtually from the start the couple saw themselves as a "team" with a shared vision of how they wanted to make a positive difference in society. Their mutual commitment was, Meghan observed, "what got date two in the books."

She recalled: "It was one of the first things we started talking about when we met was just the different things that we wanted to do in the world and how passionate we were about seeing change."

As with his brother's engagement interview, the spirit of their late mother hovered over the occasion. On that November day in 2010 the focus was on Diana's own engagement ring, which William had carefully carried with him before he proposed to Kate Middleton during a holiday in Kenya. This time small diamonds from Diana's jewelry collection decorated Meghan's engagement ring, which was dominated by a conflict-free diamond from Botswana, the country where they fell in love. They were incorporated into Harry's design so that she would be there to "join us on this crazy journey."

Just as William had said in his own engagement interview, Harry, too, felt his mother's absence on these special days. The prince was clear about how she would have responded to her American daughter-in-law. "They'd be thick as thieves, without question. I think she would be over the moon, jumping up and down, you know, so excited for me."

Certainly there was a real sense of destiny for Harry about his romance with Meghan. As he admitted: "The fact that I fell in love with Meghan so incredibly quickly was sort of confirmation to me that everything—all the stars were aligned, everything was just perfect. It was this beautiful woman just sort of literally tripped and fell into my life, I fell into her life."

Meghan's engagement interview was worlds away from the shy, blushing days of Lady Diana Spencer and Prince Charles and his comment "whatever loves means," which skewered his romantic reputation forever. It was also different from the more formal and conventional affair when Prince William and Kate Middleton faced the cameras. Then, a visibly, and understandably, nervous Kate deferred to William in her responses. Not this time. Meghan was warm, affectionate, and supportive, more at ease with the media than her royal fiancé. "A breath of fresh air" was a common view.

The rapturous reception to the news of the engagement suggested that this indeed was a popular match and that the country, beset by Brexit angst, still loved a good romance. Naturally the Queen and Prince Philip were "delighted," especially as the match cemented the monarchy's acceptance for generations to come. Prince William and the Duchess of Cambridge were "very excited" while the Duchess of Cornwall described Meghan as a "star." "America's loss is our gain," she said.

Prime Minister Theresa May commented that the engagement marked a "time of huge celebration and excitement," while Barack and Michelle Obama "wished them a lifetime of joy and happiness together." The king of Twitter, President Trump, remained silent about the first American since 1937 to marry into the royal family. Meghan's parents said they were "incredibly happy" for their daughter, while her TV father, actor Wendell Pierce, gave Harry his blessing.

As for her screen lover, Patrick J. Adams, he joked on Twitter: "She said she was just going out to get some milk." He later added his genuine thoughts: "Your Royal Highness, you are a lucky man and I know your long life together will be joyful, productive and hilarious." There was one victim in a day of smiles and laughter. While she had been able to bring Guy, her beagle, to London to live with her, her second dog, Bogart, a labrador-shepherd mix, was deemed too old to travel. He had been sent off to spend his final days with Meghan's friends.

There were other forfeits, too. Following the public announcement, she resigned from her position as global ambassador for World Vision Canada and stepped back from her involvement with gender equality and women's empowerment in organizations like United Nations Women and One Young World. Now that she was inside the wrought iron palace gates, she had to play by their rules.

Politics in particular is firmly out of bounds. Meghan has previously used her celebrity to back Hillary Clinton, lament Brexit, and attack Donald Trump as "misogynistic" and "divisive." Such strident opinions will be muted by palace protocol that aims to prevent royals—not always successfully—from publicly expressing views on political figures, parties, and issues.

Her communications secretary, Jason Knauf, told around a

hundred journalists who arrived for a briefing at Buckingham Palace that, after touring the country, her withdrawal from her existing humanitarian work would give her a "clean slate" to judge where to invest her time and talent. It will be a struggle and a test for a woman who has grown used to enjoying a public platform. As a friend of Meghan's noted: "She is going to bring a lot of diversity and new ideas, new ways of doing things. She is not just going to blend into the royals."

During their engagement interview, Prince Harry hinted at the future direction the royal couple may take, working with young children in Commonwealth countries where her mixed-race heritage will be a positive asset. In April the Commonwealth Heads of Government Meeting, known as CHOGM, took place, giving Harry the chance to introduce his bride-to-be to some of the heads of state of the fifty-two countries in attendance in central London. It was a primer for Meghan's future role inside the royal family— and her first taste of a state banquet at Buckingham Palace.

A royal insider said: "Prince Harry will definitely have a role to play, and now he is marrying Meghan Markle, CHOGM would provide the perfect opportunity for her to find out more about the Commonwealth."

Amid the back-and-forth about her future royal career, there has also been talk of family matters, Harry saying in their engagement interview that the time for children would be "in the near future."

Though Meghan upon marriage will be conferred with the appellation Her Royal Highness and become a duchess—the smart money is on Sussex—she is going to retain her American citizenship at least for the time being. This means she is still eligible to pay American taxes. In parallel, she is going to apply to become a British citizen, a process that can take up to three years. The application culminates in a quiz about British history and culture. Given her poor performance in that television quiz back in July 2016—where she was tested on cockney rhyming slang and the national animals of the British Isles—few thought she would do well.

She would not be the only one. After all, a YouGov survey showed that when the quiz was given to a group of Brits, half of those under the age of twenty-four flunked the exam. Some respondents thought that Hawaii was part of Britain and that National Insurance was used to pay for supermarket home deliveries. Other questions on the $65 test, such as what is Vindolanda (a Roman fort north of Hadrian's Wall) and the Statute of Rhuddlan (the annexation of Wales to England), left even social historians baffled.

There were other life changes as well. As she and Harry were marrying in St George's Chapel at Windsor Castle under the auspices of the Church of England, Meghan, whose father is Episcopalian and whose mother is Protestant, the faith she was born into, had to be baptized and confirmed before the May celebration, a procedure that is seen as an "important milestone of faith." Her former religious studies teacher at Immaculate Heart, Maria Pollia, has no doubts that Meghan will "utterly astound and delight" clerics from the Church of England when she undertakes her studies in preparation for her induction into faith. "She will understand the liturgy and sacrament, not to mention demonstrating the depth of her theological appreciation."

From the beginning, the couple was determined to have control over the wedding day itself. As their communications director, Jason Knauf, said:

"The couple of course want the day to be special, celebratory moment for their friends and family. They also want the day to be shaped so as to allow members of the public to feel part of the celebrations too and are currently working through ideas for how this might be achieved. This wedding, like all weddings, will be a moment of fun and joy that will reflect the characters of the bride and groom. Prince Harry and Ms. Markle are leading the planning process for all aspects of the wedding."

It will have relieved Tom Markle Senior to know that the royal family was paying for the flowers, reception, the service, and the music. He or Meghan would only have to shell out for her dress.

It was like a rebirth: a new religion, a new country, a new culture, a new language (sort of), and certainly a new career. In making a new beginning with the man she loved, she was also giving up a lot. She could never again wander down to the shops without a bodyguard, never take her dog Guy for a walk on her own, never tell the world about a passing thought or fancy on Twitter or Facebook. In short, her life would never be the same again.

Almost overnight she and Prince Harry were the most famous couple on the planet and "Megan Markle" the most googled name of 2017. She had been blessed with a gift, a gift that would challenge and fulfill her, giving her the kind of access and influence she never dreamt of. Her next test was how to use that gift wisely.

13

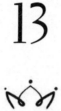

The Billion-Dollar Bride

The moment Meghan Markle said, "I will," you could almost hear the cash registers singing. Within minutes of committing to the royal family, the recently retired actor spawned a one-woman industry to rival any Hollywood blockbuster.

Everything from the coat, dress, and boots she wore for her engagements to her eye shadow, nail polish, and sweaters—even her cute turned-up nose—was copied, imitated, advertised, and sold. She was big business, very big business, the fairy dust of royalty boosting fashion brands, tourism, and even plastic surgery. The white wool coat by Canadian company Line the Label that she famously wore on the day of her engagement announcement sold out within minutes, leaving eager customers no option but to add their names to the four-hundred-strong wait list. It was relaunched the following spring when it had been renamed "The Meghan."

Meghan mania gripped the nation. Newspapers printed special supplements about the life and times of Britain's newest "Mega Star," to steal the *Sun*'s headline. In a declining industry, the hope was that Meghan, like Diana before her, was the new golden goose who could lay profitable circulation eggs.

Step aside, Kate Moss, there was a new queen of the High Street in town. Everything Meghan touched or wore transformed lives—and bottom lines.

The niche sunglasses firm Finlay and Co. was able to open a shop in Soho, Central London, on the back of a surge in sales after she wore their shades on her first public outing with Prince Harry in Nottingham. The company sold £20,000 worth of glasses within twenty-four hours, thanks to Meghan's Midas touch.

Again, when she carried a £500 tote bag produced by a small Edinburgh-based company called Strathberry, stock ran out within an hour.

Strathberry cofounder Leeanne Hundleby couldn't believe her luck. A couple of weeks before, acting on impulse, she had sent Meghan a selection of handbags and was thrilled to see her product given the royal seal of approval. "It's just amazing, it really is the greatest," said a company spokesman. "We're suddenly incredibly busy and we are so excited."

For Meghan, her induction into the royal family was an opportunity to influence her new army of fans by wearing the labels of ecologically and ethically minded designers, as well as companies that have a philanthropic element in their business ethos.

She previously used her blog The Tig to promote such brands as Conscious Step, a sock company that plants twenty trees for every pair sold, as well as the Neshama Project, a California-based jewelry business that donates a percentage of profits to Innovation: Africa. She had always known that being with Harry would give her a megaphone, and even if she was having to step back from her charity work while her future was being ironed out, she was determined to use it and communicate the messages that mattered to her in any way she could.

Careful and considered, Meghan is completely aware that anything she wears, be it makeup, clothes, a new hairstyle, or jewelry has an impact. She has to think strategically. During her days on

Suits she got used to being looked at and discussed. But this was a whole new level of scrutiny. She has the personality to cope, describing herself as someone who likes to think things through, to pause before she jumps in. As she admits: "I give things a lot of thought and I try to be as sensitive and thoughtful as possible to how it'll make someone feel."

For example, during her visit to Cardiff she carried a bag by DeMellier, a British label that funds lifesaving vaccines through their sales, and a cruelty-free coat by Stella McCartney, an animal-rights activist as well as a topline designer. As Meghan once noted on her blog: "It's good if you are fabulous but great if you do something of value to the world." Not everyone was impressed. Columnist Amanda Platell snarked: "There's a thin line between doing good and signalling how virtuous you are. We live in an age of social media, but the Windsors are NOT the Kardashians."

Whether she wants to or not, Meghan has become a one-woman walking, talking advertising board, everything she wears pored over and then sold online. Websites such as Meghan's Mirror have been created expressly to cash in on the Markle sparkle. These sites are effectively online stores devoted to all things Meghan, selling and shipping with just a few clicks, and in the case of Meghan's Mirror, using the same e-commerce site, Reward-Style, as The Tig in its heyday. The editor of Meghan's Mirror, Christine Ross, explained that Meghan's popularity was because her style was relatable to the everyday woman.

Ironically, when she was running her own website she was getting a share of the pie. Now she doesn't earn a penny, though the rewards are much greater.

This total, head-to-foot commercialization of a royal princess is a far cry from the days when a bored Buckingham Palace press officer would grudgingly hand out a piece of paper describing what the Princess of Wales was wearing that day—and if you were lucky, it included the name of the designer. During the 1980s,

Diana rarely wore High Street, preferring designers like Arabella Pollen; Victor Edelstein, who made the famous dress Diana wore when she danced with John Travolta; and later, in her years of independence, the unfussy creations of Catherine Walker. When she did occasionally step out in a High Street brand, such as an elephant-themed ensemble from the upmarket German fashion chain Escada, she faced criticism from the fashion elite.

Even if online shopping had been available in the Diana years, the cost and exclusivity of her clothing would have prevented her adoring female fans from dressing like the late princess. Of course, for years copies of royal dresses have been run up cheaply and quickly. When Wallis Simpson was married in June 1937, for example, she was furious to learn that her carefully crafted wedding dress, by the American designer Mainbocher, was copied and on sale within hours of the wedding pictures being released. In those days *cheap* was a relative term, and even the designer knock-offs were beyond most budgets.

In her own quiet way Kate Middleton began the fashion revolution in the House of Windsor by deliberately wearing accessible and affordable clothes, mixing these with high-end designer labels. The Reiss brand, for example, was a regular staple. She was the first proletarian princess, the palace and the High Street working in harmony, her styles and choices imitated from Maidenhead to Madison Avenue. "Catherine is stylish in affordable clothes and accessories," noted Reiss brand director Andy Rogers.

Meghan has taken it a stage further, using the semiology of fashion to focus on little-known ethical brands. It was an interest she had long before she met Prince Harry. At the 2014 One Young World conference, for example, Meghan made a point of befriending Ali Hewson, wife of U2's Bono, because she wanted to learn more about her ethical clothing line and makeup lines, Edun and Nude.

Ironically, when Meghan did dress like a princess, wearing a

£56,000 gown by London-based Ralph & Russo for her formal engagement portraits, she was criticized for her extravagance. First in line was her half sister Samantha, who wondered how she could spend so much on a dress when her father, Tom Senior, was supposedly in need of a financial helping hand. Meghan was discovering, as Diana and Kate had before her, that whatever you choose to wear, someone always has a better idea. The stunning black-and-white photographs taken at Frogmore House, the royal burial ground inside Windsor Castle, by fashion photographer Alexi Lubomirski were a reminder of the charm and appeal exerted by this couple. "Meghan's sheer glamour marries Hollywood to the House of Windsor," declared the normally sober London *Times*. As Lubomirski commented: "I cannot help but smile when I look at the photos that we took of them, such was their happiness together."

While the royal family were not manning the checkout tills, they had approved the sale, at gift shops in Kensington Palace, Sandringham, and Buckingham Palace, of mugs, gold-plated spoons, bookmarks, notepads, and postcards all adorned with the smiling image of Meghan and Harry. When about one thousand £20 ($27) ceramic mugs commemorating the engagement went on sale following the announcement, they were sold out within twenty-four hours. Every hotel and guest house in the vicinity of Windsor Castle was booked long before the May wedding, while the English tourism board was expecting a huge influx of visitors— around 350,000 extra tourists came to Britain during the royal wedding of William and Catherine. If visitors could not get a decent view of the happy couple, there were plenty of professional Harry and Meghan lookalikes to take their place, for a fee.

As for other happy couples, online wedding planner Bridebook reported that inquiries for castles and honeymoons in Botswana had risen dramatically, while sales of diamond engagement rings à la Markle had gone up by a third. Bridebook chief executive

Hamish Shephard commented: "Meghan and Harry's nuptials will boost both the wedding industry and the British economy. We're expecting a huge increase."

Overall, the London *Times* reckoned that the royal family would contribute £1.8 billion ($2.44 billion) to the British economy during 2018. Of that total, valuation consultancy Brand Finance estimated that the royal wedding could be worth £1 billion ($1.4 billion) to the economy and, post-Brexit, help improve Britain's relationship with the United States. The chief executive of Brand Finance, David Haigh, said: "The last royal wedding had an electrifying effect on people's attitude to the monarchy and Britain, and this will impact even more because it has taken things to a global level with Harry marrying a glamorous American."

Away from these frothy financial figures, on December 1, a week after the engagement announcement, Meghan had her first introduction to her new world when she traveled to Nottingham, meeting and greeting members of the public during an official royal engagement. It was just like walking along the red carpet, except colder, wetter, and with no red carpet.

Unlike Catherine, the Duchess of Cambridge, whose first engagement was christening an offshore lifeboat at a modest ceremony in Anglesey, North Wales, Meghan was thrown in at the deep end, thousands of people waiting for hours under chilly leaden skies for a glimpse of the Hollywood princess. Though the focus was on a visit to a center linked to the World AIDS Day charity, everyone wanted to see the bride-to-be. She looked a tad nervous, as well she might, and Harry frequently put his arm around her and whispered encouragement in her ear. Introducing herself as Meghan, she quickly got used to the English default conversation, chatting about the weather. (In LA it's the freeway traffic.) She thanked people for waiting in the cold, accepted sweets, hugs, kisses, comparisons to Princess Diana, and flowers, but declined selfies, even though if there were an Olympics for selfies, Meghan would be a gold medalist—the royal bride-in-waiting was learning fast.

Inside the AIDS center they met with victims and organizers, Meghan impressing them with her natural empathy. Chris O'Hanlon, who has HIV and works with Positively UK, a charity that helps people recently diagnosed with the disease, found the couple easy to talk to, sincere, and attentive. His verdict: "Not only will she make a good addition to the royal family, she will make an excellent ambassador to any of the causes she puts her heart and mind to."

The royal couple went on to watch a hip-hop opera, where Harry told a fellow ginger-headed man that being with Meghan was "Great, unbelievable." They left Nottingham folk all aquiver, Meghan having scored a bull's eye in Robin Hood's hometown. Complimenting Meghan on her "charm and ease," columnist Jan Moir cooed: "What an impressive debut. Meghan Markle was not born to be a princess, but she moves with ease in her brave new world."

With internet searches for Meghan Markle outstripping those for the recently released iPhone 8, it seemed that everyone wanted to dial into the charismatic Ms. Markle, including the Queen, her family, and her staff. Prince Harry made an edited YouTube version of *Suits* to show the Queen and Prince Philip so that they could understand more clearly what their grandson saw in her. The monarch was impressed enough to wave long-standing rules that only the royal family gather at Sandringham for Christmas. She extended an invitation for Harry's fiancée to join the clan. It was an acknowledgement of the changing times, as the couple have effectively been living together for more than a year. QUEEN BENDS THE YULES FOR MEGHAN punned the *Sun* headline.

The first stage of Meghan's Christmas royal progress was to join the Queen and Prince Harry for the annual Christmas staff party at Windsor Castle. Hundreds of footmen, maids, butlers, and gardeners jostled for position to snatch a brief chat with Meghan, who worked her way slowly around the room. One guest said: "She asked everyone their name and what they did—she was a natural."

No sooner had she met the staff than Harry was driving her to Buckingham Palace, where, on December 20, the extended royal family—all seventy of them—gathered for lunch. Though it is a family affair, it is still a royal family affair, and there is a hierarchy to follow of who bows to whom and who curtsies to whom. Meghan, for instance, had to curtsy to her future sister-in-law, the Duchess of Cambridge, and also to the Countess of Wessex, as Prince Edward was in the room. (Interestingly, if he had been absent she would not have had to flex her knees.) Diana's brother, Charles Spencer, recalled that on one occasion there was so much bowing and curtsying, he ended up bowing to a bemedaled footman.

For a girl from California, where casual is king and the average American proudly bows to no man, this occasion must have been perplexing, not to say a little troubling. Here she was, a standard bearer for gender equality, curtsying to all and sundry. Of course, everyone was dying to meet the new arrival, so along with curtsying, it was a frenzy of handshaking and "How do you do" and "So pleased to meet you."

When they were seated for lunch, Meghan found herself between her future father-in-law, Prince Charles, and Peter Phillips, an event organizer and the only son of the Princess Royal. They pulled crackers together, and Meghan put on a paper crown and joined the others reading out corny jokes as they tucked into turkey and all the trimmings.

A royal source was quoted as saying: "She was obviously a bit nervous at first, but she soon relaxed with Harry's help as he introduced her to everyone and then she really enjoyed it."

The lunch, however, is destined to be remembered for all the wrong reasons, as Meghan's near neighbor, Princess Michael of Kent, who lives in apartment 10 in Kensington Palace, just across from Nottingham Cottage, arrived at Buckingham Palace sporting a blackamoor brooch, a piece of sixteenth-century Venetian jewelry that is now considered racist for its depiction of slaves. As Meghan is biracial and this was her first encounter with the wider royal family, Princess Michael's decision was considered particularly offensive. The seventy-three-year-old princess apologized profusely and promised not to wear the brooch again.

"The brooch was a gift and has been worn many times before," a representative for Princess Michael said in a statement. "Princess Michael is very sorry and distressed that it has caused offense."

Princess Michael, whose husband is a cousin of the Queen and whose father was a member of Hitler's Nazi Party, is no stranger to racial controversy. When she was at a New York restaurant in 2004, she had a run-in with a group of African American diners, reportedly telling them to "go back to the colonies." In order to restore her reputation, she gave an extraordinary TV interview in which she described passing herself off as a "half caste African" in her youth to experience life among these "adorable special people" as she traveled around South Africa and Mozambique.

But Meghan had more to worry about than her new neighbor's ill-advised behavior. Her beloved rescue dog Guy broke both his back legs in an accident. Though the beagle mix was on the mend after receiving treatment from TV "Supervet" Professor Noel Fitzpatrick at his Surrey clinic, it meant she left Guy behind to recuperate when, on Christmas Eve, she and Harry drove to Sandringham to spend Christmas with the royal family.

Though there were enough bedrooms in the majestic pile— Sandringham has 270 rooms—Meghan and Harry accepted William and Catherine's invitation to stay with them at their newly renovated country home, Anmer Hall. It was more relaxed, the

"Fab Four," as they have now been dubbed, becoming closer with every passing day.

Though it was fresh and exciting for Meghan, Christmas at Sandringham has a regular soothing rhythm, like one of the many grandfather clocks that dominate the corridors. On Christmas Eve, following afternoon tea, the royal family open their presents, German style. Then it's church on Christmas morning, to the main house for lunch, and then everyone watches the queen's Christmas broadcast. Boxing Day, the day after Christmas, sees a pheasant shoot on the estate's flat acres.

At four o'clock on Christmas Eve, all the family gathered in the wood-paneled drawing room for the queen's favorite meal of the day, afternoon tea. Small sandwiches, home-baked scones, muffins, and cakes were on offer along with Earl Grey tea and the queen's special Indian blend.

After a short rest, they all came together again in the white drawing room at six o'clock to open presents, which were laid out on cloth-covered trestle tables, with a name card marking each family member's pile of goodies.

Princess Margaret's ex-husband Lord Snowdon once described the scene as "total uproar" as everyone tore open their gifts. The royal adults don't buy expensive presents but rather joke items or whimsical gifts. One year Harry gave the Queen a shower cap with the printed phrase "Ain't life a bitch" on it. Another year he gave her a singing Big Mouth Billy Bass, which now has pride of place on the piano in her Balmoral study. In her day, Diana was once given a pair of false plastic bosoms while Princess Anne received a monogrammed doormat. One report suggested that Meghan got into the zany spirit, giving the Queen a singing hamster, which, apparently, the corgis eyed dolefully.

Once the merriment had subsided the family headed back to their bedrooms to dress for dinner—long dresses for the ladies, black tie for the men. At eight o'clock on the dot the family gather once more for pre-dinner drinks. The Queen arrives at 8:15 for her evening tipple, a dry martini.

The Duchess of York once recalled: "Christmas can be exhausting, not least because you sometimes change seven times in 24 hours. You never let the Queen beat you down for dinner, end of story—to come in any later would be unimaginably disrespectful."

This Christmas Eve the banquet consisted of Norfolk shrimp, Sandringham estate lamb, and a pudding of tarte Tatin. During their starters, the family pulled another round of their bespoke crackers decorated with silver or gold crowns. Like everyone except the Queen, Meghan crowned herself with the paper hat.

On Christmas Day Meghan enjoyed a light breakfast with Harry, William, and Kate at Anmer Hall as George and Charlotte excitedly opened their presents.

Then it was over to the Big House for the walk to nearby St. Mary Magdalene Church. This year the Queen, age finally getting the better of her, arrived by car, accompanied by the Duchess of Cornwall.

Warned beforehand about the biting Norfolk winds, Meghan dressed stylishly but warmly in a Sentaler cream baby alpaca wool wrap coat, suede boots, and a brown beret-style hat. The three-thousand-strong crowd, some of whom had been waiting in the freezing conditions for hours, cheered as Meghan, Harry, William, and Catherine walked by. Meghan smiled, waved, and even playfully stuck her tongue out.

As luck would have it, the best photograph of the day was taken not by a professional cameraman but by single mother Karen Anvil, age thirty-nine, whose picture of the royal quartet easily paid for her own Christmas.

When they came out of church it was time for Meghan's first public curtsy as the Queen walked back into her chauffeur-driven Bentley.

For the first time, Meghan looked visibly nervous, clinging to her fiancé's arm as she dropped a wobbly bob, a rictus grin on her face. A smiling Kate—a seasoned veteran of such occasions—showed how it should be done, dropping the perfect relaxed curtsy.

Then it was time to thank those who had waited for so long. The most well-wishers could hope for was a handshake and a brief "Happy Christmas."

Some, though, went further to win a moment in the royal sun. Among the crowd were a large number of Americans, some from a nearby US Air Force base. Student Michael Metz from Wisconsin used the occasion to propose to his Texan girlfriend Ashley Millican, the crowd cheering as Michael went down on one knee. When Harry and Meghan heard about their betrothal, they offered their congratulations. "It was amazing, like a fairy tale," said Michael.

Back at the main house the royal family sat down for the traditional Christmas turkey and all the trimmings, the bountiful repast eaten within ninety minutes so that the family could watch the queen's Christmas broadcast at three o'clock sharp. This year Meghan got an oblique shout-out when the Queen mentioned welcoming new arrivals into the family.

In the evening the television is turned off and the royal family plays traditional games such as charades. The Queen is an excellent mimic, particularly of political figures, including several American presidents whom she has met over the years.

On Boxing Day the royal men lead the guns out to the fields where hundreds of pheasants, specifically reared for this sport, are slaughtered. William and Harry love shooting—Princess Diana called her boys "the killer Wales"—and enjoy spending the day outdoors in field sports. Not this year. For the first time Harry left his guns in their cases. Perhaps he had already had his fill. He had been shooting in early December, flying to Germany for a weekend of boar hunting with a group of pals, the shooting party organized by German aristocrat Franz-Albrecht Oettingen-Spielberg, known as the Boar Terminator.

His absence from the fields of Sandringham was notable—and duly noted, the *Sun* tabloid pointing the finger of blame at his California fiancée. "Gun-der the thumb already?" they asked.

Vegetarian fashion guru Stella McCartney was in the running to make Meghan's wedding dress—Meghan being a fan of her clothes anyway—which perhaps indicated the general direction of Meghan's thinking.

At least Harry had another excuse. He had to be in London to prepare for his stint as the guest editor of the *Today* program, the flagship BBC morning radio show. He had been given a clear editorial palette, deciding to highlight causes close to his heart, notably youth violence, mental health, social media in society, the armed forces, conservation, and the Commonwealth. He had lined up a number of big hitters, including his father, Prince Charles, who called Harry "my darling boy" and discussed the "untold horrors" caused by climate change, and former American president Barack Obama, whom he had interviewed at the Invictus Games in September at the Fairmont Hotel in Toronto.

Before the interview began, a clearly relaxed Obama jokingly asked if he should speak with a British accent. He also wondered if he should speak faster than usual because he was a "slow speaker."

The prince replied: "No, no not at all. But if you start using long pauses between the answers you're probably going to get the face."

When Obama asked to see "the face," Prince Harry gave him a stern look. "I don't want to see that face!" retorted a laughing Obama.

The conversation covered topics including Obama's memories of the day he left office and his hopes for his post-presidential life, including his plans to focus on cultivating the next generation of leaders through the Obama Foundation. With an oblique swipe at the man who took his job, former President Obama said irresponsible use of social media was distorting the public's understanding of complex issues.

In a quick-fire round of questions, he was asked which program he preferred, *The Good Wife* or *Suits*. The ex-president replied: "*Suits*, obviously."

A whimsical piece in the *Times* caught the mood of the broadcast. "The man who was once naughty Harry, drunken Harry, Boujis Harry, has left behind the fleshpots. Now he is Saint Harry who spends his time toiling among the needy and making outreach radio in which he speaks to those others ignore. The injured. The depressed. The Prince of Wales."

Fortunately, the Radio Four presenters had backed their way into a scoop: Harry's engagement had been announced long after they had arranged for his stint as a guest editor. The news angle was the upcoming nuptials.

Boxer Anthony Joshua, who was interviewed by the prince, offered to be his best man, while presenter Sarah Montague quizzed Harry about Meghan's first Christmas with "the Firm." "It was fantastic, she really enjoyed it," he said. "We had great fun staying with my brother and sister-in-law and running around with the kids. I think we've got one of the biggest families that I know of, and every family is complex as well. She has done an absolutely amazing job."

So far, so endearing. As the interview wound down he remarked: "She's getting in there, and I suppose it's the family she's never had."

Cue foot in mouth. Prince Philip would be proud.

14

Invitation to a Wedding

Retired Army captain Prince Henry of Wales walked straight into a fusillade of criticism when he told the world that the Windsors were the family that Meghan Markle never had.

The Markles galloped straight into action, Meghan's half sister Samantha leading the charge. "Actually she has a large family who were always with her and for her," she thundered. "Our household was very normal, and when dad and Doria divorced, we all made it so it was like she had two houses."

For once her brother, Tom Junior, who generally had little time for his elder sister, went into battle on her side.

"My father will be extremely hurt. He dedicated the majority of his time and everything to her. He made sure that she had what she needed to be successful and get to where she's at today." As far as the pundits were concerned Harry "dropped a clanger, a howler" by commenting on the family set up of his future in-laws. In his defense, he was basing his account on that presented to him by his fiancée. When she was growing up, she felt little sense of family—after all, her parents separated when she was only two. That was her truth, no matter what others believed.

Within days the plotting and in-fighting among the Markle clan suggested a heavily conflicted family. Samantha continued to tout her upcoming book called *The Diary of Princess Pushy's Sister* but insisted that its title was intended to mock the tabloids and that she's proud of her sister. She made a tearful television appearance to ask for Meghan's forgiveness and speak of her hope that she would be invited to the wedding. There were stories that she was being paid by a TV company to sail to England—her medical condition makes flying difficult—to host a red-carpet event outside Windsor Castle. Then she hit back at suggestions that her retiring father would not be speaking at the wedding. "He should not be deprived of the right that fathers have to give a proud speech at the wedding. That's not patriarchy that's poetry."

Meanwhile Samantha's estranged brother, Tom, was finding all the media scrutiny difficult to bear. His girlfriend, Darlene, ended up in jail overnight after an overly boisterous, boozy New Year's Eve celebration at their Oregon home, the second time since Meghan and Harry's relationship went public that police made an arrest at his house. Previously he was arrested in January 2017 for the "unlawful use of a weapon and menacing." The charges were dropped. Tom later suggested that a member of his own family had sold the story to the press. As he admitted: "All this attention has been really hard on the family."

Finally, the man at the center of so much speculation, Meghan's elusive father, Tom Markle Senior, was tracked down to his Mexican hideaway by an enterprising British tabloid reporter. Though he accepted a congratulatory bottle of champagne, the retired lighting director gave little in the way of illumination as to his plans. He said he was "pleased and delighted" with the news of his daughter's engagement, later describing Harry as a "gentleman."

The ghosts from Meghan's past kept arriving to haunt her. A warring family was one thing, a former husband out for his pound of flesh was quite another. She was less than thrilled to learn that her ex-husband, Trevor Engelson, had sold a pilot comedy drama to Fox TV, which he was slated to produce, based on the idea of a recently divorced man whose wife has married into the royal family. The comedy conflict focuses on the estranged couple bickering over access to their children. He had the idea when he was discussing his checkered love life with fellow producer Dan Farah.

Whether or not the show is ever broadcast, Meghan will have to get used to being made fun of. She has already been introduced as a character in the no-holds-barred Channel Four comedy *The Windsors*. Comedian Kathryn Drysdale plays her as a relentless name-dropper, while Harry is so dumb he cannot even read. And speaking of dumb, the US cable network Lifetime announced that it would release *Harry and Meghan: The Royal Love Story* just before the wedding. Their previous royal offering, titled *William and Kate: The Movie*, which they produced in 2011, was described by the *Guardian* newspaper as "toe-curlingly, teeth-furringly, pillow-bitingly ghastly."

What was no laughing matter was the decision by Meghan's lifelong friend Ninaki Priddy, who was her maid of honor at her first wedding, to sell her photograph albums and story to the highest bidder, receiving a six-figure sum for her memories. Given the longevity of their relationship, Meghan may have expected more loyalty. Unlike Priddy and other members of the Markle family, her mother remained a publicly silent but supportive presence, advising and discussing the details of the wedding with her daughter.

Indeed, Meghan and Harry had to tune out what she calls "the noise" and focus on the job at hand—organizing their wedding. Unlike her first marriage, which she left largely in the hands of a wedding organizer in Jamaica, Meghan wanted to control every detail, the big day reflecting what their spokesman described as the "fun, laughter and love" of their "fairy tale."

The first item on the agenda was the guest list. It was going to prove trickier than either of them expected. The first indications were when Harry was asked if his friends Barack and Michelle Obama were getting a stiff white envelope. He was uncharacteristically evasive, saying that nothing had been decided.

The elephant careering around the royal chapel was Donald Trump. When he was a Republican candidate, Meghan had made her disdain for him perfectly clear, telling talk show host Larry Wilmore in May 2016 that she would stay in Canada if he were elected. Her then publicist Ken Sunshine is a senior figure in the Democratic Party, and she herself donated to the campaign toward electing Hillary Clinton as the first female president.

Six weeks later, Prince Harry entered her life and her political world went straight to the back burner—though after their second date together she still registered her disappointment when Britain voted to leave the European Union, posting an Instagram snap of the famous placard "If EU leave me now, you take away the biggest part of me." Fast-forward to February 2017, when a story appeared in US *Weekly* magazine revealing that Harry was not a fan of President Trump, not by a long shot.

The *Sun* newspaper went further, suggesting that Harry thought Trump "terrifying" and a "threat to human rights." He supposedly called on the same words reportedly used by Trump's secretary of state Rex Tillerson to describe the president of the United States: "A moron."

While Kensington Palace refused to comment on anonymously sourced stories, alarm bells were ringing in Whitehall. By now, every diplomat in the world knows that Trump is a narcissist who bears a grudge. With Britain in a state of post-Brexit paralysis, Prime Minister Theresa May needed all the help she could get to land trade deals, and North America was a prime target.

The last thing she wanted was a popular prince taking potshots at the US president. Not that he seems to have noticed. When

Trump was asked by Piers Morgan in a TV interview in January about the royal couple, he said he wasn't aware if he had been invited to the wedding but wished the couple well. When Piers helpfully reminded him that Meghan was not a fan, accusing him of being a "divisive misogynist," Trump seemed unruffled: "Well, I still hope they are happy."

Closer to home, there were other ticklish decisions about whom to invite. While Meghan's own family is fractured, there are also rifts in the royal family, which the wedding may help to heal. The Duchess of York, who is divorced from Harry's uncle Prince Andrew, was not invited to the wedding of Prince William and Catherine Middleton. She later confessed to Oprah Winfrey that the snub left her feeling "so totally worthless." A palace source indicated that this time around, Sarah Ferguson will indeed be going to the wedding of the year. "Harry and Meghan have total control over who goes to the wedding and there was never an issue at the Palace about Sarah being invited," noted a palace official.

The thorny issue of the guest list—St. George's Chapel can accommodate eight hundred—was just one of the items on their wedding agenda. As they had chosen the day of the FA Cup football final to say their vows, they had to ensure that William, as both president of the Football Association and Harry's best man or supporter, was able to attend the nuptials before driving to Wembley Stadium in North London, where he would be meeting the teams and presenting the trophy.

Once that logistical headache was resolved, the couple went to Monaco, flying coach to see in the New Year with friends. Then Harry flew alone to Botswana as part of his work for the Rhino Conservation charity, leaving Meghan at Nottingham Cottage with her friend Jessica Mulroney, a bridal consultant who flew in from Toronto to help with arrangements. They had loads of ideas to discuss. As the wedding represents the symbolic union of two nations, there was debate how about best to integrate the red, white, and blue of the Union Jack and the Stars and Stripes. Naturally Meghan wanted it to be classy—her favorite word—not cheesy. The flowers in the chapel, her dress, and even the tiara she will borrow from the queen's collection were all ways of symbolizing the theme of two nations united.

When she visited the Chapel and looked around the magnificent fourteenth-century building, after pinching herself, she'd have been forgiven for perhaps wondering what it would be like to have her Emmy-winning father in charge of the lighting for the TV broadcast. With an expected audience of 2 billion, it would have been the biggest gig of his career—and no doubt he would have preferred to have a behind-the-scenes role. And what would he have thought about his Valley Girl daughter getting her own coat of arms? Fancy that.

One concern was aircraft noise. With so many aircraft taking off and landing from nearby Heathrow Airport, the world's busiest, Meghan worried that the billions at home wouldn't be able to hear the service. As many an American tourist has wondered, why on earth did they build Windsor Castle so near Heathrow? During the big day would air traffic control at least divert aircraft onto a different flight path so that everyone could hear her say, "I do"? The Civil Aviation Authority answered in the affirmative, agreeing to move all flights away from Windsor for "security and safety" reasons.

Meghan certainly wouldn't be saying the traditional "love, honor, and obey," as did the Duchess of York when she became Prince Andrew's wife and Sophie Rhys Jones when she married Prince Edward. She will follow the lead of Diana and Kate, who promised to "love, comfort, honor, and keep" her royal spouse.

Decisions, decisions, decisions. The couple wanted to surprise their family and friends with "quirky and imaginative" elements. The Middleton sisters had led the way; in 2011 Catherine installed a posh ice cream van and burger stalls at Buckingham Palace for her evening reception, while her sister, Pippa, brought in table tennis tables for her nuptials. She played a match with tennis star Roger Federer, who then took on Catherine, William, and Harry.

As fun as all this was, the centerpiece for the last great royal wedding for a generation was Meghan's wedding dress. Like every bride, royal or not, she wanted to keep the wedding dress secret, only unveiling the unique creation on the big day. With a royal bride, the chosen couturier goes to extraordinary lengths to keep the design and fabric under wraps. Sarah Burton, who designed Kate's wedding dress, put up net curtains in her studio, changed the door code, and banned cleaners from the building. Other royal couturiers have burned samples and shredded pencil drawings to leave no clue for the beady eyed. For Meghan's wedding dress the bookies' favorite was the queen's designer, Stewart Parvin, who made the wedding dress for Zara Phillips, daughter of the Princess Royal. Other runners and riders included Erdem, Roland Mouret, Victoria Beckham, and of course Stella McCartney.

In anticipation of Meghan's final appearance on *Suits* and the royal wedding hoopla, *Suits* producers released a trailer for the climax of season 7, which featured Meghan in a wedding dress. After all the twists and turns of their relationship, Meghan's character, Rachel Zane, was about to marry her on-screen lover, Mike Ross. This was indeed art imitating life, and the show's producers knew that the ratings would be as happy and glorious as Meghan's real-life affair.

While the world eagerly sought scraps of wedding information, this time Meghan wasn't giving out any clues on her social media platforms as she had during the very early days of her royal romance. She had already closed The Tig the previous March, but in January 2018 she went further, closing all her social media platforms—Instagram, Twitter, and Facebook—and removing all her pictures and comments.

During their lifetime she had accumulated a substantial fan

club, with 1.9 million followers on Instagram, 350,000 on Twitter, and 800,000 likes on her Facebook page. This decision outraged her fans, who began a petition to have the sites reinstated. The petition, which was started by Sabrina A., who also runs the website Meghan Maven, argued that by shutting down these accounts the royal family was cutting off the chance to reach an entirely new audience.

She has a point. The royal family's website enjoyed one million more hits in the months after Meghan formally joined the royal family. After all Princess Beatrice, the Duchess of York's eldest daughter, has a Twitter account, and other European royals, notably Princess Charlene of Monaco and Princess Madeleine of Sweden, have personal sites on social media. Then there is that other American princess, the former Sarah Butler, now Princess Zeid of Jordan, who has her own Twitter account, which focuses on worthy topics such as global learning, refugee relief, and disaster philanthropy. Her slogan is "Determined that mothers and newborns survive and thrive everywhere."

In recent months, information regarding Meghan and Prince Harry has been shared through Kensington Palace and official royal family accounts. Eventually Meghan may want her own vehicle to promote her work and chosen causes. Her fans argue that it should be launched via her existing base.

If she still had her social media accounts, she would have had a few choice words to say about the controversial decision by Simon Dudley, leader of the council borough that is home to Windsor Castle, asking the police to ensure that "aggressive" homeless beggars were removed from the castle surroundings before the big day.

His comments were described as inappropriate, and there were calls for his dismissal. Ironically the fight broke out in early January just as Megan was getting down to wedding details with Jessica Mulroney. As Meghan's first-ever charity commitment was to the homeless in downtown LA when she was a teenager, and Jessica is cofounder of the Shoebox project, which has so far donated ninety-one thousand boxes of toiletries to homeless women living in shelters, there was no need for a hotline to Kensington Palace to gauge the reaction. Moreover, as both Prince William and his late mother are and were patrons of Centrepoint, the charity for youth homelessness, the council leader could not have picked a target more likely to arouse regal ire.

While the fight rumbled on, Meghan and Harry made their second joint official visit, touring the social enterprise radio station Reprezent 107.3 FM in Brixton, South London, home to many of the capital's Afro-Caribbean community. As the excited crowd chanted, "We love you," Meghan smiled, waved, and blew kisses. When the noise reached a ragged crescendo, she coyly put her hand in front of her mouth.

During her tour of the station, which trains hundreds of young people every year in media and related skills, the gender equality campaigner singled out presenter YV Shells, asking the twenty-four-year-old if he was the guy who supported women DJs, empowering women and creating a space that is not so male driven. "I think that's incredible," she said.

Inevitably, attention focused on what she was wearing—a £45 bell-sleeve black wool sweater, a staple from the midmarket Marks and Spencer clothing and food chain. It was a marked contrast to the £56,000 dress she wore for her engagement portrait.

On a walkabout outside, she met with American students Jennifer Martinez and Millicent Sasu from Baltimore. Jennifer approved of the American import: "She's black, she's white, she's an actor, she's American. She brings a bit of everything and has so many different qualities. She brings so much to the table."

Not everyone thought so. During her time on the TV reality show *Celebrity Big Brother*, former member of Parliament and committed Christian Ann Widdecombe described Meghan as "trouble," the former MP saying that she was "worried about the background and attitude" of Harry's fiancée.

Matters got uglier as racist remarks made by the girlfriend of Henry Bolton, leader of the pro-Brexit UK Independence Party, were made public. In a series of text messages, glamour model Jo Marney told a friend that Meghan would "taint" the royal family with "her seed" and pave the way for a "black king." She went on to say that she would never have sex with "a negro" because they are "ugly." Many of the party's front bench spokesmen walked out in protest when Bolton refused to quit.

He was eventually ousted after a vote by the party's shrinking membership. The vote took place before the alarming revelation in February that an envelope containing a white powder and a racist letter was sent to Meghan and Prince Harry at Kensington Palace. While the white powder was deemed harmless, it brought back memories of the anthrax scares in the US a week after the 9/11 attack in 2001, when various senators and others were sent the deadly powder through the mail by, it was believed, an American biodefense scientist. This domestic terrorism left five dead and seventeen others affected by the anthrax spores, the incident so alarming that it enabled mischief makers to cause chaos and disruption for the price of a postage stamp.

The incident, which was officially treated as a race hate crime, was a further example, if any more were needed, that racial prejudice was still a potent issue in multiracial Britain. These sensitive subjects of race and color were issues that concerned those who wondered what happened inside the royal palaces once the cameras and microphones are switched off.

The answer is perhaps surprising: class rather than color is the great divider. Though the Duchess of Cambridge now seems part of the royal wallpaper, it wasn't always the case. She has faced much more prejudice from those on the inside, the first commoner for four hundred years destined to be queen, than the biracial Californian. When she and William were students together at the University of St. Andrews in Scotland, Kate was seen by royal courtiers simply as the girl who encouraged him to stay on when he had a well-publicized wobble in the first semester. She was viewed as a perfectly pleasant middle-class girl, who, at some point, would marry someone of her own class when she had finished her degree. When casual friendship morphed into romance, it is safe to say that royal courtiers were stunned. "She got in under the wire," said one.

Once she started moving in his circle of aristocratic friends, she faced snide remarks and out-and-out bigotry. The focus was on her mother, who was raised in a council house in Southall and snagged a job working as a flight attendant: "Doors to manual" was the cry of William's snooty pals. It didn't help Catherine that, in the early days, William was sending mixed messages about her. His ambivalence gave others the chance to criticize and snipe. Not so Harry. From the get-go he was certain that Meghan was the one. No ifs or buts. It has left no room for anyone inside the palace to raise an eyebrow at his choice of bride—commoner or not. It is fair to say that eyebrows have remained studiously unraised. The lead has been taken from the top, and that lead has been entirely positive.

Indeed, even though she has only been officially engaged since November 2017, it is as if she has always been part of the family. Meghan has only made a handful of public appearances, but she is well on the way to being accepted as a bona fide National Treasure. By the time she traveled to Wales a week after her visit to South London, she was well into her stride, the slight reticence that had characterized her first couple of engagements replaced by a relaxed manner and a willingness to have fun, to go with the flow.

During their walkabout at Cardiff Castle—where Meghan

exhibited spot-on sartorial diplomacy by sporting black jeans from the small Welsh brand Hiut Denim—Meghan described herself as a "super lucky woman" and even joked with two fans that the Welsh city would be a "fun" location for a bachelorette party. Unlike her first outing, she felt confident enough to pose for selfies, signed an autograph for one star-struck schoolgirl, and described her husband-to-be as a "feminist." She was even presented with a wooden Welsh love spoon as an early wedding gift.

Meghan mania reached fever pitch by the time she and Harry arrived at Star Hub community leisure center in the economically deprived area of Tremorfa. Meghan was soon surrounded by youngsters desperate to meet her. They were given their cue by Harry, who told them: "Let's all give Meghan a group hug!"

Her visit was a triumph, with even tabloid hacks going all misty eyed about her performance. "Centuries of royal traditions melted away as the US actress brought the warmth of modern celebrity to adoring crowds," opined the *Sun's* Jack Royston.

After the Cardiff visit Harry took Meghan on a short drive to meet the "other woman" in his life, his former nanny and companion, Tiggy Legge-Bourke, who had mentored the princes following Diana's divorce and subsequent death. For Meghan, who winces every time one of her own family opens their mouths, it was a chance to get to know and understand the woman who had such a striking impact on the upbringing of the man she was due to marry.

Though she would never meet Harry's mother, reminders of her influence and presence were everywhere. Meghan's first evening appearance was at Goldsmiths' Hall in the City of London which, by extraordinary coincidence, was where Lady Diana Spencer also undertook her first evening engagement in the run-up to her wedding at St. Paul's Cathedral.

A generation on and now Diana's youngest son was taking

his own bride-to-be. They were guests of honor at the Endeavour Fund Awards, set up by Harry's Royal Foundation, to celebrate and honor the achievements of wounded, injured, and sick servicemen and servicewomen who have taken part in remarkable sporting challenges over the last year. A veteran of awards ceremonies, Meghan was cool and poised, unfazed when the envelope containing the winner of the award "celebrating excellence" went missing for a few seconds while her copresenter hunted for the errant piece of paper. "I am truly privileged to be here," she told a specially invited audience of former service personnel and their families. Unlike Diana, who arrived for her first evening engagement in a low-cut dress that she almost spilled out of when she got out of the car, Meghan opted for a sleekly sophisticated Alexander McQueen trouser suit. The nineteen-year-old Diana would have surely been in awe of such confident self-assurance—in some ways, the groomed and camera-ready Meghan was the woman Diana always strived to become.

Yet much also connects them. Both women shared a humanitarian mission, albeit on a vastly different scale, both charismatic and glamorous, and both recognizing that they were invested with a power to do good in the world.

However, when Diana broke through the barriers of class and ethnicity on both sides of the Atlantic, her appeal as a celebrity lay as much in her vulnerability as her star status. She was all the more attractive because of that susceptibility, especially to women with unhappy marriages. Her social work, visiting those in hospices on their last lonely journey, was therapeutic, as healing for her as it was for those she comforted.

The word *vulnerable* does not immediately spring to mind when assessing Meghan's many splendid qualities. Empathetic, certainly but also self-possessed, sophisticated, and poised, equally at home on a podium making a speech or on a photo shoot. She is a flag bearer for a new generation of confident, assertive women, determined to kick through the glass ceiling.

Time and again Meghan has proved herself a team player, embracing her new family and her new country with enthusiasm. This California girl may inwardly wince at the idea of bending the knee, miss all those opportunities to take stylized selfies, and rage at the near impossibility of finding a ripe avocado or a decent hot yoga studio in central London, but she will survive and thrive. She will struggle over the pronunciation of Derby, Leicester, and Torquay, and learn that Brits prefer to sneer than do sincere and that irony is not a device to press your designer shirts. She will learn, sometimes painfully, that while we share the same mother tongue, the British and Americans are very different people.

Her presence inside the royal family is a challenge and an opportunity.

Long before Prince Harry transformed her life, Meghan had articulated what was effectively her manifesto for her future life. Following a visit to Rwanda, she wrote on The Tig: "My life shifts from refugee camps to red carpets, I choose them both because these worlds can, in fact, coexist. I've never wanted to be a lady who lunches—I've always wanted to be a woman who works. And this type of work is what feeds my soul and fuels my purpose."

For all that, her very presence inside the royal family will make the monarchy seem more inclusive and relevant to multicultural Britain even as the nation struggles to come to terms with diversity in a post-Brexit world.

The image of the Queen and Meghan's mother, Doria Ragland, an African American, standing outside St. George's Chapel together, will be a symbolic moment, one the descendant of a slave, and the other the longest-serving monarch in British history. Meghan, who has already proved herself to be an immensely popular choice of bride, will compliment her husband and the august institution she has married into, bringing a freshness, diversity, and warmth to the chilly corridors of Buckingham Palace.

Her many fans and admirers are eager to watch the next episode of her great royal adventure.

With her smarts, sophistication, beauty, and talent, Meghan represents the American Dream of having it all, achieving her success by dint of hard work and ability. Her life intersected with Prince Harry's at a point where he had proven himself worthy of respect, in spite of, not because of, the privileges bestowed upon him by dint of birth and heritage. While they may have come from different countries, backgrounds, and cultures, their union is undoubtedly the crowning symbolic achievement of the special relationship between a monarchy and a republic.

Appendix

The American Princesses

Famously, there have been Hollywood film stars, notably Grace Kelly and Rita Hayworth, who have married into royalty.

Notoriously, there have been divorced Americans, namely Wallis Simpson, who married the British king Edward VIII and sparked a constitutional crisis in the House of Windsor.

Controversially, there has even been a biracial American who wed a European prince.

Uniquely, Meghan Markle is the only divorced, biracial American actor to marry into the British royal family.

She may be unique, but she is not alone. Over the last two hundred years some thirty-five Americans have married right royally, American money, bloodline, and celebrity shoring up and sustaining the life of regal houses around the world.

Crumbling dynasties have been revived by the arrival of a fresh face from the New World. Meghan Markle was a princess waiting to happen, a figure straight out of central casting who has made the House of Windsor seem relevant and inclusive in multiracial Britain.

For all of her freshness, glamour, and star quality, she still follows a well-trodden path.

Since Betsy Patterson married Jerome Bonaparte, the youngest brother of Emperor Napoleon, in Baltimore in 1803, several dozen American girls have lent their fortunes and their faces to ancient dynasties.

Though Betsy was the daughter of Maryland's richest man, her wealth and beauty counted for nothing in the eyes of Napoleon. She was not royal, and so the marriage proved to be a short one, Napoleon refusing to allow her to land in France when his brother attempted to bring his pregnant trophy wife back home. She finally gave birth in London, but Jerome never saw his son and the couple was doomed never to meet again. Shortly afterward, on his brother's orders, Jerome was made King of Westphalia and married a German princess. Untitled ladies from the colonies were still below the salt.

GRACE KELLY

The legendary and beloved Hollywood film star Grace Kelly was a very different proposition. She was welcomed with open arms by France's neighbor Monaco and is universally credited with having saved the principality's ailing royal house.

Grace epitomizes what America can bring to foreign crowns— glamour, fame, grace, and a desire to give back. She could serve as a template for Meghan Markle's own royal journey.

Born in 1930, she enjoyed a comfortable East Coast upbringing in a prominent Catholic Philadelphia family. Like Meghan, she starred in school plays, but though she had two uncles working in movies, her father, a former Olympic gold medalist, disapproved of her going into acting, which he considered only one step above prostitution.

She defied him and, perhaps, made her small screen debut

in *The Swan*, where she played a princess. Much in demand on TV—like Meghan—she made headlines when she appeared on the big screen in the seminal cowboy movie *High Noon*, which starred Gary Cooper.

By now high-profile and highly prized for her classic blonde ice-maiden looks, she won an Oscar for her role in *The Country Girl*, playing opposite Bing Crosby and William Holden. Her legendary status was assured with three Alfred Hitchcock movies, *To Catch a Thief*, *Dial M for Murder*, and *Rear Window*. Perhaps appropriately, her final film, released in 1955, was named *High Society*, for she had been transformed from a Hollywood star to a European princess.

Renowned these days as a sunshine destination for Europe's jet set, in the 1950s the tiny principality of Monaco was struggling for existence. It had a seedy reputation. "A sunny place for shady people," as novelist Somerset Maugham memorably described this stretch of the Mediterranean coastline. Prince Rainier, the twenty-six-year-old scion of the Grimaldi family who had ruled the principality since 1297, realized that he had to attract rich backers if the pocket-sized country was to expand beyond its almost total reliance on its famous casinos. The Greek shipping magnate Aristotle Onassis, later famed for his marriage to Jackie Kennedy, widow of the assassinated US president, was one of his key advisers.

In the summer of 1955, Grace Kelly was at the Cannes Film Festival in the south of France promoting *The Country Girl*. Rainier, desperate for some positive publicity and urged on by Onassis, agreed to a photo shoot with the Hollywood star at his palace.

Her encounter with her future husband lasted a mere forty-five minutes, but they began secretly corresponding. Seven months later, Rainier arrived in the US, and around Christmas suddenly announced the royal engagement.

Hollywood insiders viewed the match as a cynical business

arrangement masterminded by Onassis. As film producer Robert Evans recorded in his memoirs: "The right bride could do for Monaco's tourism what the coronation of Queen Elizabeth did for Great Britain." However, the majority saw their union as a fairy-tale match, a beautiful Hollywood princess whisked away to a magical hillside kingdom by the azure sea.

In April 1956 the couple were married in Monte Carlo, the wedding lavishly covered by the world's media and watched by a television audience of some 30 million. By contrast the, coronation of Queen Elizabeth was watched by 20.4 million, then a record. From that moment Monaco commanded the world's attention as a glamour spot, with the new princess the jewel in its crown. There soon followed the birth of the couple's three children—Princess Caroline, Prince Albert, and Princess Stephanie. The dynasty was secure.

Eventually life in the goldfish bowl of a tiny principality proved suffocating as far as Grace was concerned. In 1962 she managed to convince a reluctant Rainier to support her fourth collaboration with director Alfred Hitchcock, accepting the lead role in the movie *Marnie*. The prospect of her return to the big screen triggered a firestorm of publicity in the United States but at the same time a rush of sanctimonious disapproval among the Monégasques. They did not want their princess playing the part of a kleptomaniac. Rainier changed his mind. In the end Tippi Hedren took the part of Marnie, much to Princess Grace's disappointment.

Her experience might give Meghan pause. For Meghan, to be separated from a profession she has pursued so determinedly all her adult life must inevitably present similar psychological challenges and engender comparable feelings of alienation. Like Grace, Meghan has given up much—her acting career, her philanthropic work, and her very successful website, all those vital elements that helped define her as a woman. Their absence will inevitably leave a gap in her heart that may not be entirely filled by her royal duties.

For a woman who was so adept at using social media to project her taste, choices, and political and social views, it will be hard to come under the umbrella of Kensington Palace and go along with their reign of silence. A similar example is Queen Letitia of Spain. Before she married King Felipe, she was a journalist and commentator, used to expressing her sometimes controversial views on mainstream Spanish television. After her marriage, silence. It was difficult for her to leave that life behind, and in the early years she did struggle. She was naturally assertive, but she had to allow her husband to take the lead. As far as Meghan is concerned, the good news is that she has adapted to her elevated social position.

In the case of Grace Kelly, she substituted her career with her philanthropic work, notably the launch of a very successful charity, AMADE Mondiale. The aim of this worldwide charity is to protect the "moral and physical integrity, and spiritual well-being, of children throughout the world without distinction of race, nationality, or religion, and in a spirit of complete political independence." A charity, indeed, after Meghan's own heart. When Princess Grace died in September 1982 at age fifty-two, she left behind a heartbroken husband and family and a grieving principality that had come to adore and revere their Hollywood royal.

RITA HAYWORTH

Actor Rita Hayworth, known as the Hollywood "love goddess," was another famous film star who caught the eye of a prince, on this occasion Prince Aly Khan, the son and heir of the impossibly rich Aga Khan III, the leader of the world's Ismaili Muslims.

Their union caused a sensation, especially as Hayworth had been married twice before, first to a used car dealer who became her agent and then to legendary Hollywood director Orson Welles. Khan, who was divorced, had a reputation as a lover of speed, sex, and showmanship.

Dark, dashing, and flirtatious, the playboy prince drove cars faster, raced horses harder, and loved women more recklessly than any other man. He was a lawyer, soldier, big-game hunter, and diplomat, though it is his skills in the bedroom for which he is still renowned. "A copper-skinned bedroom bombshell," wrote one biographer, "the ultimate lady-killer of his day."

It was Aly Khan's dalliance with the Prince of Wales's mistress Lady Thelma Furness that ended their entanglement and opened the way for Wallis Simpson to occupy the vacant position. It was, however, during his dalliance with Pamela Harriman, later US ambassador to France and one-time daughter-in-law of Winston Churchill, that Aly met Rita Hayworth, at the time one of Hollywood's greatest stars and pinups. He made her his princess.

Predictably, the union between the Brooklyn-born actor and the royal playboy lasted only a matter of months. Hayworth left her royal husband during a three-month visit to Africa and headed to Hollywood to patch things up with Orson Welles.

They were together long enough for Hayworth to present him with a daughter, Princess Yasmin Aly Khan, who today is known as a philanthropist and influential advocate in the fight against Alzheimer's disease, the illness that claimed her mother in 1987, at age sixty-eight.

DUCHESS OF WINDSOR

Nothing illustrates how much society and the royal family have changed than the life and loves of Wallis Simpson, the twice-married woman from Baltimore who rocked the throne of England in 1936 when King Edward VIII abdicated rather than reign without the help and support of the woman he loved. If Prince

Harry and the divorced actor Meghan Markle had fallen in love in those days, they would not have been allowed to marry. The stigma surrounding divorce was not just an issue for the royal family; it permeated society as a whole. During the 1920s and 1930s divorce was unthinkable and expensive. Wallis's uncle Sol told her firmly that no member of the family had divorced in three hundred years. She traveled to France and China in search of a cut-rate divorce from her first husband, aviator Win Spencer, and then spent years jumping through administrative hoops before she finally was free, in December 1927. When Meghan divorced in 2013 after two years of marriage, she simply signed a form stating that she and her first husband, Trevor Engelson, had "irreconcilable differences," paid a small fee, and went her own sweet way.

In Wallis's day even remarriage was difficult. After she divorced her second husband, shipping broker Ernest Simpson, she and the former king had to wait a frustrating and seemingly endless six months in separate countries before they could marry.

Just to twist the knife, while the royal family agreed that the once and former king could be titled His Royal Highness the Duke of Windsor, they specifically withheld the HRH appellation from the duke's bride. In their eyes, she was only grudgingly royal. The royal family referred to her as "that woman." It caused a family rift that lasted until the duke died. Though she is a divorcée, no such restriction applies to Meghan Markle, who will be Her Royal Highness from the moment she says, "I do." A full-throated member of the first family.

As a gender equality campaigner, Meghan will be the first to appreciate that in Wallis's day, few women went to college and only slightly more took paying jobs. She was from a generation where marriage was the only recognized path to social acceptance and financial stability.

Where Wallis and Meghan would recognize one another is in their unquestioned ability as networkers. Wallis's social triumph was to import the American tradition of the cocktail hour, where her growing circle of mainly American friends dropped in to her apartment in Bryanston Court, near Marble Arch, which she shared with her second husband Ernest Simpson, for drinks and conversation for an hour or so in the early evening. She had the knack of fixing a decent cocktail for their guests—and in a prod at the English she made sure that her drinks were ice cold.

Word got around and her salon attracted businessmen, journalists, lawyers, and eventually a smattering of aristocrats and minor royalty. After meeting the Prince of Wales at a weekend house party hosted by his mistress Viscountess Furness, the future king also became a regular, often staying for dinner.

The modern-day equivalent to the salon is Instagram, Facebook, Twitter, and a personal blog—and Meghan, who also enjoys a cocktail (especially dirty martinis) has used her blog, The Tig, to convey her passion for food, travel, beauty, and fashion combined with her advocacy for women's rights and gender equality. While Wallis's currency was cocktails and parties, Meghan's was shared confidences—with blog posts that give glimpses into her life on the road, suggest remedies for homesickness, and thoughtful lists of books she recommends (including some by Donna Tartt, Stephen King, and Lena Dunham). By the time she closed down her internet portals following her engagement last November, her Instagram site had accumulated 1.9 million followers.

In spite of the distance in decades, where Wallis, Meghan, and, for that matter, Princess Diana reigned supreme was in the power of fashion. The so-called revenge dress worn by Princess Diana for a charity event at the Serpentine Gallery on the night Prince Charles admitted his adultery on prime-time television will go down in history as an iconic moment that defined their marriage and revealed her liberation as an independent woman.

Wallis, too, used her wardrobe as a weapon, her sleek, crafted style in sharp contrast to the homely fashions preferred by her enemy, the queen mother, whom she called "Cookie," as she apparently resembled a cook.

While she acknowledged that she was no great beauty, she made sure that her clothes reflected the standing of her husband as ex-king, preferring to wear such designers as Mainbocher, the American designer who made the iconic wedding dress, Chanel, Givenchy, Balenciaga, Elsa Schiaparelli, and Dior. "The duchess loves Paris because it is not too far from Dior," drawled the duke wearily on one occasion. As royal jewel historian Suzy Menkes remarks: "She worked even harder than her husband at being elegant, punishing herself by existing on little more than a single egg when her weight shot up two tiny ounces. In that absolute dedication to appearance she belongs to an era when a woman dressed to please, rather than tease, her man. There is something eternal about her style that still resonates today."

Her signature style—sophisticated, classic, and glamorous— ensured that she regularly topped the list of the world's best-dressed women. What became known as the Windsor style—a neat but fluid silhouette—ensured that she was able elegantly to display her diamond bracelet; her flamingo brooch covered with rubies, sapphires, emeralds, and diamonds; and the other jewelry showered upon her by her doting husband. She amassed such a collection that it made history when it was auctioned at Sotheby's Geneva in 1987, a year after her death, fetching $50 million—a record for a single-owner jewelry collection at the time. Elizabeth Taylor, Joan Collins, and Charles, Prince of Wales, were among the bidders.

The extravagance of her wardrobe and her lifestyle—the Windsors employed around twenty-five full-time staff attired in royal livery at their mansion in the south of France—was in marked contrast to the utilitarian ethos of the House of Windsor back in Blighty. Living well and graciously was her best revenge on the royal family who had turned their back on her and her husband.

Though much has been made of Meghan's slave heritage, she is not the first biracial woman to join European royalty. In 1958 a mixed-race baby was born in Bocas del Toro, Panama, to Javier Francisco Brown and Silvia Maritza Burke. The family moved to New York, where their daughter, Angela Gisela Brown, proved to be a talented student. She went on to study fashion at Parsons School of Design, where, as their outstanding pupil, she was presented with the Oscar de la Renta Gold Thimble Award.

She started her own fashion label, A. Brown, before working for the fashion house of Adrienne Vittadini. In 1997, at a party in New York Angela, then thirty-nine, met a banker who was eleven years her junior. Eventually it emerged that he was also a royal, Prince Maximilian of Liechtenstein—the smallest royal nation in Europe, but the richest. After dating for two years, they married in January 2000 at the Church of St. Vincent Ferrer in New York. Among the five hundred guests were members of the royal House of Liechtenstein, including Max's parents, Prince Hans-Adam II and Princess Marie; other members of his family; as well as representatives from other European royal houses. Though this was the first-ever multiracial royal wedding, it went almost unnoticed in the world's press.

The couple's only child, Prince Alfons Constantin Maria of Liechtenstein, was born in London in May 2001. Though the family feature occasionally in Panamanian and South American media, they remain largely under the radar in Europe.

While Prince Max heads a major investment company and makes the occasional speech on the environment, the royal couple, like the rest of the family, stay out of the limelight. A statement from the royal Palace in Verduz, the nations's capital, rather says it all. "The Liechtenstein family is a private family, and this applies to any charities that they are involved in." While the curious might catch the royal family strolling on the beach at their Panama holiday home in Playa los Destiladeros, they would rarely if ever see them on a public platform.

Though Meghan has much in common with Grace, Rita, Wallis, and Angela, the American royal she most closely matches is the former Sarah Butler, now Princess Sarah Zeid. Not only did she qualify with the same degree, international relations, from an American college, she works for the United Nations and devotes her life to often difficult and draining humanitarian work. When she married she changed her religion, her country, and her culture— just like Meghan. Born in Houston, Texas, she was educated in London and then attended college in Houston at the University of St. Thomas. Armed with a master's degree in development studies, she joined the United Nations in New York, focusing on peacekeeping and children's issues.

While working there she met Prince Zeid bin Ra'ad Zeid al-Hussein of Jordan. Educated at Cambridge University and Johns Hopkins University in Maryland, he married Sarah Butler in Jordan's capital, Amman, in 2000. They have four children— Prince Ra'ad, born in 2001; Princess Hala, born in 2003; Princess Azziza, born in 2009; and Prince Zaid in 2011. Princess Sarah, now forty-five, continues her good works by raising awareness for causes including Every Newborn Action Plan, the White Ribbon Alliance for Safe Motherhood, and the Women's Rights Division at Human Rights Watch.

Charming and committed to the work of the UN, in 2014 Prince Zeid was appointed United Nations High Commissioner for Human Rights. In December 2017 Princess Sarah visited Africa in her capacity as the UNHCR Advisor on Gender, Forced Displacement, and Protection. She went to witness the humanitarian work being done in war-torn South Sudan, meeting displaced persons in refugee camps and visiting orphanages. Then she went on to visit more refugees settled in camps inside Kenya.

She recalled: "Everywhere we went, people were pleading for peace, for the opportunity to go back home and restart their normal life. I am truly humbled by the stories I have heard—stories of enormous courage, resilience and perseverance."

She is also cochair of Every Woman Every Child, described as "an unprecedented global movement that mobilizes and intensifies... action by governments to address the major health challenges facing women, children and adolescents around the world."

On her Twitter account, @PrincessSaraZR, she describes herself as "determined that mothers and newborns survive and thrive EveryWhere!" In one tweet she touchingly paid tribute to her husband: *So very proud of #Zeid. He and @UNHumanRights have worked so hard and been so strong.*

It has been a remarkable life so far, leading others by her example. Such is his admiration for his American wife that whenever Prince Zeid makes a speech, he tries to mention his American wife by name.

While Princess Sarah Zeid is from Meghan's generation, it is another American, Lisa Halaby, who is probably the best known royal philanthropist. Born in Washington, DC, to a rich and accomplished family—her test pilot father headed Pan American World Airways—she worked in several countries before she found herself in Amman, the capital of Jordan.

There she met King Hussein of Jordan, whose wife had recently died, and in June 1978 they married. The king was forty-three, and Queen Noor, as Lisa became known, was twenty-seven. Of all Americans who married into foreign royalty, Queen Noor did more to help those less well-off than any other, working tirelessly in establishing a range of charitable foundations until the king's death in 1999.

She alarmed many conservatives inside the Arab kingdom with her focus on women's rights, economic development, and environmental protection. When the king died, her grace and warmth touched many Jordanians. President Bill Clinton described her as a "daughter of America and Queen of Jordan who made two nations proud."

Another American queen, albeit of a much smaller country, was San Francisco–born socialite Hope Cooke, who by chance met Palden Thondup Namgyal, the heir to the throne of the tiny mountain kingdom of Sikkim, in a hotel lounge during a summer trip to India. He married the twenty-two-year-old student in 1963 and two years later became the king, or chogyal, after the death of his father. After a referendum in 1975, the population voted to join neighboring India and thus abolish the monarchy. As a result, the queen of Sikkim left behind the king, from whom she had become estranged, and took their two children back to New York, where she set up a new life in Brooklyn, finding work and contentment as a writer, historian, and lecturer.

Other notable American women who have married right royally include Jackie Kennedy's kid sister Caroline Lee Bouvier, who married a Polish count in 1959 and became Princess Lee Radziwill, clinging to the title after their divorce after fourteen years of married life. Nearer Meghan's own age is model Kendra Spears, who is the youngest American princess. Born in Seattle in 1988, by the time she was at college she was juggling her studies with the demands of the fashion world.

Introduced to the forty-two-year-old Prince Rahim Aga Khan by supermodel Naomi Campbell, Kendra was whisked off her feet in a whirlwind courtship and married in the beautiful Bellrive Castle in Geneva in 2013. They have two children, and she is now known as Princess Salwa Aga Khan.

While the list of Americans marrying into foreign royal families is as varied as it is long, only one American family can claim to have two princesses among its ranks. As Americans have discovered over the last two centuries, it does help if you have deep pockets. Billionaire businessman Robert Warren Miller enjoyed watching two daughters marry into royalty: Marie-Chantal Miller wed Prince Pavlos, the Crown Prince of Greece—a country without a monarchy, it should be added—and her younger sister, furniture designer Alexandra, is married to Prince Alexander von Furstenberg. The third of the Miller sisters failed to make it a royal flush, but she did snag a member of the famous Getty family.

Finally, you can have all the money and titles in the world, but nothing can stop that moment of magic when two people connect across a crowded room—as Prince Harry and Meghan Markle discovered. They were not the first royals to experience that moment of magic. When Florida-born Kelly Jeanne Rondestvedt was in a New York restaurant with a group of girlfriends she spotted a handsome man across the room. He looked at her, they connected, and in 2009, the brilliant investment banker and the talented lawyer were married. The lawyer is one of Harry's cousins, Prince Hubertus, heir to the Saxe-Coburg and Gotha royal house, which was, incidentally, the surname of the British royal family until 1917.

Kelly Jeanne Rondestvedt took the title Hereditary Princess Kelly of Saxe-Coburg and Gotha, and the couple and their three children live happily ever after in their the magical Schloss Callenburg in Coburg, Germany.

As Prince Harry might say, "the stars were aligned."

Acknowledgments

Sometimes it helps to be in the right place at the right time. My wife, Carolyn, is from Southern California, and for some of the year I live in Pasadena, a few miles northeast of downtown Los Angeles. When Meghan Markle's engagement to Prince Harry was announced, it was remarkable how many local people had stories about the *Suits* actor. Pasadena was truly Meghan Markle central; Edmund Fry, owner of Rose Tree Cottage, a piece of England in the town, served her tea; her old boyfriend, now a Realtor, sold a house just across the street; parents sent their children to the schools where Meghan has either studied or performed at. Local photographers had boxes of slides with unseen shots of the royal-in-waiting. And talking about waiting: the Hippie Kitchen, where she volunteered as a teenager, was just a short drive away, as was nearby Glendale, where comedian Natasha Pearl Hansen, herself Norwegian and African American, amused audiences with a stand-up routine based around her unusual biracial upbringing.

So, starting in Pasadena, I would like to thank my friend Dr. Wendy Kohlhase for introducing me to the enthusiastic and helpful staff and administrators at Immaculate Heart High School. School president Maureen Diekmann and Callie Webb delved deep into the archives stored in the basement to discover all matters Markle, while senior teachers Christine Knudsen and Maria Pollia added their insights with regard to their former pupil. My thanks, too, to photographer John Dlugolecki for uncovering a charming series of shots of Meghan as she blossomed into a beautiful young woman.

Gigi Perreau, a Hollywood child star herself and Immaculate Heart alumni, and Emmanuel Eulalia, director of drama at St. Francis High School in La Cañada, described Meghan's emerging talent. Elizabeth and Dennys McCoy spoke warmly of the young Meghan, while the thoughts of Catherine Morris, Jeff Gottrich, and the staff at the Hippie Kitchen, who work tirelessly to help those without a roof over their head, were much appreciated.

With regard to Meghan's complicated and extensive family tree, I would like to thank genealogists Elizabeth Banas and Gary Boyd Roberts, historian Christopher Wilson, as well as Professor Carmen Harris, University of South Carolina, Upstate, who put the lives of her ancestors in context. Family members Tom Markle Junior, Roslyn Loveless, and Noel Rasmussen all helped tease out her equally complicated upbringing, while several friends, including Leslie McDaniel and others who remain anonymous, added their perspective. Tameka Jacobs and Leyla Milani talked perceptively about the girl they knew from the *Deal or No Deal* days, while several members of the crew of *Suits*, who for professional reasons did not want to be named, also pitched in.

I would also like to thank Professor Prochaska and Trevor Phillips, OBE, former chairman of the Equality and Human Rights Commission, for their views on her impact on the monarchy and the country. I have discussed this issue with other former members of the royal household who have understandably asked not to be named.

My thanks too to Samantha Brett, author of *Game Changers*. A huge thank-you too to my researchers, Phil Dampier in

London and the indefatigable Lisa Derrick in Los Angeles. Without the consummate professionalism, too, of my editors Gretchen Young in New York and Fiona Slater in London, as well as the dedication of editorial assistant Katherine Stopa, we would never got over the finish line.

Finally, a big shout-out to all my Pasadena friends, acquaintances, and neighbors, whose thoughts, suggestions, and advice energized this whole project.

Pasadena
March 2018

About the Author

Andrew Morton is one of the world's best-known biographers and a leading authority on modern celebrity and royalty. His sensational 1992 biography, *Diana: Her True Story*, which was written with the intimate cooperation of the Princess of Wales and for the first time revealed her conflicted secret life, became an international bestselling phenomenon. Since then Morton has gone on to write *New York Times* bestsellers on Monica Lewinsky, Madonna, David and Victoria Beckham, Tom Cruise, and Angelina Jolie. His most recent works include *17 Carnations*, on Edward VIII, later Duke of Windsor, and Wallis Simpson's relationship with the Nazis and the big royal cover-up, and *Wallis in Love*, the groundbreaking biography of Wallis Simpson. The winner of numerous awards, he divides his time between London and Los Angeles.